In Search of
the New South

In Search of
the New South
The Black Urban Experience
in the 1970s and 1980s

Edited by
Robert D. Bullard

The University of Alabama Press
Tuscaloosa and London

Copyright © 1989 by
The University of Alabama Press
Tuscaloosa, Alabama 35487
All rights reserved
Manufactured in the United States of America

Library of Congress Cataloging-in-Publication Data

In search of the new South: The black urban experience in the 1970s and 1980s/
  edited by Robert D. Bullard.
      p.   cm.
  Bibliography: p.
  Includes index.
  ISBN 0-8173-0425-8 (alk. paper)
    1. Afro-Americans—Southern States.   2. Southern States—Race
relations.   I. Bullard, Robert D. (Robert Doyle), 1946-
E185.92.I5 1989
305.8'96073'075—dc19   88-20911

British Library Cataloguing-in-Publication Data available

To the struggling
Third World people
in America

Contents

Foreword   ix
Delores P. Aldridge

Acknowledgments   xi

Introduction: Lure of the New South   1
Robert D. Bullard

1 **Blacks in Heavenly Houston**   16
Robert D. Bullard

2 **New Orleans:** A City that Care Forgot   45
Beverly Hendrix Wright

3 **Atlanta:** Mecca of the Southeast   75
Robert D. Bullard and E. Kiki Thomas

4 **Memphis:** Heart of the Mid-South   98
Sandra Vaughn

5 **Birmingham:** A Magic City   121
Ernest Porterfield

6 **Blacks in Tampa**   142
Robert A. Catlin

Conclusion: Problems and Prospects   161
Robert D. Bullard

Notes   174

Select Bibliography   190

Contributors   196

Index   197

Foreword

Much has been written about the emergence of the South as a changed land. For a sizable segment of the region's population, however, the "New South" has been more illusion than reality. This is especially true for the region's largest minority group, blacks. Blacks were systematically discriminated against under the Jim Crow system of the Old South. This system relegated blacks to second-class citizenship. The residuals of southern apartheid are with us in the New South, as demonstrated by the present-day inequities in education, employment, income, housing and residential amenities, the judicial system, and a host of other areas.

This book, edited by Robert D. Bullard, focuses on the extent to which blacks have shared in the New South's growth and prosperity. The authors of this book are drawn from diverse academic disciplines. All of the contributors, however, share the common background of growing up black in America. Moreover, all of the authors have chosen to live and work in the New South.

Although gains were made during the seventies through the mid-eighties, millions of the region's blacks, as the authors agree, remain outside the mainstream. Beginning in the mid-seventies, a number of books focused on the southern Sunbelt and its cities. A survey of these books include: Kirkpatrick Sale, *Power Shift: The Rise of the Southern Rim and Its Challenge to the Eastern Establishment* (1975); David C. Perry and Alfred J. Watkins, eds., *The Rise of the Sunbelt Cities* (1977); Richard M. Bernard and Bradley R. Rice, eds., *Sunbelt Cities: Politics and Growth since World War II* (1983); and Franklin James et al., *Minorities in the Sunbelt* (1984). While the aforementioned books describe the major changes that occurred in the region during the seventies, none provides an indepth analysis of these changes on the black population in the South, as a distinct part of the larger transformation. Moreover, the Black Belt within the Sunbelt and the New South was largely ignored in the academic arena and among popular media.

This book, *In Search of the New South*, clearly documents the black experience from the seventies through the mid-eighties, a crucial period of the South's history. It is both contemporary and timely since the South continues to be a favorite point of destination for new industry and in-migrants from other regions of the country. A case study analysis of six major cities, that is, Houston, New Orleans, Atlanta, Memphis, Birmingham, and Tampa, provides substantial documentation that the benefits and burdens associated with economic development, industrial expansion, and new jobs were not uniformly distributed across the various segments of the region's population.

Each of the case study cities has a "story" to be told. More often than not, these stories revolve around blacks' struggle for civil rights, political empowerment, and economic parity within the larger society. White racism and institutionalized discrimination created and maintained the dual society—black and white, separate and unequal—in the South as well as in the rest of the nation.

This work is a significant contribution, for its subject matter spans many audiences, including the general public, public officials, city planners, civil rights groups, and individuals who are concerned about social change and equality. It is written in a style that facilitates easy integration into both undergraduate and graduate curricula, for example, urban studies, ethnic studies, planning, social and public policy, urban and community sociology, and public history. In sum, the book provides a timely and insightful analysis of the black experience in the New South.

Delores P. Aldridge
Atlanta, Georgia

Acknowledgments

This book grew out of some long and sometimes heated discussions that took place at professional meetings in the South. The special panel sessions held during the 1986 meeting of the Association of Social and Behavioral Scientists in Jackson, Mississippi, and the 1987 meeting of the Mid-South Sociological Association in Memphis were useful vehicles for black scholars who live and work in the region to interact and share their ideas for this volume. Special thanks must go to my fellow contributors and their institutions. Without their valuable insights this book would not have been possible. They were patient and understanding of the demands and delays that often occur during a collaborative project.

The bulk of the work was completed while Robert D. Bullard was on the faculty at Texas Southern University in Houston. The final editing was performed at the University of Tennessee. A hearty thanks is extended to L. Alex Swan, a fellow sociologist and dean of the College of Arts and Sciences at Texas Southern University, who provided moral support and release to complete the work on this project. Linda McKeever Bullard typed the draft and Billy J. Turner proofread much of the manuscript, for which we are grateful.

In Search of
the New South

Introduction
Lure of the New South

Robert D. Bullard

The lure of the South has been a topic of much discussion in recent years. This interest was triggered largely as a result of the social, economic, and demographic changes that occurred in the 1970s. The South became a center of growth and economic expansion. Growth in the southern region during this period was stimulated by a number of factors. The 1980 *Report of the President's Commission for a National Agenda for the Eighties* delineated five basic explanations for these changes: (1) a climate pleasant enough to attract workers from other regions, and the "underemployed" work force already in the region; (2) weak labor unions and strong right-to-work laws in many southern states; (3) cheap labor and cheap land found in the South; (4) its attractiveness to new industries, such as electronics, federal defense, and aerospace contracting; and (5) aggressive self-promotion or booster campaigns by southern states and their cities, which targeted businesses that were looking for places to relocate.[1] Sociologist John D. Kasarda offered similar factors for the South's "turnaround from a net exporter of people to a powerful human magnet."[2] He asserts:

> In addition to . . . investment advantages . . . there are a variety of interrelated factors that have played a role: (1) a growing, footloose, sunseeking retirement population that has private pensions, social security payments and other sources of income not tied to a place of work; (2) the spread of central air conditioning that allows more comfortable summertime living and working conditions; (3) lifestyles that are more oriented to recreation and year-round outdoor activities; (4) changing racial attitudes that permit blacks and Hispanics new opportunities to participate in the economic and social institutions of the South; (5) a more progressive political atmosphere in the metropolitan South; (6) generally lower living and amenity costs; and (7) a dramatic improvement in the quantity and

quality of the region's consumer services, financed by rising personal income.[3]

The South in the 1970s desperately attempted to rid itself of the image of a socially and economically "backward" region. The region was vigorously promoted as the "New South." However, many of the problems that characterized the postindustrial economy endured in southern metropolises. Emerging industries and technical fields did not provide a major source of new jobs for the blacks who were concentrated in central cities. Both in-migrants and incumbent residents of the region who had marginal skills generally found themselves in the growing unemployment lines. Individuals who did not have the requisite education often became part of the emerging underclass. The new prosperity in the South heightened status differences between blacks and whites. The shift of population and jobs to the suburbs contributed to the ghettoization of central-city blacks and exacerbated many existing urban problems (for example, poverty, unemployment, social dislocation, family instability, welfare dependence, crime, etc.).[4] Poverty in the South represented a source of "cheap labor." The large pool of nonunion labor was also part of the so-called good business climate.

Many household heads whose jobs only paid the minimum wage had to work an extra job just to pull themselves above the poverty level. Uneven development within the region's central cities and suburbs and companies' systematic avoidance of areas that had large concentrations of blacks heightened the social and economic inequalities between blacks and whites.[5] Moreover, white racism permeated nearly every institution in the region. This persistent problem caused many writers to challenge the existence of a New South. Chet Fuller, a black journalist, traveled across the South in the late seventies and discovered that "the much touted progress of some southern cities is more illusion than reality."[6]

The New South was portrayed as booming with industrial growth and expanding employment opportunities that were once closed to the black masses. The New South was marketed as a changed land where blacks could now share in the American Dream. Fuller argues:

> It would be possible for me to believe in this New Land had I . . . not seen the countless flesh-and-blood people behind the government unemployment statistics, desperately trying to find work in Atlanta and south

Georgia, Charlotte, Greensboro, and Wilmington, North Carolina, Anderson, Columbia and Charleston, South Carolina, and across Alabama and Mississippi. . . . Power has not changed hands in the South, not from white hands to black hands. Economics is the great controller. Economics is money is power is still white. Until we realize that and move to cooperate more fully with one another to take greater control of our economic destiny, there will be no New South.[7]

It is within this context that this book attempts to explore the changes that took place in the South between the 1970s and the mid-1980s. The study explores the distribution of benefits associated with economic development, industrial expansion, and business growth in the South. It also analyzes the distribution of burdens (negative side effects) that resulted from rapid growth: pollution, land use conflicts, crowding, spiraling housing costs, and other threats to the quality of life. It does not matter what the region is called, the New South or the Sunbelt, its growing black underclass has endured, along with the other problems that usually accompany fiscally strained urban centers, such hindrances as a dwindling tax base, inadequate public services, loss of low- and moderate-income housing, strained employment markets, rising crime and drug problems, and business closures in low-income and minority areas.

A number of unanswered questions remain. To what extent have blacks in the South benefited from growth in the New South? Did the boom of the seventies pass over the region's black community? Did black population gains translate into comparable economic and political gains? What impact did the economic recessions, or the "bust" period of the early 1980s, have on blacks' progress in the South?

A case study approach was used in selecting and analyzing social, political, and economic data on six large southern cities: Houston, New Orleans, Atlanta, Memphis, Birmingham, and Tampa. Each case study was written by an individual who resided in the study city. A general outline was provided to the contributors in an attempt to facilitate an even coverage of issues related to the black experience.

Defining the South

The boundaries of the South have been defined in different ways by a host of journalists, social scientists, and government bureaucrats. For ex-

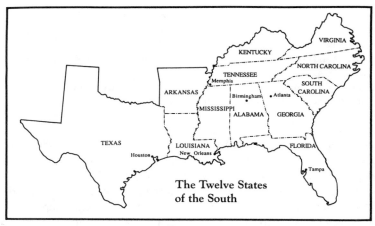

The Twelve States
of the South

Figure 1.

ample, the U.S. Bureau of the Census has defined the South as a statistical entity comprising sixteen states and the District of Columbia. However, the South is more than a statistical entity because of its distinct history, culture, and development pattern. Because this book is about changes that have occurred in the Old South, a broad belt that stretches from Virginia to Texas, it seems logical to define the New South on the basis of state boundaries (see Figure 1). The South thus includes twelve states: Virginia, North Carolina, South Carolina, Georgia, Florida, Kentucky, Tennessee, Alabama, Mississippi, Arkansas, Louisiana, and Texas.

The South has the largest population of any region in the country. More than 64.9 million inhabitants, nearly one-third of the nation's population, lived in the South in 1980. All of the southern states experienced a net in-migration during the seventies. The South during the 1970–80 period also grew at a faster rate than the nation as a whole. The nation's population grew by 11.4 percent between 1970 and 1980; the South's population expanded by 21.9 percent during the seventies.[8]

The southern region also has the largest concentration of blacks. In 1980, there were more than 12.2 million blacks living in the South. Blacks represented nearly one-fifth (18.9 percent of the South's population (see Table 1.1). The 1970–80 period saw the region's black population increase by nearly 18 percent, and six of the southern states

Table 1.1
Black Population in the South by States, 1980

State	Total Population (× 1,000)	Percent Change 1970–80	Percent Black 1980	Percent Change in Black Population 1970–80
Virginia	5,347	15.0	18.9	17.1
North Carolina	5,882	15.7	22.4	17.1
South Carolina	3,122	20.5	30.4	20.2
Georgia	5,463	19.1	26.8	23.4
Florida	9,746	43.5	13.8	28.8
Kentucky	3,661	13.7	7.1	12.1
Tennessee	4,591	16.9	15.8	16.9
Alabama	3,894	13.1	25.6	10.2
Mississippi	2,521	13.7	35.2	8.7
Arkansas	2,286	18.9	16.3	6.2
Louisiana	4,206	15.4	29.4	13.8
Texas	14,229	27.1	12.0	22.2
Total	64,948	21.9	18.9	17.8

Source: U.S. Bureau of the Census, *State and Metropolitan Area Data Book 1982* (Washington, D.C.: U.S. Government Printing Office, 1982).

(Mississippi, South Carolina, Louisiana, Georgia, Alabama, and North Carolina) had black populations that exceeded 20 percent.

The South has always been home for a significant share of the black population. More than 90 percent of black Americans lived in the southern states at the turn of the century. A little more than one-half (53 percent) of all blacks were living in the South in 1980—the same percentage as in 1970.[9] In an effort to improve their life situations, millions of rural blacks migrated from the South to other regions of the nation. From the mid-forties to the late sixties, nearly 4.5 million more blacks left the South than migrated to it. Beginning in the mid-seventies, however, the number of blacks moving into the South exceeded the number departing for other regions of the country. For the period 1975–80, more than 415,000 blacks moved into the South, while only 220,000 left the region (or a net in-migration of 195,000 blacks), thereby reversing the "longstanding black exodus."[10] The 1980–85 period, however, witnessed more than 324,000 blacks leaving the South, but more than 411,000 moved into the region. These new migrants were generally better educated and had higher incomes than the population found in the region.[11] The income gap between black college-educated migrants to the South and their white counterparts has all but disappeared. However, many of the incumbent residents of the region have far too few skills and too little education, factors that limit their access to these largely white-collar and professional positions.

The South has averaged a net of some 87,000 blacks through migration since 1980. This reverse migration stream is "indicative of the changing social, political, and economic structure of the South."[12] As industry and jobs relocated to the region, job seekers were soon to follow. The movement of blacks to the southern United States is expected to continue as more nonagricultural jobs are added to the region's economy. For example, more than 17 million new jobs were added in the South between 1960 and 1985, compared to 11 million jobs added in the West, and a combined total of 13 million jobs added in the Midwest and Northeast.[13]

The six largest standard metropolitan statistical areas (SMSAs) in the South (as defined in this book) are Dallas–Ft. Worth, Houston, Atlanta, Miami, Tampa–St. Petersburg, and New Orleans. These are eighth, ninth, sixteenth, twenty-first, twenty-fourth, and thirty-third, respectively, in population among all the nation's SMSAs. Blacks make up a significant share of the region's metropolitan and central-city population. For example, the data in Table 1.2 show the distribution and percentage of blacks in selected SMSAs. Blacks comprised one-third of the population in the Memphis, Jackson, and New Orleans metropolitan areas in 1980. Blacks made up one-fourth of the Birmingham, Richmond, and Atlanta SMSAs. The Miami and Atlanta SMSAs registered the largest percentage increase in the number of blacks between 1970 and 1980. The black population in metropolitan Miami grew by 47.8 percent in the seventies, while blacks in the Atlanta SMSA increased their numbers by 43.5 percent during this same period. On the other hand, the Birmingham metropolitan area experienced the smallest increase in its black population in the 1970s. Birmingham's black population grew by only 8.2 percent between 1970 and 1980.

George Hall in his speech "Statistical Portrait of Black America" summarized the trends that were taking place as blacks moved south-

Table 1.2
Black Population Change in Selected Metropolitan Areas in the
Southern United States, 1970–80

SMSA	Black Population 1980	Percent Change in Black Population 1970–80	Percent Black 1970	Percent Black 1980
Houston	528,510	35.5	19.5	18.2
New Orleans	387,422	19.6	30.9	32.6
Memphis	364,253	17.2	37.2	39.9
Atlanta	498,826	43.5	21.8	24.6
Dallas–Ft. Worth	419,200	26.9	13.9	14.1
Miami	280,434	47.8	15.0	17.2
Birmingham	239,673	8.2	28.8	28.3
Richmond	174,529	20.9	26.4	27.6
Tampa–St. Petersburg	145,688	28.7	10.4	9.3
Charlotte	138,661	23.1	20.2	21.8
Jackson	126,202	30.8	37.2	39.4

Source: U.S. Bureau of the Census, *State and Metropolitan Area Data Book 1982.*

ward: (1) the black population continued to be geographically concentrated; (2) the number of states with black populations of one million or more increased from nine in 1970 to twelve in 1980, and over one-half of these states were in the South; and (3) southern cities of 100,000 or more attracted blacks in significant numbers.[14] A distribution of nineteen cities in the South with the largest black population is presented in Table 1.3 Four of these cities (Atlanta, Birmingham, New Orleans, and Richmond) have black majorities. The black populations in Savannah, Memphis, and Jackson approached the 50 percent mark in 1980.

The challenges that southern cities must face rest with how their resources, that is, housing, jobs, public services, political representation, etc., are shared with blacks and other ethnic minorities, who historically have not gotten their fair share of the region's economic advances.[15] Gurney Breckenfeld describes the problems of the Deep South as follows:

Numerous pockets of poverty remain, especially in black rural parts of the Deep South. In its Sunbelt expansion, industry has tended to build

Table 1.3
Cities in the South with the Largest Black Population, 1980

City	Total Population	Black Population Number	Black Population Percent of Total
Houston, TX	1,595,138	440,346	27.6
New Orleans, LA	557,515	308,149	55.3
Memphis, TN	646,356	307,702	47.6
Atlanta, GA	425,022	282,911	66.6
Dallas, TX	904,078	265,594	29.4
Birmingham, AL	284,413	158,224	55.6
Jacksonville, FL	540,920	137,324	25.4
Richmond, VA	219,214	112,357	51.4
Nashville-Davidson, TN	455,651	105,942	23.3
Charlotte, NC	314,447	97,627	31.0
Jackson, MS	202,895	95,357	47.0
Norfolk, VA	266,979	93,987	35.2
Fort Worth, TX	385,164	87,723	22.8
Miami, FL	346,865	87,110	25.1
Shreveport, LA	205,820	84,627	41.1
Louisville, KY	298,451	84,080	28.1
Baton Rouge, LA	219,419	80,088	36.5
Mobile, AL	200,452	72,568	36.2
Montgomery, AL	177,857	69,660	39.2
Savannah, GA	141,390	69,241	49.0
Tampa, FL	271,523	63,835	23.5

Source: U.S. Bureau of the Census, *We the Black Americans* (Washington, D.C.: U.S. Government Printing Office, 1986).

new factories where it can find surplus white labor and has avoided places with a high ratio of poor and unskilled blacks. [16]

Many communities with large black populations were passed over during the height of the economic push southward. Economic growth patterns in the Deep South generally occurred along racial and geographical lines. As a result, millions of rural and urban blacks in the South are racially and economically segregated from the expanding job centers in the region. The plight of black southerners has been exacerbated by the combination of economic recession (and depressionlike conditions in many black communities), federal budget cuts, growing tension among individuals competing for limited jobs and other scarce resources, and the federal retreat on enforcement of civil rights and antidiscrimination laws.[17]

Residents of many southern cities have experienced hardships not unlike those faced by northern ghetto residents. The urban ghettos in the South have been as difficult to eliminate as those in the Northeast and Midwest. Moreover, many southern cities are well on a course of experiencing the social and fiscal problems similar to the urban centers in other regions of the country. Southern cities now attract more low-income migrants than they lose. The crime rates of major southern cities are among the highest in the nation. The populations in New Orleans, Miami, and Birmingham, for example, have a higher "hardship rating," as measured in terms of unemployment, dependency, limited education, crowded housing, and poverty, than Cleveland or Detroit.[18] Falling oil prices in the 1980s have further weakened the economic base for many of the communities that were tied to this industry. The population in the Gulf Coast states (Texas, Louisiana, Mississippi, and Alabama) and in Oklahoma have been hit especially hard by the international oil glut, while other parts of the country have benefited from lower energy costs.

There is little doubt that the South experienced substantial population gains in the decade of the seventies. A major part of the population increases can be pinpointed to two states: Florida and Texas. Florida, for example, led the South's population gains in the 1970s, growing by 43.4 percent. Texas, on the other hand, gained the most people, with more than three million persons added to its population between 1970 and 1980. The 1980 census revealed that, for the first time in the history of the United States, more than one-half (52 percent) of the nation's population lived in the South and West census regions.[19]

The South and West also had the fastest-growing metropolitan areas in the nation. The ten fastest-growing metropolitan areas during the seventies are presented in Table 1.4. Five of these fast-growing metropolitan areas are located in the South. The Houston SMSA, for example, gained more people than any other area; it gained more than 906,000 new residents during the 1970–80 period. The Dallas–Ft. Worth SMSA was second, with 597,000 persons gained in the same period. California had four of the ten fastest-growing metropolitan areas in the country: Ana-

Table 1.4

Population Gains in the Nation's Ten Fastest-Growing Metropolitan
Areas, 1970–80

	Population (× 1,000)			Percent Change
SMSA	Total Population 1980	Population Gains 1970–80	Percent Black 1980	Black Population 1970–80
Houston	2,905	906	18.2	35.5
Dallas–Ft. Worth	2,974	597	14.1	26.9
Phoenix	1,509	537	3.2	46.3
Anaheim–Santa Ana– Garden Grove	1,932	511	1.3	148.4
San Diego	1,861	504	5.6	68.3
Tampa–St. Petersburg	1,569	480	9.3	28.7
Atlanta	2,029	434	24.6	43.5
Riverside–San Bernardino–Ontario	1,558	419	5.0	69.8
Los Angeles–Long Beach	7,447	405	12.2	23.7
Ft. Lauderdale– Hollywood	1,018	398	11.2	46.7

Source: U.S. Bureau of the Census, *State and Metropolitan Area Data Book 1982.*

heim–Santa Ana–Garden Grove; San Diego; Los Angeles–Long Beach;
and Riverside–San Bernardino–Ontario. Florida had two metropolitan
areas to make the top ten list, including the Tampa–St. Petersburg and
Ft. Lauderdale–Hollywood SMSAs.[20]

Housing Construction and Occupancy Trends

Housing construction in the South grew by more than 40 percent in
the seventies. Home construction in a number of southern SMSAs barely
kept pace with housing demand in the seventies. High demand contributed to the rise in housing costs. The value of owner-occupied housing
rose most rapidly in metropolitan areas where demand for home ownership was strongest, namely, the South and West. Median family income

more than doubled between 1967 and 1979, while the price of single-family homes tripled over the same period. Median sales price of homes nationally rose from $20,000 in 1967 to over $60,000 in 1979. In 1975, one-half of the nation's white families and one-third of the nation's black families could afford the average price of a home, which sold for $36,750. But by 1979, less than one-half of the nation's white families and less than one-fourth of the nation's black families could afford the average price of a house (new and older homes), which sold for $57,000. An even smaller percentage of the nation's families could afford the price of a new home in 1979; only 15 percent of white families and 10 percent of black families could afford the average price of a new home, which sold for more than $70,000.[21]

Home ownership continues to be an integral part of the American Dream. The United States has made significant gains in the area of promoting home ownership. Prior to World War II, for example, America was primarily a nation of renters: only 45 percent of all housing units then were owner occupied. Over two-thirds of the nation's households currently own their homes. The shift from a nation of renters to that of homeowners has not been equally distributed across all population groups. Specifically, blacks as a group have not fully shared in the benefits that accrue to home ownership. Black home ownership rates have continued to lag behind that of whites.

Black home ownership rates have increased over the past four decades. Only 23 percent of black households owned their homes in 1940, compared with 46 percent of white households. The 1960 home ownership rates increased to 38 percent for blacks and to 64 percent for whites. Black home ownership rates increased from 42 percent in 1970 to 44 percent in 1980; white home ownership rates were 65 percent in 1970 and 68 percent in 1980.[22] The major factors that contributed to boosting home ownership were rising income, high rates of marriage and household formation, and federal government programs and tax incentives designed to facilitate home purchases.

Black home ownership grew at a faster rate than for whites during the seventies. Black homeowners numbered around 2.6 million in 1970 and 3.7 million in 1980, or a 45-percent increase. On the other hand, the number of white homeowners rose from 37 million to 46.7 million, or a 26-percent increase between 1970 and 1980.[23] Black home ownership rates also vary by region. The black home ownership rate is highest in

Table 1.5
Home Ownership Rates by Census Region, 1980

| Census Region | Home Ownership Rate (percent) | | | Difference in Percentage Points Whites-Blacks |
	All Households	Whites	Blacks	
Unites States	64.4	67.8	44.4	23.4
Northeast	59.0	63.3	31.1	32.2
North Central	68.8	71.6	44.1	27.1
South	67.0	70.7	50.5	20.2
West	60.3	72.4	39.9	32.5

Source: U.S. Bureau of the Census, *State and Metropolitan Area Data Book 1982.*

the South. This regional difference has existed for some time. The regional differences in black home ownership actually increased in the past four decades as a result of larger gains made in ownership by southern blacks. For example, over 24 percent of blacks in the South owned their homes in 1940, compared with 19 percent of blacks in the North and West. The rates in 1960 showed that 42 percent of blacks in the South and 35 percent of blacks in the North and West owned their homes. Comparable figures for 1970 revealed that 47 percent of blacks in the South and 36 percent of blacks in the North and West were homeowners. [24]

The 1980 black home ownership rates were consistent with the earlier pattern. More than one-half of the blacks in the South owned their homes in 1980. Black home ownership rate was 44.4 percent in the North Central region, 39.9 percent in the West, and only 31.1 percent in the Northeast (see Table 1.5) The gap between black ownership in the South and the Northeast was more than 19.4 percentage points in 1980. While black ownership lagged behind that of their white counterparts in all four census regions, the black-white home ownership gap was smallest in the South.

Black home ownership rates in southern SMSAs were generally higher than the national home ownership rate for blacks (see Table 1.6). For example, 54 percent of the black households in the Jacksonville, Florida, SMSA and nearly 53 percent of the blacks in the Birmingham SMSA

Table 1.6

Home Ownership Rates and Housing Gains in Selected Southern
Metropolitan Areas, 1980

| SMSA | 1980 Home Ownership Rate (percent) | | Housing Units (× 1,000) | | |
	Total SMSA	Blacks	1980	1970	Percent Change
Houston	58.8	47.2	1,160	673	72.4
New Orleans	53.8	35.2	455	346	31.6
Memphis	60.3	47.3	332	256	29.8
Atlanta	61.4	41.8	769	515	49.2
Dallas–Fort Worth	62.3	46.6	1,174	810	45.0
Birmingham	67.6	52.9	320	254	26.2
Jacksonville, FL	65.4	54.0	290	174	66.6
Richmond	63.6	49.5	241	140	41.7
Nashville–Davidson	65.1	45.4	319	231	38.4
Tampa–St. Petersburg	63.9	49.9	745	432	72.5

Source: U.S. Bureau of the Census, *State and Metropolitan Area Data Book: 1982* (Washington, D.C.: U.S. Government Printing Office, 1982).

owned their homes in 1980. Just under one-half of the blacks in the Richmond, Memphis, and Houston metropolitan areas were homeowners.

Much of the housing growth during the seventies occurred in the metropolitan areas of the South. The South added over 2.9 million housing units in the 1970s. The West added 2.5 million units, the North Central region added 1.3 million units, and the Northeast added the fewest with 859,000 units. While most of the southern SMSAs experienced growth in their housing stock during the seventies, the largest increases (number of new units) were registered in the Houston, Dallas–Ft. Worth, and Tampa–St. Petersburg metropolitan areas. These three SMSAs were classic examples of the southern Sunbelt housing boom. Home builders could barely keep up with the demand for single-family homes in these three areas. The Houston metropolitan area, for example, was the leader in the absolute number of housing units added during this era. More than 487,000 new housing units were added in the Houston area between 1970 and 1980, or a 72-percent increase.

Even with all of the housing construction taking place in the southern United States, black southerners were still more likely to be ill housed than their white counterparts. The South was the only region that showed a marked difference between black and white housing quality. As late as 1975, over 15 percent of black households and 3 percent of white households in the South had incomplete plumbing facilities; by contrast, only 2 percent of the black and white housing units in the North and West had incomplete plumbing.[25]

A large portion of the housing in the rural South remained inadequate. This was especially the case of housing in the southern Black Belt counties of the Old South. The term *Black Belt* originally referred to the black soil in the area, which was very suitable to agricultural production. It was later known for the large concentration of blacks who lived along the broad belt that stretched from South Carolina through Georgia, Alabama, Mississippi, and Louisiana, to East Texas. Black housing inadequacy was by no means limited to the rural areas. This problem has been increasing in the region's large urban centers. Many unincorporated black communities in the South have been annexed as part of the region's expanding metropolitan areas. However, annexation of black communities into southern cities has not guaranteed these communities a share of the housing and residential amenities provided to other city residents. Racial discrimination still exists and often influences allocation of housing and other city services.[26]

Finally, the boom in the South during the 1970s provided millions of families and individuals a chance to acquire a stake in the American Dream. However, a sizable share of the black community in the South was untouched by the new growth and new prosperity. The benefits that accrued to new industries locating in the region were not equally spread across all segments of the population. Additionally, southern ghettos expanded their boundaries at the same time that the region was experiencing a housing boom. Many of the southern ghetto areas now easily rival those of the North in terms of poverty, crowding, youth unemployment, crime, and other social problems. One need only to visit Houston's Fourth and Fifth Wards, Atlanta's Vine City, or the black ghettos in Tampa, Birmingham, Memphis, and New Orleans to see the picture of poverty. These and other black communities were passed over by the boom of the seventies. The economic recessions of the 1980s have pushed them even further down the economic pecking order and have locked many of their residents in an unending cycle of poverty.[27]

Institutionalized discrimination continued to deny a significant portion of the South's population an equitable share of the region's wealth. This pattern prevailed in the Old South, as well as in the heyday of the region's growth and boom period of the 1970s, the era of the New South, and in the bust period of the mid-eighties. A large and growing black underclass remains outside the economic mainstream.[28] While many of the overt manifestations of racial discrimination no longer exist, the more subtle forms of discrimination have produced similar results.

The above discussion has offered a backdrop for exploring the changes that have taken place in the six southern cities that form the basis for this study. The first city to be discussed in this volume is Houston. It is fitting for Houston to lead, since it is the region's largest city and has the South's largest black community.

1
Blacks in Heavenly Houston

Robert D. Bullard

Historical Background

Houston to many observers was the premier Sunbelt city during the seventies. The city was founded in 1836 by two New York businessmen, Augustus and John Kirby Allen, and was a "raw and explosive town where economic competition was ruthless."[1] The Allen brothers were sure that the newly settled town would attract settlers from across the region. The black presence has been in Houston from the very beginning. The townsite was cleared by black slaves and Mexican laborers because it was feared that "no white man could have worked and endured the insect bites and malaria, snake bites, impure water, and other hardships."[2] The black slave population in the city remained small up until the 1860s. The black slaves worked largely as domestic servants. However, small numbers of blacks worked in the trades and on the wharves.[3] After Emancipation Day in Texas (June 19, 1865, or "Juneteenth"), a steady stream of blacks began migrating to Houston to fill the growth demand for labor.[4]

Many newly freed slaves migrated to Houston and settled in a part of the city's Fourth Ward, which was later referred to as Freedmen's Town. Houston's Freedmen's Town neighborhood became the hub of black community life in the city. The area became a thriving center of black business, commerce, and cultural activity during the twenties. More than 95 percent of the city's black-owned businesses were found in the Fourth Ward.[5] San Felipe Street (later renamed West Dallas Street) was the heart of the neighborhood's business district. This neighborhood had its own community facility, Pilgrim Temple, which provided offices for the city's black professionals, social and cultural events, and the office of the Houston Negro Chamber of Commerce. This black landmark was demolished in the sixties as a result of construction of Interstate 45 and the elevated streets.

Unrestrained capitalism served as a magnet to attract settlers from all over the country. Houston's population grew from a mere 2,396 residents in 1850 to over 44,633 in 1900.[6] One of the early boosters of Houston as a city of opportunity for blacks was *The Informer*, a black weekly newspaper. The newspaper took an aggressive stance in selling blacks on Houston. *The Informer* in the 1920s underscored the idea that blacks could expect "unexcelled industrial opportunities" in the city, which it affectionately tagged "Heavenly Houston."[7] The growing black population in the city intensified the prejudices of whites toward blacks. The era of Jim Crow was set into motion to control blacks and to institutionalize racial discrimination. Despite the evils of Jim Crowism, blacks were sold on the idea of Heavenly Houston and continued to migrate to the city. Houston's black workers were restricted primarily to traditional "Negro jobs" as domestic servants, yardmen, and unskilled laborers. Racism permeated every institution in the city, including housing, education, employment, and politics.

Over the years, blacks gradually lost control of the land in the Freedmen's Town and the Fourth Ward through delinquent taxes, foreclosures, sale of heir property, and outright swindles. The bulk of the black property was lost during the Great Depression. By 1930, most of the land had passed from the hands of former slaves and their descendants. The fifties, sixites, and seventies saw a rapid deterioration of the neighborhood and the out-migration of its young and better-educated residents. Although few blacks owned property in the Fourth Ward in 1985, a legacy of the neighborhood lives on in its churches. The most notable church in the area is Antioch Baptist Church, which is listed in the National Register of Historic Places. Antioch Baptist Church dates back to the 1860s and is the oldest black Baptist church in Texas.[8] The church's first full-time pastor, Reverend John "Jack" Yates, was a well-known and respected leader in Texas. Antioch Baptist Church and another black church, Trinity Methodist Church, were instrumental in purchasing the land for Emancipation Park in 1872 to commemorate the freeing of the slaves in Texas. Emancipation Park endures as a landmark in Houston's black community and serves as a main site for the city's annual Juneteenth celebration.

In addtion to the Fourth Ward, other wards have special meaning for

Houston's black population. For example, the Third and Fifth wards both have a rich history as black neighborhoods. Just as West Dallas Street was strongly associated with Houston's Fourth Ward, Dowling Street and Lyons Avenue were likewise associated with the Third Ward and Fifth Ward, respectively. These two wards emerged as predominantly black areas as a result of increased housing demands and population increases in the post–World War II era. The boundaries of these neighborhoods later expanded as black families sought housing in other areas. Blacks in the 1960s began to move southward from the Third Ward and northward from the Fifth Ward. The concentration of the city's black population along this corridor, northeast to southeast, could still be found in the mid-eighties.

Smaller black neighborhoods were also found on the periphery of the city. These neighborhoods were often isolated and received few, if any, city services. Some of the black neighborhoods that were found on Houston's fringe included Chocolate Bayou Estate, Blue Ridge, Sunnyside, Pleasantville, Galena Manor, Carvercrest, Bordersville, and Riceville.[9] Henry A. Bullock, a well-known sociologist at Texas Southern Univeristy, described Houston's black neighborhoods as areas that are "more than sheer aggregates of people" but are areas where "the people have strong loyalties."[10]

Strong competition and rivalries developed among Houston's black neighborhoods. Rivalry was probably most pronounced in athletic competition between neighborhood high schools. Athletic competition between Phyllis Wheatley High School of the Fifth Ward and Jack Yates High School of the Third Ward epitomized this neighborhood rivalry. Competition between these two schools represented something more than a sports event or game but, indeed, represented the entire neighborhood. These schools were the "flagship" institutions of their respective neighborhoods and commanded a great deal of loyalty from the local residents.

Population and Metropolitan Growth

The Houston metropolitan area was composed of nearly 2.9 million persons in 1980. There were over a half million blacks in the Houston area, or 18.2 percent of the six-county (Harris, Fort Bend, Brazoria,

Table 2.1
City of Houston Total Black Population, 1900–1980

Year	Total Population	Black Population	Percent Black
1900	44,633	14,608	32.7
1910	78,800	23,929	30.4
1920	138,276	33,960	24.6
1930	292,352	63,337	21.7
1940	384,514	86,302	21.4
1950	596,163	125,400	21.0
1960	938,219	215,037	22.9
1970	1,232,802	316,552	25.7
1980	1,595,138	440,346	27.6

Source: U.S. Bureau of the Census, *Census of Population and Housing* (Washington, D.C.: U.S. Government Printing Office, 1900–1980).

Montgomery, Liberty, and Waller counties) metropolitan area. Houston's population stood at 1.6 million persons, with over 440,346 blacks, about 28 percent of the city population, in 1980. The city's black population has been expanding since the turn of the century. For example, there were 14,608 blacks in Houston, or 32.7 percent of the city's population, in 1900 (see Table 2.1). While Houston's black population increased over the years, early black population growth was outpaced by the large in-migration of whites and the city's aggressive annexation of outlying areas. It was not until 1960 that the percentage of blacks in the Houston population actually showed an increase. Houston's black community during the seventies was the fastest-growing and largest black community in the South. Its black population grew from 316,551 in 1970 to 440,346 in 1980, a 39-percent increase.

The Houston metropolitan area included nearly 1.2 million housing units in 1980, up from 673,000 in 1970. Most of the new single-family home construction occurred in the western half of the city and in the suburban areas where land was less expensive. Many of Houston's black households remained "trapped" in older and deteriorating neighborhoods during this period. Moreover, the housing market response to increased competition for limited resources placed low-income and black residents at a disadvantage in securing decent and affordable housing.

Such factors as housing discrimination, loss of rental housing stock in the central city, high cost of single-family homes, and rediscovery of near-town neighborhoods diminished the housing choices available to inner-city blacks.

Recent data on home ownership reveal that nearly one-half (47.2 percent) of the Houston area blacks owned their homes in 1980, compared with nearly two-thirds (62.8 percent) of the whites in the Houston metropolitan area.[11] While the overall housing picture boomed in Houston during the seventies, a sizable segment of the area's population continued to be ill housed. This was especially the case for the city's black and brown communities. More than 20 percent of the city's households were inadequately housed in the 1970s. The city's blacks were twice as likely to be inadequately housed when compared with the area's whites.[12]

Housing and Residential Patterns

Residential segregation became the dominant housing pattern early in Houston's history. Racially identifiable neighborhoods became more pronounced "during the period of 1875 to 1930 where there were two separate societies (black and white) connected only by economic necessity."[13] A 1929 Houston City Planning Commission report strongly endorsed rigid separation of the races. The report stated that "because of long established racial prejudices, it is best for both races that living areas be segregated."[14]

Houston's black community, though it is no longer confined to the wards, remains residentially segregated from the larger community. Houston's black community is located in an hourglass-shaped belt that extends from the south central and southeast portions of the city into the north central and northeast sections of the city. Blacks live largely in the eastern half of the city, with smaller enclaves in northwest and southwest Houston. The city's black population is residentially segregated in historically black neighborhoods, as well as in those that have recently undergone racial transition due to "white flight." More than 93 percent of the city's blacks lived in black majority areas in 1970. By 1980, Houston's segregation level had declined by 12 percentage points; still, 81 percent of Houston's blacks lived in areas where blacks were in the majority.[15]

The black population in the Houston metropolitan area is confined largely to neighborhoods in the central city. While blacks have been moving to the suburbs, the black share of Houston's suburban population actually declined during the 1960–80 period. For example, the black share of Houston's suburban population dropped from 12 percent in 1960 to 8.8 percent in 1970. Blacks comprised only 6.2 percent of Houston's suburban population in 1980.[16] Suburban housing construction in the seventies expanded housing options largely for white Houstonians.

Black suburbanization often meant successive spillover from black neighborhoods or an extension of the segregated housing patterns that typified the central city.[17] Many blacks who moved to Houston's suburbs have been resegregated. A number of suburban neighborhoods that were racially integrated in the seventies have become predominantly black in the eighties. This was especially true for a number of neighborhoods in the South Main and Hiram Clarke areas as well as in northeast Houston. A number of older black suburban enclaves have been encircled in a "sea of whiteness." Residents of these older settlement areas received few benefits from the rapid buildup in housing during the seventies. Houston's Riceville and Bordersville neighborhoods are classic cases of black areas that were left out of the city's construction boom. These two neighborhoods lacked running water, sewer and gas hookups, sidewalks and paved streets, storm drainage, and regular garbage pickup as late as 1980.[18]

The rediscovery of near-town neighborhoods (accelerated by such factors as the rising energy costs, the spiraling cost of housing construction and previously owned homes, and the desire to live close in) resulted in much-improved physical amenities in a number of inner-city Houston neighborhoods. However, neighborhood revitalization efforts often fostered racial and ethnic exclusion as well as residential displacement of incumbent residents. Revitalization activities were undertaken in a number of Houston neighborhoods, including the Binz, Heights, Montrose, Sixth Ward, Harrisburg, and Third Ward areas. Revitalization activities affected a disproportionate number of elderly, minority, and renter households.[19]

Near-town neighborhoods in Houston became "hot" in the seventies. In short, neighborhoods that were once given up as families made their move to the suburbs were reclaimed and "gentrified." Low- and moderate-income families who could not afford to purchase housing in these neighborhoods were caught between the rising housing costs that resulted from increased demand and the dwindling supply of low-cost housing.[20] The fears and anxieties of being displaced were prevalent in several black Houston neighborhoods. Residents of Houston's Riceville, Bordersville, Fourth Ward, and Third Ward neighborhoods, for example, all shared the common struggle of trying to maintain a sense of residential stability while their areas were under siege from commercial encroachment.

A classic example of a neighborhood under siege is Houston's Fourth Ward. The fate of the city's oldest black neighborhood has been uncertain for several decades because of the small number of homeowners in the neighborhood. As blacks gradually lost ownership rights to the land in the neighborhood, they lost leverage in determining the future of the area. The neighborhood is adjacent to Houston's central business district and occupies some of the most valuable real estate in the city. The incumbent residents of the Fourth Ward are vulnerable to residential displacement, since the vast majority of residents are black, poor, elderly, and renters. The neighborhood has been allowed to decline over the years with few infrastructure improvements. Some commercial and residential development has occurred on the southern edge of the neighborhood, but for the most part, the Fourth Ward stands as one of the worst urban ghettos in the nation.

Houston's Fifth Ward has not escaped the effects of long-term neighborhood decline. The Fifth Ward lies in the heart of Texas's Eighteenth Congressional District and is just north of Houston's central business district. The development of this neighborhood dates back to the early 1860s, with major growth taking place during the late nineteenth and early twentieth centuries.[21] By the onset of World War II, the neighborhood changed from predominantly white to predominantly black. Residents of the neighborhood often referred to the area as "Fifth Ward Texas," since it was Houston's most-populated black neighborhood.[22] In 1950, more than 40,680 blacks lived in the Fifth Ward. The neighborhood once boasted a thriving retail area along Lyons Avenue. The social and economic vitality of the area was severely disrupted with the construction of two major freeway systems, Interstate 10 and U.S. Highway 59. Many residents were physically cut off from the core of the Lyons Avenue–Jensen Avenue commercial district.

As blacks gained access to public facilities and businesses throughout the city, many of the black-owned firms along the Lyons–Jensen commercial corridor declined. Black business entrepreneurs no longer had a captive clientele of black customers, as had existed during the days of legalized segregation. A substantial number of businesses closed their doors or moved to other locations. Crime and fear of victimization accelerated the disinvestment cycle and the atmosphere of economic abandonment.

The Fifth Ward was included in both the city's Community Development Block Grant program and its Economic Development Target Area program. However, residents have received few benefits from either one of these programs. Such problems as a shrinking supply of low-cost housing, high rates of unemployment and underemployment, inadequate public services, and industrial encroachment in its residential area are still critical concerns in the city's Fifth Ward. Although the neighborhood may have more than its share of problems, there still exists a strong determination of its residents to survive and make their neighborhood a better place to live.[23] Given the adversities and hardships that exist in the neighborhood, the area continues to make its mark on the social, cultural, and political lives of blacks in the city.

The enduring problem of discrimination operated in limiting the housing options available to black households. The city passed a Fair Housing Ordinance in 1975, seven years after the federal Fair Housing Act of 1968. A total of 1,617 housing discrimination complaints were filed with the city's Fair Housing Division between 1975 and 1983. More than 75 percent of these complaints were filed by blacks, while blacks comprised only 28 percent of the city's population in 1980.[24]

Housing discrimination complaint acctivity in the 1970s came largely from renters. The volume of complaints also corresponded to the growth patterns within the city. For example, housing discrimination complaints were more frequent in the southwestern quadrant of the city, where multifamily housing construction was concentrated. Conversely, complaint activity was lowest in areas of high minority concentrations and in areas that experienced a decrease in housing units.[25]

Housing for low- and moderate-income families did not increase dramatically in the past decade. In 1978, Houston had a total of 8,702 low-income housing units that received some type of housing subsidy.[26] However, more than 22 percent of the city's households could have qualified for housing assistance. The Houston Housing Authority's waiting list for public housing has averaged more than 5,000 persons since the mid-seventies. Houston had a total of 9,893 units of subsidized housing in its 1983 inventory. The local housing authority managed 4,077 units of public housing in fifteen developments. It also provided rent subsidies for an additional 5,816 housing units. Overall, the Houston Housing Authority served more than 25,000 persons in 1983.[27]

Economic Change

Houston as late as 1980 had the twenty-third-lowest cost of living of the twenty-five major metropolitan areas in the United States. In addition, the Houston SMSA ranked fifteenth nationally on per capita income in 1978, a jump from seventy-sixth place in 1969.[28] The relatively low cost of living combined with the potential for earning an above-average income made Houston an ideal place for those seeking expanding opportunities in the 1970s. The median income of black Houstonians in 1980 was $15,442, while the median income for whites in the city was $25,669. This represented a $10,227 income gap separating the two groups.[29] The average black Houston family earned approximately 60 percent of what its white counterpart earned in 1980. The median income of black Houston families, however, compared favorably with the national median income of all families in the United States, which was $19,908. Houston's black median family income was nearly 77 percent of the national median.

The poverty rate in Houston was close to the national average in 1980, which was 12 percent. Blacks in Houston were nearly three and one-half times as likely to be found in poverty as were their white counterparts. A little over 6 percent of the area's whites fell below the poverty level, compared with a little over 20 percent of black Houstonians. The more than 117,000 poor blacks make up a sizable portion of the area's population.

Poverty exists as a social problem amid the sparkling glass and steel towers of Houston. The problems that accompany urban poverty are not new to Houston. Houston's black poverty pockets are the invisible Houston, a city hidden within the well-publicized city of traffic and shopping centers. City leaders for years refused to participate in federal urban renewal programs for fear of government "interference" from Washington. Efforts to ameliorate the problems of the poor in low-income Houston neighborhoods, through such programs as Model Cities and Community Development Block Grants, have achieved mixed results.[30] The Community Development Block Grant (CDBG) program was established under Title I of the Housing and Community Development Act of 1974 by the U.S. Congress, and the city of Houston became involved in the CDBG program in 1975. Houston received more than $251 million in grants during the period from 1975 to 1986. Local program administrators have had trouble spending the poverty funds fast enough. This has been a constant criticism from the U.S. Department of Housing and Urban Development. The Houston CDBG program has had minimal effect in reversing the physical decline of the city's low-income and minority areas.

The federally funded local jobs program under the Comprehensive Employment and Training Act of 1973, CETA, was another program designed to help Houston's hard-core unemployed and underemployed become full-time workers in better-paying jobs. Houston's CETA program was supposed to locate and process its clients, make them "job ready," provide skill and on-the-job training, and locate and place its clients in jobs. The program had marginal, if any, effect on the wage scale and employment status of its participants. Participants in the CETA program often remained unemployed or in low-paying, dead-end jobs such as picking up litter and debris along roads, cutting grass, and other unskilled laborer positions. In many cases, the "trained" workers were no better off than prior to their training. Houston's CETA program was mired in controversy that often centered on the handling of funds, the selection of participants, and the cost-benefit of the federal manpower training program.

The problems that afflicted Houston's manpower program were not unique, since they were present in a number of other cities. They were in fact so widespread that Congress, in 1983, enacted the Job Training Partnership Act as a replacement for CETA. Houston's CETA program was phased out in 1984, and the Houston Job Training and Partnership Council (HJTPC) program took its place. The HJTPC program emphasized privatization and voluntarism in creating a partnership between business and government. The program served 12,000 individuals and placed more than 5,000 individuals in private-sector jobs in 1985. The HJTPC program exceeded its predicted job placement by 15 percent in 1985.[31]

Row houses, also known as "shotgun" houses, in Houston's Fourth Ward, 1983. (Photograph by Earlie Hudnall)

The commitment to eliminate poverty has diminished over the years at the federal and local level and has been manifested in the indiscriminate budget cuts for social programs. These programs can be cut or monies diverted to projects outside CDBG target areas because the poor have few allies in decision-making positions. Houston's CDBG program for the years 1980–85 has seen a 29-percent reduction in funds. Congress funded the program through 1988; after that no one knows what federal support will be given to cities. Budget cuts within Houston's city government because of revenue shortfalls have reduced needed services, such as neighborhood clinics and capital improvement projects in low-income areas.

Houston during the seventies was a leader in the creation of jobs. The Houston SMSA, for example, added more than 669,700 new nonagricultural jobs between 1970 and 1980. The Houston area produced more than 107,700 new jobs in 1978 (its peak year); 93,300 new jobs in 1979; and 59,700 new jobs in 1980. The employment gains were concentrated in finance, insurance, real estate, services, and the trade industries. The Houston area unemployment rate during this same period averaged significantly lower than the national average. The unemployment rate for the Houston SMSA was 4 percent in 1979, 3.3 percent in 1980, and 4.2 percent in 1980.[32] The area's black workers, however, were still more likely to be unemployed than were white workers. The distribution of blacks in the Houston area work force also differed from that of whites (see Table 2.2). Twenty percent of the area's blacks were employed in service occupations, compared with less than 10 percent of Houston area whites. On the other hand, whites in metropolitan Houston were two times more likely than blacks to have managerial and professional occupations in 1980.

The sluggish economic conditions that had existed in the black Houston community during the seventies were worsened by the economic recessions of the early eighties. The unemployment rate for Houston's whites was 6.5 percent in 1982, compared with 11.2 percent for blacks. The 1983 unemployment rate for whites increased to 7.6 percent, while the black unemployment rate skyrocketed to 22.7 percent the same year.[33] Black workers were three times more likely to be unemployed than their white counterparts. The unemployment gap between blacks and whites actually widened during the 1982 recessions. The black unemployment rate was 4.7 percentage points higher than the white rate in

Antioch Missionary Baptist Church (founded 1866), 1984 with downtown skyline in the background. (Photograph by R.D. Bullard)

1982, but was 15.1 percentage points higher in 1983. Black Houstonians have been troubled with double-digit unemployment through the mid-eighties. Nearly one-fifth (19.2 percent) of Houston's black work force, compared with 8.9 percent of the white work force, was unemployed in 1986.

Houston during the seventies was the economic bright spot in the region. This was the case for job creation and business expansion. On the other hand, the city's sluggish economy in the first half of the 1980s produced a record number of business failures and bankruptcies. For many, Houston in the eighties became "Busttown." Economic hard times, however, were not new to many of the city's older black neighborhoods. The neighborhoods of the Fourth and Fifth wards, Settegast, Acres Homes, Sunnyside, and Carverdale were all passed over during the city's boom era.

Black Houstonians not only had difficulty finding employment but also had to contend with the "last hired, first fired" phenomenon that often

Table 2.2
Employed Persons Sixteen Years Old and Over by Occupation for
Blacks and Whites in the Houston SMSA, 1980

Occupations	Whites (percent)	Blacks (percent)
Managerial and professional	27.6	13.5
Technical, sales, and administrative	35.7	28.2
Service occupations	7.6	20.5
Crafts, operatives, and laborers	28.3	36.9
Farm, forestry, and fishing	0.8	0.9
Total all occupations (number)	1,101,920	232,871
Total percent	100.0	100.0

Source: U.S. Bureau of the Census, *General Social and Economic Characteristics: Texas*
(Washington, D.C.: U.S.Government Printing Office, 1983).

becomes an active policy of employers during economic recession. This
is the case for both private- and public-sector employers. The task of
coming up with an employee layoff plan during economic hard times is
complicated by seniority systems and affirmative action programs. However, because of institutionalized discrimination, seniority does not nec-

Local protest against apartheid and South African Airways, 1983. (Photograph
by R.D. Bullard)

U.S. Congressman George "Mickey" Leland, 1983. (Courtesy of Texas Southern University Archives)

essarily translate into job security for black workers. In a budget-cutting measure, the city of Houston laid off 770 employees in July 1986. Most of these city workers were from the health, library, parks, and solid waste departments (workers at the lower end of the city's pay scale and heavily minority). Nearly 60 percent of those laid off were black. Whites constituted 47 percent of the city's work force, but only 18 percent of those laid off were white.[34]

The lingering economic recession had a devastating effect on many once-stable moderate- and middle-income black neighborhoods. These neighborhoods in the mid-eighties were replete with foreclosures, for-sale signs, boarded-up storefronts, empty strip shopping centers, business failures, and thousands of idle black job seekers. The economic woes exacted a heavy toll in terms of social and human costs.

The 1970s did see Houston's black-owned businesses make some impressive gains despite the economic recessions. The national ranking of black business firms (by the number of businesses) in the Houston SMSA shifted between 1977 and 1982. For example, the number of black businesses in the Houston SMSA ranked seventh in 1977 and fifth in 1982.[35] Houston ranked fourth among major cities in terms of (1) the number of black-owned firms, (2) the number of black-owned firms with paid employees, and (3) the gross receipts generated by black-owned business enterprises. Houston's black-owned firms grew from 5,104 in 1977 to 10,019 in 1982 (see Table 2.3). The gross receipts generated by Houston's black businesses jumped from $141 million in 1977 to more than $283 million in 1982.

The city's black firms continued to be clustered around the services and retail trade businesses. Services and retail trade firms accounted for nearly two-thirds of Houston's black-owned business enterprises in 1977 and 1982. The distribution of black-owned business enterprises in Houston mirrored the national trend of underrepresentation in manufacturing, wholesale, finance, insurance and real estate. As black communities across the nation attempted to stimulate reinvestment and redevelopment activities in declining areas, black lending institutions took on added importance. Black lending institutions (banks, savings and loan associations, and mortgage companies) provided needed loans to black homeowners and business entrepreneurs in redlined neighborhoods. There were forty-eight black banks in the nation in 1980. Three of these black banks were located in Texas: Riverside Bank in Houston, First Texas Bank in Dallas, and National Security Bank in Tyler. The eco-

Table 2.3
Distribution of Houston's Black-Owned Firms, 1977–82

| Industry | 1977 | | 1982 | |
Classification	Number	Percent	Number	Percent
Agricultural	—	—	90	0.9
Construction	498	9.8	679	6.8
Manufacturing	39	0.8	52	0.5
Transportation and utilities	757	14.8	1,052	10.5
Wholesale trade	24	0.5	53	0.5
Retail trade	1,203	23.5	2,162	21.6
Finance, insurance, and real estate	214	4.2	409	4.1
Selected services	2,047	40.1	4,235	42.3
Other industries and not classified	322	6.3	1,287	12.8
Total	5,104	100.0	10,019	100.0

Source: U.S. Bureau of the Census, *1982 Survey of Minority-Owned Business Enterprises: Black* (Washington, D.C.: U.S. Government Printing Office, 1982).

nomic recessions of the early and mid-eighties had a devastating effect on two of them. National Security Bank in Tyler was declared insolvent in 1982, and Riverside Bank in Houston closed its doors in 1985. Houston celebrated its 150th birthday in 1986, the much-publicized sesquicentennial, without a single black-owned bank.

Houston's Riverside Bank was founded in 1963 and was located in the heart of the city's Third Ward. It was the nation's twenty-eighth-largest black-owned bank in 1980, with assets of $15 million. The bank increased its assets to $18.3 million in 1982, making it the twenty-fifth-largest black-owned bank in the country at the time.[36] While Houston's black community emerged as the largest of its type in the South, Riverside Bank was one of the smallest black banks in the region.

Hard economic times, combined with low black patronage, figured largely in the demise of Riverside Bank. Low black patronage can be attributed largely to the social changes that occurred in the sixties. When Riverside Bank was founded in the early sixties, civil rights issues were on the national agenda, but Houston lagged behind cities that were in

Houston Police Chief Lee P. Brown, 1983. (Courtesy of Texas Southern University Archives)

the forefront of the civil rights movement. Houston's black leadership was conservative compared with the leaders in such cities as Birmingham, Montgomery, Atlanta, Memphis, Nashville, and Richmond; this was apparent in the fact that Houston was one of the only major cities in the nation that did not explode in the sixties, even after the assassination of Dr. Martin Luther King, Jr., in 1968. Strong loyalties between Houston's large and conservative black community and its black bank never materialized. The opposite was true in Richmond, which had a black bank as early as 1903; Nashville, in 1904; Atlanta, in 1921; and Memphis, in 1946.

Public accommodation concessions were made by city government and local white-owned businesses to black Houstonians in the sixties. These concessions further weakened the economic bond between Riverside Bank and the black community. The black community expanded and became more decentralized, moving outside the traditional wards, in the seventies and eighties. This population expansion was in part due to the in-migration of individuals from outside the region and from the adjoining states, individuals who had little knowledge of or few loyalties to Riverside Bank or the city's other black-owned businesses.

Houston in 1983, for the first time, had two firms to make the coveted *Black Enterprise* "Top 100 Black Businesses" list: Smith Pipe Companies (ranked fourteenth) and Frenchy's Po-Boy (ranked eighty-ninth). Smith Pipe, an oil supply firm, boomed with the Houston economy. The company in 1980 had sales over $48 million, making it the seventh-largest black-owned business in the nation. The oil glut and economic recession beginning in 1981 had a dramatic impact on small oil supply firms, including Smith Pipe. Smith Pipe's sales dropped to $35 million in 1982[37] and plummeted to less than $4 million in 1983.

Frenchy's Po-Boy, a fast-food chain specializing in Louisiana Creole-style chicken, replaced Smith Pipe as the largest black business in Houston in 1983. Frenchy's Po-Boy's sales totaled $8.3 million in 1982 and $9.5 million in 1983. This fast-food chain expanded from its original location in the heart of Houston's Third Ward (between Texas Southern University and the University of Houston) to locations throughout the Houston metropolitan area. By the summer of 1984, there were eleven locations in the Houston area. The economic recessions in 1985 and 1986, however, forced Frenchy's Po-Boy to close several restaurants because of falling sales.

Many black-owned businesses flourished under the the city's segregated system. The strategy of "integration" dealt a severe blow to many small black business owners who under Jim Crowism had a captive clientele. However, desegregation of public facilities, department stores, and lunch counters became a reality in the 1960s. The next barrier to come down was desegregation of the city's dual public school system.

School Desegregation

Educational institutions in Houston, as was true in most of the South, were segregated along racial lines. This was true for elementary, secondary, and postsecondary schools. Educational facilities for blacks were often underfunded, neglected, and poorly staffed. Racial segregation in education—separate and unequal facilities—institutionalized advantages for whites at the expense of blacks.

Higher education for blacks in Houston began in 1927 with the creation of Houston Colored Junior College, which operated under Houston's school board.[38] The junior college in 1934 was changed to a four-year institution and became Houston College for Negroes. Houston College for Negroes operated from 1934 to 1947, when it became a state-supported institution and was renamed Texas State University for Negroes.

The creation of Texas State University for Negroes as a state-supported institution for blacks was a reaction to the threat of a lawsuit by the National Association for the Advancement of Colored People (NAACP). In 1945, the NAACP was looking for a black plaintiff to challenge Texas's segregated university system. Heman Sweatt volunteered to serve as the test case for the NAACP, which targeted the University of Texas's policy of excluding blacks from its law school.[39] Sweatt, a mail carrier and a graduate of Wiley College in Marshall, was active in the local NAACP and in the National Alliance of Postal Workers, which at the time was fighting discrimination against black postal workers. These activities reinforced Sweatt's ambition to become a lawyer.[40]

While the team of NAACP lawyers was engaged in court litigation, the Texas legislature in March 1947 passed Senate Bill 140, which established a "Negro University" that would include a law school, to be located in Houston. Thus, Texas State University for Negroes was created in an effort to keep Heman Sweatt out of the University of Texas law school and, in essence, was an extension of Jim Crowism. The school's name was changed in 1951 to Texas Southern University (TSU).

The U.S. Supreme Court in *Sweatt v. Painter* resolved this case on

June 5, 1950, when it ruled that Heman Sweatt must be admitted to the University of Texas law school. The Supreme Court ruling also compelled the University of Texas and similar state institutions to admit blacks to graduate and professional schools. Two black students enrolled in the University of Texas graduate programs in the summer of 1950: Horace Heath enrolled in a doctoral program in government, and John Chase enrolled in the architecture program. Heman Sweatt enrolled in the University of Texas law school in the fall of 1950.

The *Sweatt* v. *Painter* decision was an important precedent for the famous *Brown* v. *Board of Education* decision, which in 1954 overturned the "separate but equal" doctrine established by the high court's 1896 decision in *Plessy* v. *Ferguson*. It is somewhat ironic that TSU's law school is named in honor of Thurgood Marshall, the NAACP attorney who led the challenge to Jim Crow education. Despite the Thurgood Marshall School of Law's rather dubious beginning in 1947, it has produced more than two-thirds of the black practicing attorneys in Texas.

Just one block from TSU is University of Houston, another state institution. Scott Street has served as the unofficial line of demarcation between the mostly black TSU and the mostly white University of Houston. Enrollment at TSU peaked during the mid-seventies with 9,500 students. However, the school experienced a steady enrollment decline in the late seventies through the mid-eighties. The major contributors to the decline involved the substantial drop in international student enrollment (mostly Iranians) and the tripling of tuition and fees for state institutions under guidelines passed by the Texas legislature. The predominantly black TSU was severely hurt by the tuition increase because a disproportionately large share of its students come from low-income families. The university's enrollment was close to 8,000 in 1985.

The desegregation of Houston's public schools began in 1956, two years after the landmark U.S. Supreme Court decision of *Brown* v. *Board of Education*. The NAACP filed a lawsuit on behalf of two black girls, Beneva Williams and Delores Ross, to break up the city's dual public school system. The Houston Independent School District (HISD) in 1960 was ordered by the federal court to begin a "grade-a-year" desegregation plan based on "freedom of choice." The freedom of choice plan did little to desegregate the city's schools. The federal courts in 1970 ordered HISD to develop a new model for breaking up the dual system of public education. The district submitted a modified plan in which "pairing" black and white schools was held out as a solution. This plan was later rejected by the courts because Hispanics, who at the time were counted as whites, were paired with blacks. The courts later ruled that Hispanics, or "browns," had to be considered as a separate racial/ethnic group. The district's desegregation plan was again modified with primary emphasis placed upon the majority-minority transfer program and magnet schools.[41]

The HISD experienced a dramatic demographic transition from a white majority school district in the late sixties to a predominantly minority (blacks and Hispanics) district in the eighties. The HISD experienced a 62.8-percent decline in its white pupil enrollment between 1968 and 1980. In 1970, 49.9 percent of the students were white, 35.7 percent were black, and 14.4 percent were Hispanic.[42] By the fall of 1987, only 16.3 percent of the district's students were white, 41.9 percent were black, 38.9 percent were Hispanic, and 2.9 percent were of other races (see Table 2.4). On the other hand, the Houston area suburban school districts have largely white student populations (see Table 2.5).

The desegregation of Houston's public schools has been a long and controversial struggle. Much of the controversy has centered around minority teacher hiring, teacher assignment in poor and affluent schools, and the quality of the educational programs in one-race minority schools. The Houston Area Urban League, in 1978, and black sociologist Kenneth Jackson, in 1983, observed that Houston's black and Hispanic schools have more teachers with less experience than do their white counterparts.[43]

A number of factors have contributed to the increasingly political overtones of education administration in the district: teacher discontent, teacher hiring and termination, school closings, pupil transfers, and the polarization of the school board along ideological and racial lines. The local school board administration has often been accused of trying to guarantee employment of white teachers by manipulating the so-called Singleton ratio, which refers to a 1970 court decree by the U.S. Fifth Court of Appeals decision in *Singleton v. Jackson Municipal Separate School District*. The court mandated a specified black-to-white ratio to be maintained in every school in the system. Moreover, the court required nondiscrimination in employment, demotions, and dismissals. The Singleton ratio was thus designed to protect black faculty from wholesale dismissals following desegregation attempts. The Houston school board

Table 2.4
Pupil Enrollment in the Houston Independent School District,
1970–87

Year	Total Enrollment	Race of Students (percent)			
		Black	Brown	White	Other
1970	241,138	35.7	14.4	49.9	—
1971	231,922	37.5	15.6	46.9	—
1972	225,397	39.4	16.6	44.0	—
1973	216,981	41.2	17.9	40.4	0.5
1974	211,547	41.9	19.0	38.6	0.5
1975	211,408	42.6	20.3	36.5	0.6
1976	210,025	43.1	21.8	34.2	0.9
1977	206,998	44.0	22.8	32.1	1.1
1978	201,960	45.0	24.2	29.4	1.4
1979	193,906	45.3	25.6	27.3	1.8
1980	194,043	44.9	27.8	25.1	2.2
1981	193,702	44.3	29.7	23.3	2.7
1982	194,439	44.1	30.9	21.7	3.3
1983	194,467	44.1	32.4	20.3	3.2
1984	187,031	43.6	34.2	19.0	3.2
1985	193,889	43.0	36.0	17.6	3.4
1986	193,855	42.6	37.4	16.9	3.1
1987	191,831	41.9	38.9	16.3	2.9

Source: Houston Independent School District, "Pupil Enrollment Data 1970–1984," Pupil Enrollment Division (1987).

adopted the Singleton ratio in February 1970, calling for all HISD schools to have 65 percent white teachers and 35 percent black teachers (the ratio could have a variance of 5 percent). The hiring practices of HISD was challenged in 1983 by Barbara Mathews, a black science teacher. The case was filed in U.S. District Court by attorney Linda McKeever Bullard. The lawsuit alleged that HISD engaged in racial discrimination when it turned down Mathews, who had more than four years of teaching experience, for a science position (an area where there is a national shortage of teachers) that was later given to a white. Bullard asserted that "hundreds of black college graduates are turned away while they're [HISD] recruiting whites for 'white only' positions."[44] The lawsuit

Table 2.5
Ethnic Composition of Houston and Suburban School Districts, 1980

School District	Total Enrollment	Ethnic Composition of District (percent)			
		White	Black	Hispanic	Other
Aldine	32,683	68.0	15.0	15.9	1.1
Alief	14,549	82.5	2.7	7.8	7.0
Channelview	4,366	90.0	1.0	9.0	0.0
Clear Creek	18,451	92.2	1.9	3.6	2.0
Crosby	2,398	55.0	43.0	2.0	0.0
Cypress-Fairbanks	20,233	86.9	4.2	5.7	3.1
Deer Park	8,211	91.4	0.2	7.9	0.5
Galena Park	11,648	74.0	8.0	18.0	0.0
Goose Creek	15,363	71.0	13.0	16.0	0.0
Houston	194,043	25.1	44.9	27.8	2.2
Huffman	1,878	98.0	0.0	2.0	0.0
Humble	10,700	94.5	1.7	2.7	1.1
Katy	8,899	90.0	3.0	5.0	2.0
Klein	16,751	92.0	4.0	2.4	1.6
LaPorte	6,145	82.2	7.1	9.6	1.1
North Forest	17,731	14.8	85.2	0.0	0.0
Pasadena	36,483	74.8	1.7	20.9	2.6
Pearland	5,218	83.9	0.7	15.1	0.3
Sheldon	3,835	89.7	2.0	7.8	0.5
Spring	11,347	91.7	2.8	4.1	1.4
Spring Branch	34,611	86.1	2.9	6.8	4.2
Ft. Bend	18,500	64.0	16.0	17.0	3.0
Tomball	2,980	91.0	6.0	2.0	1.0

Source: Texas Educational Agency, "Pupil Enrollment Data" (1980).

was settled out of court in 1985. In 1985, HISD began recruiting teachers from as far away as Canada and Ireland to remedy its teacher shortage problem.[45] The school district's hiring policies have been called "insulting and racist" by some of its black teachers.[46] For example, faculty hiring breakdown within HISD in 1982 revealed that 673 teachers had been hired during the summer. The ethnic composition of these teachers showed that 68 percent were white, 9 percent were black, and 28 percent were Hispanic.[47]

Houston's public schools were officially declared desegregated when
U.S. district judge Robert O'Conor ruled in 1981 that HISD was a "uni-
tary" system; this court ruling meant that HISD had done everything
possible to desegregate its schools (even though a substantial number of
the district's schools remained "one-race" schools). After more than
twenty-eight years, *Ross v. HISD*, the lawsuit that was filed by the
NAACP against HISD, was finally settled out of court in the fall of
1984. A major point in the NAACP's argument had been equal access of
minority students to the ditrict's magnet school programs. While blacks
made up more than 44 percent of the district's students, only 14 percent
of the students enrolled in the district's magnet programs were black.
The settlement agreement went to the heart of this matter, targeting district inner-city magnet schools' ratios at 60 percent minority and 40 percent white (from 50–50), and 65 percent minority and 35 percent white
after July 1985. The settlement also dealt with the issue of minority faculty recruitment.

The struggle for quality education will likely remain a key battleground because legislation, court orders, and settlement agreements have
not ended the disparate conditions under which minority students are
educated. There is continued concern that Houston's nonmagnet inner-
city schools have become "invisible" or forgotten institutions because of
the district's effort to stem white flight. Education of black children has
become a hot political issue that is not expected to go away. The political
struggle continues as blacks attempt to increase their representation on
the local school board, city council, county commissioners court, state
legislature, and other elective positions.

Black Politics

Black Houstonians have come a long way since Dr. Lonnie E. Smith,
a prominent black dentist from the Fifth Ward, was refused a ballot in
the 1940 "all-white" Harris County Democratic primary. The legal challenge to the "white primary" system culminated in the 1944 U.S. Supreme Court decision *Smith v. Allwright*, which outlawed this practice.[48]
However, it was fourteen years after *Smith v. Allwright* that the first black
was elected to a public office in Houston. Hattie Mae White, a former
schoolteacher and the wife of a prominent black doctor, was elected in

1958 to the HISD board. Asberry Butler was later elected to the HISD board in 1964. One year after the passage of the Voting Rights Act of 1965, Barbara Jordan was elected to the Texas State Senate, and Curtis Graves was elected to the Texas State House of Representatives. Judson Robinson, Jr., whose father was one of the city's pioneering black business entrepreneurs, became the first black elected to the Houston city council in 1971. The foundation for the election of these black officials was laid by such pioneering black community activists as Carter Wesley, Christin V. Adair, George Nelson, Moses and Erma LeRoy, Dr. Lonnie E. Smith, Fred Alston, Sid Hillard, John Butler, and other dedicated individuals who worked to make the black presence felt in the Harris County Democratic party.[49]

A little less than two-thirds (61 percent) of the blacks in the Houston SMSA were registered to vote in 1980, and only 49 percent actually voted in the November 1980 election. Houston's black community, "a sleeping giant," did show some level of awakening in the 1970s and 1980s. This was due mainly to intensified voter registration and voter education programs, the broadening of the black leadership base with the growth of the black middle class, and ethnic bloc voting.[50]

The period 1972-85 was especially important to black Houston's quest for political empowerment. Two decades after the passage of the Voting Rights Act, a total of twenty-nine blacks held public elective office (see Table 2.6). Houston's blacks in 1985 held elective offices at the city, county, state, and federal level. Blacks in 1985 were elected, for the first time, to Harris County Commissioners Court and the Harris County School Board of Trustees.

While Houston's black community made significant gains in the 1970–80 period, the community's resources in recent years have been directed largely at electing black males to office. This pattern was not inconsistent with that of the larger white society, where resources historically have been directed at electing white males.[51] This is not a small point when one considers the fact that the first black to be elected to a public office in Houston since Reconstruction was a woman, Hattie Mae White, and the first black from Houston to be elected to the Texas State Senate was also a woman, Barbara Jordan. As of January 1985, however, only six of the twenty-nine black elected officials in Houston were females. There can be little doubt that sexism exists in the black and white communities when it comes to the political process. It is not

Table 2.6
Black Elected Officials in Houston, January 1985

Elective Office or Government Body	Total All Houston Elected Officials	Number of Black Officials	Black Elected Officials
U.S. Congress	6	1	George "Mickey" Leland
State Senate	8	1	Craig Washington
State Representatives	26	5	Harold Dutton
			Al Edwards
			Larry Evans
			Senfronia Thompson
			Ron Wilson
Houston City Council	14	4	Rodney Ellis
			Anthony Hall
			Ernest McGowen, Sr.
			Judson Robinson, Jr.
Harris County Commissioners Court	5	1	El Franco Lee
Harris County Board of Education	7	1	Launey Roberts
State District Judge	48	3	Ken Hoyt
			John W. Peavy, Jr.
			Thomas H. Routt
Harris County Justice of the Peace	16	2	Betty Bell
			Alexander Green
Houston Independent School District Board	9	3	Wiley Henry
			Herbert Melton
			Elizabeth Spates
North Forest Independent School District Board	7	7	Patricia Alexander
			Abner Brown
			Elwin Franklin
			Fran Gentry
			Edward King
			Maxine Seals
			Joe Sample

uncommon to find black females comprising the bulk of workers in local campaigns. One only has to visit the black church, still an important institution in the black political structure, to see the level of women's involvement as foot soldiers. However, black female political candidates, in recent years, have fought an uphill battle in getting elected to public office in Houston and Harris County.

Conclusion

There is little doubt that Houston experienced phenomenal growth and prosperity in the seventies. However, many of its "poverty pockets," inhabited largely by the city's blacks, benefited little from the boom era of the seventies. Many of these older areas experienced economic decline during the height of the city's growth period. However, the problems of unemployment, neighborhood disinvestment, dwindling low- and moderate-income housing, and rising crime rates left once-stable black neighborhoods in depressionlike conditions. The recessions of the 1980s exacerbated the already dire economic conditions in many low-income black Houston neighborhoods. There is a clear need in Houston for economic development strategies that utilize black neighborhood resources, generate commercial investment, provide expanded job opportunities to incumbent residents, and improve the quality of life and quantity of housing for low- and moderate-income residents. The challenge that Houston must face in the future is how to more fully include its black and other minority communities in the economic and political mainstream.

The Houston black community as a whole was not mobilized during the civil rights movement of the sixties to the degree that many other black communities (for example, Atlanta, Memphis, Birmingham, etc.) in the South were. White business and political leaders in the early sixties made concessions to the city's black community, but the incremental changes that were put in place did not eliminate the evils of Jim Crow. Houston continues to be a racially segregated city in many respects. Black housing and public schools remain racially segregated.

The seventies through the mid-eighties saw a steady stream of blacks migrating to the city. Many of the migrants had few loyalties to the long-standing black institutions, such as Riverside Bank, Standard Savings and Loan, Texas Southern University, the Urban League and NAACP, and many other grassroots organizations found in the black community. Houston's black community in the seventies had the distinction as the largest and most affluent black community in the South. The city's black community, however, is one of contrasts: it has both a large black middle class and a large black underclass. Changing social and demographic characteristics of the black population and the expanding education and economic structure have provided opportunities for some but not all of the city's black residents. The gap between the black middle class and black underclass is widening. The key to the future of Houston's black community rests with the extent to which the city's poor are allowed to enter the economic and political mainstream.

2
New Orleans
A City That Care Forgot

Beverly Hendrix Wright

Historical Background

New Orleans has been described as a charming, romantic place that looks and feels a lot more European than American. Its history is also interesting and accounts for much of its charm and peculiarity. It is one of the oldest cities in the Deep South. This chapter examines black New Orleans by its history, beginning in the early 1700s and proceeding through the 1970s and middle 1980s.

New Orleans has a unique history. Because of the influence of several different cultures, it has boastfully been called the most European of American cities. Founded in 1718, its initial pattern represented a deliberate plan by French engineers. The city was designed in a gridiron pattern—symmetrical, with a central square facing the Mississippi River. Although the plans were laid in 1718, the grids were not populated until after 1800.[1] New Orleans was turned over to the Spanish in 1767 for approximately thirty years but was returned to the French in 1800. Many people assume that the architecture in the old French Quarter is French, but there were two great fires during the time of Spanish rule, and much of the city was rebuilt with Spanish regalia.

As a result of the official launching of the American slave trade, blacks began to appear in large numbers in New Orleans. The 1726 census recorded only 300 slaves living in the city, but by 1732, there were nearly 1,000 slaves living in New Orleans.[2] New Orleans was not only unique because of its European inhabitants, uncommon in most southern cities, but it also had a significant number of "free colored people." The first free blacks were recorded in New Orleans in the 1720s;[3] and by 1803, there were 1,335 free blacks living in the city.[4]

The European era came to an end with the purchase of the Louisiana

45

Territory by the United States in 1803. Although the United States acquired New Orleans, the Creoles (French and Spanish) remained in power. The city, however, was bound to become an American city. There were far too few Europeans to populate the city, and there was a continuing enclave of American settlers.

In 1810, the U.S. Bureau of the Census reported New Orleans as the largest city west of the Appalachians. There were only four cities larger than New Orleans, and they were on the East Coast—New York, Philadelphia, Boston, and Baltimore.[5] Unlike the four East Coast giants, New Orleans in 1810 was a predominantly black city. There were 5,727 free blacks, 8,000 whites, and 10,824 slaves.[6]

The transition of New Orleans to an American city was traumatic. Schisms were created (the legacy of which still symbolically remains). The Americans took the Creoles by storm. The Creoles, an educated, refined, and polite group of people, loathed the presence of the American frontiersmen with their rough manners and English backgrounds. The Americans thought the Creoles to be a rather odd group and hence began establishing their own neighborhoods in such places as the now-famous Garden District, a development on the west side of Canal Street.

The city was increasingly plagued with internal divisions between ethnic groups. These growing antagonisms eventually led to the city's division into three self-governing municipalities in 1836. The first municipality, with boundaries established between Canal and Esplanade streets (the French Quarter), was controlled by the Creoles; the second municipality, with boundaries west of Canal (Faubourg St. Mary), was governed by the Americans; and the third, with boundaries east of the French Quarter, was governed by immigrant farmers. This third municipality, however, had far less influence on the city's decision makers than did the first two.

The three governing municipalities eventually were found to be unmanageable and were later abandoned in 1852, but not without leaving tangible signs of their past existence. So great was the antagonism between the ethnic groups that the names of streets on one side of Canal Street changed on the other side. For example, Royal Street on the east side of Canal changes to St. Charles on the west side of Canal. Each municipality also had its own great hotel, its own square, and its own navigation canals.[7] Each municipality also had its own fiscal system and its own currency, called "shinplaster," which was used to pay employees.[8]

New Orleans acquired much of its charm from the intense ethnic loy-alties of its population, which curiously affected its growth. After the Civil War, New Orleans's black population experienced a dramatic in-crease. This resulted in the inability of many ex-slaves to find work or housing. Consequently, the poorest blacks lived where they could. They lived along the battures, or backswamps. Because the city of New Or-leans was built facing the Mississippi River, her course followed the great crescent bend of the river. Hence, the batture was "the area on the riv-erside of the artificial levee without flood protection and without private ownership."[9] The poorest blacks built shacks in the batture away from the dock area. These houses were, however, temporary because the river would periodically overflow and wash away the shacks.

Keeping in mind that New Orleans is a seaport town that is located at the mouth of the Mississippi and is situated below sea level, with flood-ing her main problem, it is not surprising that in all three municipalities whites occupied the highest and best land, protected by natural levees. Poor blacks lived in the backswamps, or as P. F. Lewis describes it, "the demiland on the inland margin of the natural levee, where drainage was bad, foundation material precarious, streets atrociously unmaintained, mosquitos endemic, and flooding a recurrent hazard."[10] It is along this margin that a continuous belt of black population developed.

Free blacks in New Orleans, many of whom were economically well off, originally lived and owned property in the French Quarter. After the Civil War and the onset of Jim Crow laws, however, they were pushed out of that section. Many of the blacks moved their families to the Treme, or Sixth Ward, an area adjacent to the French Quarter. As the Sixth Ward became crowded, many moved to the old Seventh Ward, an area that was contiguous to the Sixth Ward and represented a natural ex-tension of the black community. These early black residential patterns developed over the years into long-standing, traditionally black neigh-borhoods, although early New Orleans's residential patterns were pecu-liarly integrated.

Several inventions influenced the racial geography of New Orleans in the twentieth century. These included the development of the Wood pump and the expansion of the city's public transportation system through use of the streetcar. The onset of World War I brought with it a virtual halt in the construction of housing. Black residents of New Or-leans at this time lived in housing comparable to their white working-class counterparts. Blacks, however, were relegated to the less desirable homes in the backswamp area. There was also a large in-migration of rural blacks and whites, attracted by defense jobs in the city.

Paul Kellogg, in 1904, surveyed the housing conditions in New Orleans for a volunteer citizens' committee. He found the supply of available housing adequate, but unsanitary conditions were widespread.[11] Kellogg's recommendations went unnoticed until 1905, when a yellow fever epidemic appeared, mostly in those areas cited in his report. At this point, sanitation ordinances were passed, but enforcement and compliance were minimal. In 1917, A. Baldwin Wood developed a heavy pump that made it possible to drain and clear land that had previously been uninhabitable. Wood, whose discovery would greatly change the residential geography of the city, later became the director of the city's sewer and water board.

It became clear in the early 1920s that additional housing units were needed in the city. There were, however, many early barriers to the construction of new housing units. There was an apparent drive to improve housing conditions when the 1920 census showed that New Orleans had dropped from twelfth to sixteenth place in population.[12] The loss of population was blamed on the local authorities' inability to solve the housing problems of the city, resulting in many of the townspeople moving out beyond the city's boundaries.

South Carrollton Avenue was the focal point of the first systematic housing development in New Orleans. A second area of the Carrollton section, which consisted of more than 250 bungalows, was called "Little California." The developer boasted that it was exclusively Caucasian and composed of only homeowners. The Carrollton development probably marked the beginning of rigid residential segregation in the city. The onset of new housing brought with it a heretofore nonexistent residential segregation paranoia. Ralph Thayer observes that "the more desirable renting and buying areas were correlated more and more with racial exclusivity from 1920 onward."[13] The Wood pump that made the Carrollton development possible was truly a pervasive invention. It directly influenced the racial geography of the city.[14]

The expansion of the city's streetcar system also affected its racial geography. As public transportation expanded, old black neighborhoods established in the nineteenth-century backswamp areas expanded into the newly drained margins of that area.[15] The expanded transportation system made it possible for blacks to live in areas away from their jobs. The Wood pump, therefore, made it possible for whites to move to the suburbs and for blacks, with the aid of an expanded streetcar system, to move closer into the city. The black and white populations, it seems, were moving in opposite directions.

Population and Metropolitan Growth

New Orleans has experienced a loss in population in recent years. For example, the city had a population of 593,471 in 1970, but the city's population stood at 557,515 in 1980, a 6-percent decrease from a decade earlier. The city's population loss was largely a result of white flight to the surrounding parishes. The city's black population has grown over the past several decades (see Table 3.1). New Orleans's black population grew from 233,514 in 1960 to 308,149 in 1980, or a 31.9-percent increase. (On the other hand, the city's white population declined from 392,594 in 1960 to 236,987 in 1980, or a 39.6-percent decrease.) New Orleans has become an increasingly black city. Blacks made up 37.2 percent of the city's population in 1960, 45 percent in 1970, and 55.3 percent in 1980. The New Orleans SMSA, unlike the central city of New Orleans, has grown over the years.

The New Orleans SMSA (Orleans, Jefferson, St. Bernard, and St. Tammany parishes) had a population of nearly 1.2 million in 1980. Whites made up nearly two-thirds of the metropolitan population, while blacks comprised just under one-third. Although the metropolitan area's population has shown a steady increase, other SMSAs in the South far outdistanced its growth. The New Orleans SMSA was the largest in the South in 1940; it was the fifth-largest metropolitan area in the South in 1980.

The New Orleans SMSA experienced a 31.6-percent increase in its housing stock between 1970 and 1980 (a change from 346,000 units to 455,000 units). The bulk of this new housing construction took place outside the central city, in surrounding parishes and away from the black community that was concentrated in New Orleans. More than 80 percent of the blacks in the New Orleans metropolitan area lived in the central city in 1980. New Orleans's black population over the past four

Table 3.1
Population Change in the New Orleans Metropolitan Area, 1960–80

Race	1960 Population	Percent of 1960 Population	1970 Population	Percent of 1970 Population	1980 Population	Percent of 1980 Population	Percent Change 1960–80
SMSA							
White	627,231	69.1	717,739	68.6	774,421	65.2	23.4
Black	278,010	30.6	323,776	30.9	387,422	32.6	39.3
New Orleans							
White	392,594	62.6	323,440	54.5	236,987	42.5	-39.6
Black	233,514	37.2	267,308	45.0	308,149	55.3	31.9

Source: U.S. Bureau of the Census, *State and Metropolitan Area Data Book 1982.*

decades has for the most part remained segregated within the established black neighborhoods of the city.

The boundaries of New Orleans's black community have only been extended outward as pressures on the housing market have intensified. This was the case in the black population expansion in the 1960s and 1970s, when white population expansion occurred mostly in the suburbs surrounding New Orleans.[16] Some black expansion occurred in areas that were undergoing transition. However, newer housing developments or subdivisions in the New Orleans area expanded home ownership opportunities primarily for whites. This fact is reflected by black owner occupancy rates, which continue to lag behind that of whites. Only 35.2 percent of the blacks and 53.8 percent of the whites in the New Orleans SMSA owned their homes in 1980. The figures for the central city of New Orleans are even more revealing. Only 30 percent of the blacks in Orleans Parish (an area which is coextensive with the city) owned their homes. Black home ownership, nevertheless, was higher in the suburban parishes than in the central city. The black home ownership rate was 51.2 percent in Jefferson Parish, 66.2 percent in St. Tammany Parish, and 68.9 percent in St. Bernard Parish.

Housing and Residential Pattern

New Orleans's population change closely resembles that of the changes that took place in older cities in the Northeast and Midwest, that is, a growing black central-city core and a white suburban ring. However, there has been some racial integration of a few areas. Residential segregation actually declined in the decade of the seventies. More than 94 percent of the city's blacks lived in mostly black neighborhoods in 1970, compared with 76 percent in 1980. The New Orleans eastern sector is a classic example of an area experiencing transition.[17] The area has signs of racial mixtures in neighborhoods ranging from 25 to 75 percent black. A number of factors affect the housing pattern in the New Orleans area, including racial and economic discrimination, access to housing markets and employment centers, and residential choice of individual citizens.

New Orleans's blacks have been subjected to housing discrimination, although the quiet that has surrounded this issue would give one the impression that it was not a grave problem. In fact, the issue of housing discrimination did not become a public issue until the city's Urban League published its 1967 report entitled *To House a City*. The report called attention to discriminatory practices of real estate agents. It pointed to the many instances of blockbusting in white neighborhoods. Real estate agents routinely exploited the racial fears of unsuspecting whites, thereby accelerating white flight from these neighborhoods. Whites feared a black invasion would drastically reduce their property values. The study further reported that real estate agents reaped inflated profits by charging a "black tax" to blacks desperately searching for better housing.[18]

Housing discrimination practices greatly affected the housing options of blacks in New Orleans. Upwardly mobile and middle-class blacks in particular had few opportunities to buy new or improved housing. The only attempt to alleviate the housing shortage for middle-class blacks was construction of the Pontchartrain Park development in the 1950s. Housing discrimination continued to plague the city's black home seekers in the decades that followed.

The federal Fair Housing Act of 1968 was more than a decade old when efforts were taken at city hall to combat housing discrimination in New Orleans. The city established its Fair Housing Program in December 1979. Mayor Ernest Morial created this program to expedite the city's attack on all forms of housing discrimination. It operated as a service unit to provide information to the general public concerning their rights and responsibilities under the Fair Housing laws. The program investigated and monitored housing discrimination complaints. The Fair Housing Program was funded by a grant from the U.S. Department of Housing and Urban Development under the Community Development Block Grant program. The first-year Fair Housing Program report showed that only seventy-eight housing discrimination complaints had been recorded and only twenty-four inquiries had been made. The 1980–81 report, however, showed an increase in activity, with 139 complaints and thirty-one inquiries.

The New Orleans Fair Housing Office, by winning its first housing discrimination suit in 1980, made its first mark in the housing discrimination fight and increased its credibility as a force to be reckoned with for those who would use discriminatory practices in housing. One New Orleans landlord was fined $1,000 for refusing to rent to a person because of his color. The *Times Picayune* reported that the "landlord also agreed

Warren Woodfork was sworn in as chief of police of New Orleans in December, 1983, making him the first black to hold this office in the city's history. (Courtesy of the New Orleans Public Library)

to implement an affirmative action plan which reportedly would ensure that no one would be denied the right to rent his apartment because of race, color, religion, sex or national origin."[19]

The rebirth of the New Orleans central business district brought with it the rediscovery of its numerous examples of architecturally historic housing structures. Consequently, the preservation of the old flamboyant Victorian homes became an issue for the city and an alternative for new home buyers. The paradox of the situation was that these Victorian homes represented a generous source of low-income rental properties and were located in well-established black neighborhoods. Three such areas, however, were "reclaimed" by whites in the early 1970s: the Faubourg St. Mary area, the lower Garden District around Coliseum Square, and Old Algiers.[20]

Efforts to reclaim the Treme area were met with extreme resistance by local black political groups. The Tambourine and Fan black community

Ernest "Dutch" Morial became New Orleans' first black mayor when he was elected to office in 1978. (Courtesy of the New Orleans Public Library)

organization was the forerunner of this resistance movement. As a result, the reclamation of the Treme area was not nearly as successful as in the aforementioned communities. The more militant factions of that black community made open threats on local television news programs and radio stations to whites who would attempt to "invade" their community. The community organization also claimed that the Treme area had been redlined by local banks and mortgage companies, making it impossible for blacks to obtain mortgage loans for housing renovation.

The problem of housing the poor persists despite nearly five decades of federal housing programs. The Housing Authority of New Orleans was established in 1937, and in 1938, the plans for the St. Thomas (white) and Magnolia (black) projects were approved. The federal government allocated $8.4 million for the construction of these two racially segregated public housing developments.

Advanced planning allowed New Orleans to be one of the first cities to receive funds under the Wagner Act of 1937.[21] A total of ten low-in-

Mayor Sidney J. Barthelemy, a former state senator and councilman, became New Orleans' second black mayor when he was elected in 1986. (Courtesy of the City of New Orleans)

come housing projects were constructed in New Orleans from 1945 to 1965. The Magnolia development was occupied in 1941, as were the St. Thomas, Iberville, Lafitte, and Calliope developments. The St. Bernard development was occupied in 1942, the Florida development in 1946, the Desire development in 1956, Guste Homes in 1963, and the Fisher Home Development on the West Bank of the city in 1965. Only three of the ten housing developments were built exclusively for whites: St. Thomas, Iberville, and Florida.

Public housing in New Orleans has been described as good and fairly well built, when compared with other cities, although the tenants in these establishments might disagree. The city's public housing developments are occupied primarily by black tenants. Most are isolated from the mainstream of city life and exist almost as cities within themselves.[22] For example, at the time of construction, the St. Bernard housing project was located far from town beyond a raised railroad line. Transportation was limited, with access to town only by way of Elysian Fields Avenue. The Desire and Florida projects were also cut off by railroads. Residents were often inconvenienced for long periods of time while waiting for a train to pass before they could cross the tracks. The Iberville and Lafitte projects replaced the old decaying "Storyville" area. The Calliope project was developed on vacant land near an industrial area, offering a view that was undesirable for home buyers.[23]

The first projects to be constructed (St. Thomas and Magnolia) were built on land that had to be cleared of existing houses before construction could take place. These efforts caused the displacement of large numbers of people. Although over half of the persons displaced by the slum clearance efforts of the construction of the St. Thomas project were black, the new facility was for white occupancy only. The problem was compounded by the federal Public Housing Administration's requirement that for each new public-assisted unit constructed, an equivalent unit of substandard housing had to be demolished. The results of this requirement, which was viewed as a necessary evil to alleviate the problem of slum housing, were to decrease the number of low-income rental properties and to seriously handicap the ability of the displaced to find affordable housing.[24]

The early white housing projects, constructed before integration, are now occupied by black tenants. As whites reclaimed houses in previously all-black neighborhoods, blacks unable to pay the high rents secured housing in subsidized developments. The previously all-white Iberville project located close to the French Quarter, accepted blacks who could no longer afford the high rents charged for their homes in the Vieux Carré. The St. Thomas project served displaced black residents of the lower Garden District, and the Florida project facilitated the overflow of occupants of the Desire housing development.[25]

In 1980, HANO reported a total of 39,965 persons as residents of the ten city-owned housing developments.[26] In 1968, HANO had begun its scattered-sites program, designed to provide housing for the poor in units of lower density than that in conventional complexes. Within a year, a total of 1,658 scattered-site units had been occupied, 1,636 of which were in the city's home ownership program. This program allowed a portion of the residents' monthly rent to be applied to an earned-payments account, which could later be used as a down payment to purchase the unit.

The Housing Assistance Payments Program, Section 8 housing program, began in New Orleans in October 1975. This program was also designed to reduce the density of large conventional public housing developments. The goal of the program was to integrate low-income families into the mainstream of the community by housing them in standard, safe, and decent existing housing available through the private rental market. Initially, HANO received a $1.8 million contribution contract from the U.S. Department of Housing and Urban Development for its Section 8 program. These funds allowed HANO to house 1,182 low-income families. The authority was later awarded funds to place 600 additional low-income families under its Section 8 housing program.

The housing dilemma for low-income New Orleans citizens is directly related to the general condition of the city's housing stock. A 1979 survey of housing conditions in New Orleans revealed a total housing of 228,861 units. These dwellings, both owner- and renter-occupied, included a total of 54,067 occupied substandard units.[27] More than 14 percent of the owner-occupied housing units were substandard.

New housing developments in the city experienced a staggered growth pattern resulting from many factors closely linked to the economy. However, high interest rates and the shortage of land suitable for residential use surfaced as the chief obstacles to new housing starts in the seventies.

Although the geographic location gives the city an edge as an outlet to international waters, present topographic conditions require extensive drainage, site filling, and grading prior to residential construction. Attempts were made by the city government to alleviate the housing shortage for low-income New Orleans residents. Specifically, a total of 300 new housing units were constructed through the Community Development Program between 1978 and 1981. The city secured a $1 million Urban Development Action Grant to help fund the Gordon Plaza single-family housing development, where sixty-seven moderate-income homes were constructed. The Morial administration also constructed twenty-one single-family detached homes in the Gravier urban renewal area through the Community Improvement Agency and the Office of Housing and Community Development. The city renovated 587 housing units for low- and moderate-income qualified citizens. Housing for the elderly was also expanded, with the construction of the 128-unit Gordon Plaza apartments and senior citizen center and an additional 34 single-family housing unit, Satchmo Plaza.[28] Low-income blacks in the city were the greatest beneficiaries of this housing.

Economic Change

New Orleans lagged far behind such cities as Houston, Dallas, and Atlanta in terms of economic growth during the booming seventies. The major factor for industries' bypassing New Orleans was the makeup and training of the city's labor force. Arnold Hirsch asserts that the city has a "docile low-wage labor force, but is so poorly educated and inefficient that the business community considers it a deterrent, rather than an attraction, for industry."[29] Oil and tourism were the mainstay of the area's economy in the 1970s.[30]

The 1970s saw an economic surge in the city, which was directly related to a change in political leadership and philosophy. The administrations of both Moon Landrieu and Ernest "Dutch" Morial (the city's first black mayor) radically changed the role of city government. Both Landrieu and Morial won their elections with a combination of business-oriented whites and a large black vote.

Landrieu characterized himself as a development-minded mayor. In this tradition, he forthrightly obtained federal funds for improvements that had never been attempted in the past. During his administration the French Market in the historic French Quarter was renovated. Pedestrian malls around Jackson Square in the French Quarter were constructed, and the Moonwalk, a scenic walkway with a magnificent view of the Mississippi River, was created. He also sponsored the construction of the Superdome at a time when there were many disclaimers, and he strongly supported the expansion of construction in the central business district. The result of these efforts was boosted tourism, but more significantly, it meant a break with decades of economic stagnation. Landrieu's administration worked closely with the business community and the downtown establishment to forge economic development projects in the city. The city added more than 3.5 million square feet of office space in the central business district between 1970 and 1979.[31]

Moon Landrieu's administration marked the entrance of blacks in city government. Landrieu increased black civil service employment from 1,833 positions, or 19 percent of all such jobs, in 1970, to 4,304, or 43 percent of all civil service jobs, in 1978. Black city employment increased by 168.2 percent during the Landrieu administration. Moreover, many of the positions awarded to blacks were in middle- and upper-level management job categories.

When Dutch Morial became the first black mayor of New Orleans in 1978, he faced the difficult task of developing an economic base for long-term economic stability. Morial turned to the private sector and encouraged business to move forward and provide the economic growth that would be the salvation of the city. The Morial administration made significant progress in the business sector. The central business district experienced a construction boom of approximately $80 million. Office space in the central business district was in great demand, and the city had a 98-percent occupancy rate.[32]

Morial created several departments to enhance the economic future of the city. He created an Office of Economic Development to coordinate and manage the city's efforts in retaining and attracting business and industry. A citywide Economic Development Corporation was also created to provide low-cost loans as an incentive for business to stay, expand, or relocate in Orleans Parish. The mayor's International Trade and Economic Development Council was established to attract business, banks, and foreign investment. A Women's Business Enterprise Committee was organized to move women entrepreneurs into the city's economic mainstream. He also established the city's first Minority Business Enterprise Unit and a minority business counselor.

Morial increased the level of minority participation in city contracts. During May 1978, less than one month after being in office, he ordered a study of the amount of business the city had contracted with minority firms. The findings were absolutely shocking and far worse than what had been expected. Blacks had actually never done any significant business with the city. Black involvement had been limited to federal programs, where regulation mandated black participation. Morial then organized a Minority Set-Aside Program through which 10 percent of the goods and nonprofessional services (excluding construction) purchased by the city would be designated for bidding solely by small and minority businesses located in New Orleans.[33] By the end of Morial's first three years in office minorities had successfully competed for more than $10 million in contracts with the city. This $10 million represented more city business contracted with blacks and other minorities than all previous administrations combined.[34]

Although economic gains were made in the seventies, blacks in the New Orleans area remain significantly worse off than their white counterparts. This point is probably best illustrated by the latest poverty figures. The 1980 census revealed that 37.7 percent of the blacks in the New Orleans SMSA were below the poverty level.[35] On the other hand, only 9.3 percent of the whites in the New Orleans SMSA had income below the poverty level. The fact that this level of poverty exists in the New Orleans area is supported by other statistics (for example, the unemployment rate), which illuminate the quality of life for black New Orleanians.

Black unemployment in New Orleans has remained consistently higher than that of area whites. For example, black unemployment rate for the central city of New Orleans was 8.4 percent in 1970 and rose to 10 percent in 1982.[36] The city's overall unemployment rate was more than 10.5 percent in August 1986. Recession in the Louisiana oil fields helped push the state's August 1986 unemployment rate into double digits. The worldwide oil glut and Louisiana's heavy dependence on the petrochemical industry have pushed a higher percentage of households into poverty.

The distribution of the work force in the New Orleans metropolitan area varied greatly by race in 1980. For example, whites were two times

Table 3.2
Occupations of Blacks and Whites in the New Orleans SMSA, 1980

Occupation	White Number	Percent	Black Number	Percent
Managerial and professional	93,311	27.5	17,884	13.6
Technical, sales, and administrative	128,503	36.3	32,227	24.5
Service occupations	32,409	9.2	34,324	26.1
Crafts, operatives, and laborers	93,238	26.3	45,982	34.9
Farm, forestry, and fishing	2,640	0.7	1,240	0.9
Total	354,101	100.0	131,657	100.0

Source: U.S. Bureau of the Census, *General Social and Economic Characteristics: Louisiana* (Washington, D.C.: U.S. Government Printing Office, 1983).

more likely than blacks to be employed in managerial and professional occupations (see Table 3.2). Overall, more than 63 percent of area whites, compared with 38 percent of area blacks, were employed in white-collar occupations in 1980. Black workers, on the other hand, are more highly concentrated in the service occupations. Twenty-five percent of New Orleans area blacks were employed in the services and private household industries (jobs catering to tourism), but less than 10 percent of whites held similar occupations. Although the service jobs tended not to be high paying or high status, workers in these occupations experienced a degree of job stability that was absent from many other job categories in the area.

The recession in the mid-eighties brought hard economic times to New Orleans and its beleaguered city government. The city's second black mayor, Sidney Barthelemy, faced a staggering $30 million deficit when he took office in 1986. The layoff of 1,200 city employees chopped the city's deficit by an estimated $20 million. However, other more drastic measures were taken to trim another $10 million from the city budget. The city council in October 1986 passed a measure that ordered about 5,800 city employees to work four days a week at a 20-percent wage reduction through the remainder of the year.

New Orleans in 1977 had a total of 2,679 black-owned business firms, with receipts amounting to $74.7 million. The number of black-owned business enterprises in New Orleans increased to 3,563 in 1982. These firms had combined gross receipts of more than $112.7 million.[37] The best industry opportunities for black business enterprises in New Orleans were represented in the selected services category, followed by retail trade and by transportation and public utilities. These three categories represented more than 73 percent of the city's black-owned firms in 1982 (see Table 3.3).

Blacks have barely entered the wholesale trade and manufacturing industries. The large number of firms in the transportation category includes the black-owned taxi cabs, traditional to the South because of segregated cab practices of the past. The large number of retail trade industries includes small black-owned grocery and corner stores common to black neighborhoods in New Orleans. Overall, black businesses grew in number and in gross receipts between 1977 and 1982.

School Desegregation

As in other parts of the South, blacks in New Orleans were subjected to a segregated school system. New Orleans's public schools, however, had substantial integration during Reconstruction, from late 1870 until 1877.[38] It is estimated that from 500 to 1,000 black children attended schools with white children during Reconstruction.[39]

In 1883, however, the Supreme Court of the United States struck down the Civil Rights Act of 1875, and by 1890, "separate but equal" laws had been enacted and rigid segregation had become the rule in New Orleans.[40] Separate and unequal public school systems were set up across Louisiana. However, absolutely no provisions were made to support institutions of higher education for blacks. Black higher education was primarily supported by philanthropic and religious organizations.

In the years immediately following the Civil War and during Reconstruction, three colleges dedicated to the education of blacks were founded.[41] The American Missionary Association in 1869 founded Straight College, the first black institution of higher education in Louisiana and in the city of New Orleans; the Freedman's Aid Society of the

Table 3.3
Black Businesses in New Orleans, 1977 and 1982

| Industry | 1977 | | 1982 | |
Classification	Number	Percent	Number	Percent
Agriculture	—	—	49	1.4
Construction	322	12.0	337	9.5
Manufacturing	19	0.7	16	0.4
Transportation and utilities	418	15.6	433	12.1
Wholesale trade	14	0.5	18	0.5
Retail trade	683	25.5	840	23.6
Finance, insurance, and				
real estate	85	3.2	136	3.8
Selected services	985	36.8	1,336	37.5
Other industries and				
not classified	153	5.7	398	11.2
Total	2,679	100.0	3,563	100.0

Source: U.S. Bureau of the Census, *1982 Survey of Minority-Owned Business Enterprises: Black.*

Methodist Episcopal Church founded New Orleans University; and the American Baptist Home Mission founded Feland College.

In 1879, a delegation headed by P. B. S. Pinchback, a black lieutenant governor during Reconstruction in Louisiana, sponsored in the Constitutional Convention of Louisiana a movement that resulted in the establishment of a publicly funded institution in New Orleans for the higher education of blacks. Southern University was chartered by the state General Assembly in 1880.[42] It was later recognized as a land grant college by the federal government and was operated in New Orleans until 1914. The institution was then relocated to Scotlandville, just outside of Baton Rouge.

Higher education for blacks in New Orleans continued to be provided by private colleges and universities until the establishment of Southern University in New Orleans (SUNO) in 1959. Louisiana State University in New Orleans (which changed its name to the University of New Orleans in 1974) had been established a year earlier in 1958, and SUNO was established as its black counterpart. The establishment of both of

these institutions, which ran counter to the 1954 Supreme Court decision of *Brown v. Board of Education*, represented an attempt by the state
to avoid integration of its institutions of higher education by continuing
segregated facilities for blacks and whites.

The dual system of education in Louisiana, not unlike other vestiges
of segregation, has been a most difficult system to dismantle. On March
14, 1974, the U.S. attorney general filed suit against the state of Louisiana in order to enforce the provisions of the Fourteenth Amendment to
the Constitution and Title VI of the Civil Rights Act of 1964. The federal government alleged that the state of Louisiana and its agents were
maintaining a racially dual system of public education and that the state
had failed to develop and implement plans to eliminate all vestiges of a
dual system within its boundaries. The state denied the allegations and
asserted that it had maintained nonracial open-admissions policies and
nonracial employment policies. On September 8, 1981, the Justice Department and the state entered into a consent decree in settlement of
United States v. the State of Louisiana.

In summary, the consent decree ordered the state to implement
changes that would result in the dissolution of a racially dual higher education system. All predominantly black and predominantly white universities in the state were placed under the order.[43] The colleges and
universities were specifically ordered to increase student access to other-
race schools, and specific guidelines and enrollment target figures were
established for a specified period in order to ensure the accomplishment
of the prescribed goals. The colleges and universities were also ordered to
increase other-race faculty and staff members. Guidelines for implementation of prescribed goals were also outlined. Disparities in financial support for predominantly black, as compared with predominantly white,
institutions were also addressed.

The U.S. District Court for the eastern district of Louisiana reviewed
the decree and determined that it was consistent with the objectives of
the Fourteenth Amendment to the Constitution and Title VI of the
Civil Rights Act of 1964. The decree required that a monitoring committee file annual progress reports. The consent decree remained in effect until December 31, 1987. The plaintiff in 1988 requested a hearing
to extend the terms of the consent decree. To date, no ruling has been
granted on this request.

Removing the vestiges of institutional racism (for example, Jim Crowism) has been a rather difficult task. This fact is borne out by the enrollment data of the two state universities that are located in New Orleans. The Consent Decree Monitoring Committee report for August 1986 shows both an increase or no change in other-race students and faculty for the two public universities in the city. Specifically, the percentage of other-race students enrolled at SUNO increased from 0.5 in 1980 to 8.4 percent in 1985. The percentage of other-race students enrolled at the University of New Orleans (UNO) increased from 15.5 percent in 1980 to 18.4 percent in 1985.[44] It should be noted, however, that one provision of the consent decree was cross-enrollment of students at UNO and SUNO. The cross-enrollment policy has greatly enhanced other-race enrollment at both schools.

The other-race employment percentage at UNO for executive, administrative, and managerial positions decreased from 7.7 percent in 1981 to 6.7 percent in 1985. The other-race employment percentage for full-time faculty in 1981 was only 3.1 percent. Although UNO experienced a slight increase in other-race employment of faculty in 1982 and 1983, the 1981 percentages are also 3.1 percent. This figure represents no change in other-race full-time faculty employment. The other-race employment percentages at SUNO for executive, administrative, and managerial positions went from zero percent in 1981 to 10 percent in 1985. The other-race employment percentage for full-time faculty went from 23 percent in 1981 to 25.4 percent in 1985.

The predominantly black school, SUNO, has experienced its greatest difficulty in meeting other-race student enrollment figures as prescribed by the consent decree. The difficulties experienced at the predominantly white school, UNO, are the exact opposite. Goals for black faculty employment and retention, as well as the employment of blacks in executive, administrative, and managerial positions, have been much more illusive.

The New Orleans public schools have also been a bone of contention in the push for equity.[45] The district has undergone a dramatic demographic change since the late sixties. White enrollment in the district stood at 32 percent in 1968, 19 percent in 1974, and only 12 percent in 1980. The white student enrollment has decreased by approximately 500 students per year since the early eighties. The district in 1986 was 84.4 percent black, 11.7 percent white, and 4.9 percent other-race persons. Black enrollment in the district is declining, but at a much slower rate than that for whites. However, the district is losing a sizable share of its middle-class blacks to the parochial and private schools.

The school board in 1986 had a black majority. Three of the five school board members were black, including the board's president. The election of blacks to leadership positions in the district, however, has had a negligible impact on the quality of education in many of the schools in low-income black neighborhoods. The quality of education for children attending many of New Orleans's predominantly black public schools (as indicated by standardized test scores) is grossly inadequate.

Although white student enrollment in the district is quite low (less than 12 percent), white enrollment in the city's magnet and gifted/talented programs presents a different picture. White students have greater access to magnet programs than their black counterparts. In 1983, for example, there were 1,828 students enrolled in gifted and talented programs. Of this total, 66 percent were white, 29 percent were black, 4 percent were Asian, and 1 percent were Hispanic. By 1987, the gifted and talented programs enrolled 2,322 students, with an ethnic composition of 51 percent white, 42 percent black, 6 percent Asian, and 1 percent Hispanic.

It is quite obvious that more white students are exposed to the best that the New Orleans public school district has to offer than are blacks, even though blacks represent a majority of the student population. The magnet school concept and the gifted and talented programs are used primarily as a vehicle to lure whites back to public schools. The school board in its zeal to stem white flight and attract more white students may be tempted to do so at the expense of the city's largely poor and black student population. Black community residents can point to a discernible pattern of school closures in their areas, while new programs are being proposed for white areas.

The racial disparities that exist for black students in gifted and talented programs also exist for teachers assigned to the classes in these programs. Although black teachers comprise 85 percent, or 3,544 teachers, of the total number of teachers in the New Orleans public school district, there are only twenty-nine black teachers in the gifted and talented programs. However, ninety-three white teachers are assigned to the gifted and talented programs.

The ramifications of this obvious disparity in racial assignment of both black teachers and black students to gifted and talented programs in a predominantly black school system certainly suggest that the selection process perpetuates internal segregation within the larger system. This internal segregation phenomenon appears to be solidly embedded in the structure of the school system. The district's middle-class black children have greater access to the magnet and special programs for talented and gifted students than their low-income black counterparts. The city's low-income children, who make up a majority of the students enrolled in New Orleans public schools, attend schools that are largely devoid of not only whites but have few middle-class blacks. The middle-class black students who are not in magnet schools, or the "good schools" that have a reputation for gifted and talented programs and a middle-class student body, are increasingly enrolled in parochial and private schools. Catholic schools have experienced a steady increase in black enrollment since the mid-seventies. Private schools have also experienced a slight but steady increase in black student enrollment.

A growing segment of New Orleans's black middle-class, not unlike its white middle-class counterpart, has abandoned the city's public schools and, to a large extent, the infrastructure within the black community. This trend, if not reversed, will likely have severe consequences for the poor black children who are trapped in a school and community environment where failure is the norm and where positive black role models are few. This problem is exacerbated as blacks move up the socioeconomic ladder and move out of the traditional black neighborhoods. The black middle class appears to have escaped the confines of the ghetto to be reghettoized or segregated in the suburbs. The problems of the dark ghetto persist. The conditions in many of New Orleans's inner-city areas are worsened by the absence of a vibrant black middle class, from which black leadership historically has been drawn.

Black Politics

Before the Voting Rights Act of 1965, four prominent black New Orleans political organizations were established and served important functions. In 1941, Ernest J. Wright organized the first black political organization in New Orleans, the People's Defense League. Blacks' voting, however, was not a great issue at that time, and the organization expended most of its energies fighting police brutality.[46] Through the efforts of the league's voter registration and education for participation in elections drive, black voter registration increased from 400 in 1940 to nearly 27,000 in 1950.[47]

Reverend A. L. Davis organized the Orleans Parish Progressive Voters League. This organization was also one of the NAACP's voters leagues that had been established all over the South. Two other black political organizations were formed before the Voting Rights Act of 1965. The Consumer's League of Greater New Orleans was founded by Reverend Avery Alexander, and Dave Dennis organized the Crescent City Independent Voters League. The ninety-three-person membership of both these groups was mostly composed of the General Workers Local No. 1419.[48] Under the leadership of Clarence "Chink" Henry, this group became a very powerful force in New Orleans politics. Both of these organizations were also involved with voter registration and educational programs.

The Voting Rights Act of 1965 marked the beginning of real black participation and influence in the governmental process in the city of New Orleans. Voter registration increased from 36,000 in 1961 to 67,000 in 1969.[49] This increase in black voter strength from 17 to 30 percent also marked the beginning of viable black political organizations. The Southern Organization for United Leadership (SOUL) was formed in 1965 and became the dominant black political organization in New Orleans. Composed of black professionals, homeowners, and low- and middle-income residents of the Lower Ninth Ward, SOUL embraced a new political vision and supported black candidates for office. Although few members expected their candidates to win, the candidates, however, were expected to generate local black political participation.[50]

In 1966, SOUL ran its first candidate of promise, attorney Niles Douglas, for the state House of Representatives in a district that was 45 percent black. The organization's main tasks were to promote viable black candidates and to get out the voters. But SOUL's greatest political accomplishment was its successful get-out-the-vote campaign for Governor Edwin Edwards in 1971. The election of Edwards to the state's highest office greatly increased the status and importance of SOUL's prominent leaders in both city and state political arenas.

The second major black political organization to emerge was the Community Organizations for Urban Politics (COUP), which included a number of influential and highly respected black leaders. Organized in the black "Creole" part of town, COUP was composed of mostly Catholics who lived or had once lived in the Seventh Ward.

In the 1970s, SOUL and COUP became the most powerful black organizations in the city. These organizations reached prominence and gained respectability after a large number of successful political backings produced winners. In 1971, both COUP and SOUL strongly supported and worked hard to galvanize the vote in electing Moon Landrieu as mayor of New Orleans. Landrieu had been a liberal city councilman and had often been a lone champion of black causes. Landrieu won the mayoral election with approximately 40 percent of the white vote and slightly over 90 percent of the black vote. Historically, this marked the first time that a candidate for mayor in New Orleans had won by receiving more black than white votes. This fact was also not forgotten by Mayor Landrieu once he was in office. The percentage of blacks working in city government increased from 10 percent to 40 percent during the mayor's eight-year tenure.

The ability of black political organizations to mobilize the black vote increased the number of black elected officials in the city.[51] In 1970, only one black (Ernest Morial) had been elected to public office. During the 1970s, New Orleans, like many urban cities, experienced an enormous growth in its black population, with a subsequent decline in its white population. This newly emerging majority status for blacks greatly improved their political power, or their ability to determine the outcome of elections. Consequently, at the close of Moon Landrieu's eight years as mayor in 1978, blacks constituted 43 percent of New Orleans's registered voters. Subsequently, blacks began running for citywide offices against whites, and a new era of black versus white citywide elections was ushered into New Orleans politics.[52] In 1978, there were sixteen black elected officeholders in New Orleans.[53] This number grew to twenty black elected officials in 1984.[54] The number of black political organizations also grew in the 1970s to inclucde the Black Organization for Leadership Development, the Treme Improvement Political Society, and the Development Association for Wards and Neighborhoods.

The unprecedented 43-percent figure for black registered voters encouraged Judge Ernest "Dutch" Morial, of the state Court of Appeals, to run for mayor as the first black to ever declare candidacy for that office. Morial had already garnered a number of firsts behind his name. He was the first black to have been elected to the state legislature since Reconstruction, the first black graduate of Louisiana State University Law School, and the first black elected to the state Court of Appeals. He was also a former president of the New Orleans chapter of the NAACP.

Morial initially fought an uphill election battle, with many black political organizations endorsing two moderate white opponents. However, through vigorous campaigning in the black community, he garnered 58 percent of the black vote, which placed him first in the primary ahead of Joseph Dirosa, a conservative white city councilman.

In the runoff election, the black turnout was an unanticipated 76 percent. Joseph Dirosa was not popular in the black community and was generally perceived as antagonistic toward blacks. He had also campaigned as the candidate for the "little man," which many blacks interpreted as the "little white man." His position had also greatly antagonized the white business elite, who subsequently supported Morial as "the best manager of their investments."[55] Morial won the election with 97 percent of the black vote and 20 percent of the white vote, which gave him 51.6 percent of the total votes cast. Morial made history again in 1978, when he became the first black mayor of the city of New Orleans.

Morial's first four years as mayor have been described as an era of pride and accomplishments for blacks and an absolute nightmare for the white business elite. Historian Joseph Logsden succinctly describes the dilemma:

> Much of the power structure supported Morial in the runoff against Joseph Dirosa in 1977 because they thought he would accommodate them once in office. Once Dutch was elected, an impasse quickly developed. As a civil rights advocate, Morial felt it would be betrayal of his cause to allow them to influence his rule. On their side, they simply were not ready for a civil rights minded mayor. It was a clash between the civil rights movement and the white establishment that had been building for 100 years.[56]

The fiery first term of Mayor Morial, marked by much conflict with the white community, who despised what they characterized as his arrogance and his disinterest in their views and desires, led to his second term being challenged by both a white and a black candidate for mayor. William Jefferson, a black state senator and former ally of Morial, attempted to form an alliance with uptown whites to defeat Morial. Many had been former Morial supporters. He also attacked Morial on several key points of importance to blacks in the community, which had not been satisfactorily resolved. These unresolved issues, however, were not enough to sway the loyalty of a black community who had been living with unresolved issues for years under white leadership. Morial's accomplishment of becoming the first black mayor was symbolic and served as a source of pride for most blacks. Blacks also credited Morial's efforts to improve city government access to the community. They pointed with pride to the fact that black city employees increased by 11 percent during his first term, although 1,500 positions had been eliminated. Also, more than $77 million had been awarded to minority contractors.[57]

In the primary, the mayor also faced a formidable white candidate, state representative Ron Faucheux. However, Jefferson's inability to overcome the "spoiler" image in the election allowed Morial to garner 91 percent of the black vote, compared with Jefferson's 8 percent, which, although small, forced Morial into a runoff with Faucheux. This also marked the first time in the twentieth century that an incumbent mayor in the city of New Orleans had had to enter into a runoff.[58] In the end, Morial defeated Faucheux, receiving 53.2 percent of the ballots cast in this election.

Following Morial's defeat of Ron Faucheux and William Jefferson, his influence over the black electorate was unquestionable. Morial then began the long arduous ordeal of attempting to change the city charter so that he would be allowed to run for a third consecutive term in late 1985. In spite of his popularity among members of the community, Morial was defeated on this issue. With Morial out of the 1986 mayoral election, the battle between councilman Sidney Barthelemy and Senator William Jefferson ensued. This political race was significant in that it pitted two black candidates against each other for mayor of New Orleans. The percentage of black registered voters in 1986 reached 51.6 percent. This new majority of registered voters made this competition possible.

The race between Barthelemy and Jefferson also marked a change in traditional strategies and coalitions for the successful election of blacks to political office. Traditionally, and as was the case for Morial, black candidates in large cities with sizable black populations often win elections by capturing the lion's share of the black vote and by receiving a lesser portion of the white vote. Barthelemy, who at one time had been Morial's friend and ally, became an opponent of Morial, especially during the mayor's final term. He either remained silent or opposed Morial on a number of issues that were largely supported by black community members. During Morial's administration, Barthelemy took increasingly conservative stands on some city issues. Barthelemy's relationship with the white community actually strengthened during Morial's eight years in office. His many battles with Morial increased his white support, while at the same time weakening his black support. By garnering the white vote and maintaining some margin of black support, this coalition had the potential of being a winner.

Senator Jefferson, on the other hand, pursued the more traditional black–crossover white coalition. He campaigned hard in the black community, attempting to solidify the black vote, and worked even harder in the uptown white community to secure a sufficient percentage of their votes.

In the first primary, Barthelemy's strategy was threatened by a little-known white candidate, Sam LeBlanc, who had the potential of siphoning the councilman's white voter support. Barthelemy, however, was able to maintain a large enough share of his white voter base (40 percent) and received a small but sufficient percentage of the black vote (24 percent). Although black support was weak, it was enough to land him a spot in the runoff election. Barthelemy received 34 percent of the total vote, running second to Jefferson, who received 39 percent of the vote. In the end, Jefferson was unable to capture the white voter support he needed to win. Barthelemy, on the other hand, captured one-third of LeBlanc's white supporters, handing him an easy victory.

Barthelemy's successful racial coalition was a direct contrast to that of Moon Landrieu. Landrieu, who is white, won with overwhelming black support and only minimal white support. On the other hand, Mayor Barthelemy, who is black, won with overwhelming white support and only minimal black support. The white community cast the deciding vote that ran counter to the choice of the city's black majority. Although the majority of blacks favored Senator Jefferson, the white bloc vote served as a swing vote to elect Barthelemy as mayor. The results of this election sent shock waves through the black community. Racial bloc voting by the city's whites will likely impact the campaign strategies of future black mayoral candidates in New Orleans.

Blacks are now securing more elected positions in city government.

New Orleans in 1987 found itself with a black mayor, while four of the seven city council seats, nine of the city's seventeen state representatives, and three of the five school board members were black. But the real value of these accomplishments outside of the obvious symbolic value is not yet known. Electing blacks to political offices is not an end in itself. It is certainly unclear as to how effective black officeholders can be at addressing some of the enormous problems of the poor black community.[59] The black poverty level has grown unabated. The mid-eighties find nearly one-half of the city's black families in poverty; black unemployment has remained around 20 percent, with more than 50 percent of the city's teenagers unemployed; and the high school dropout rate has reached epidemic proportions.

Conclusion

Blacks have a very long history of residing in New Orleans. Socioeconomic conditions have been greatly influenced by historical events. New Orleans was a late benefactor of the economic boom of the seventies that was common in a number of other Sunbelt cities. The fact that New Orleans had a large visible underclass (mostly black, poorly educated, and marginally skilled) was a deterrent in attracting new industry to the area during the early seventies. Economic recessions in the early and mid-eighties severely limited economic growth options available to the largely black New Orleans community. Falling oil prices in the mid-eighties left many Gulf Coast communities, including New Orleans, in dire economic straits. New Orleans during those years was near fiscal collapse. The city and its mostly black work force during these hard times became more dependent on service occupations and tourism as a mainstay.

Declining birthrates and white flight to the surrounding parishes have left New Orleans's public schools with an overwhelmingly black student population. Many middle-class blacks have also opted to send their children to private and parochial schools. Competition and sometimes outright conflicts have intensified between whites and middle-class blacks over the placement of students in the city's talented and gifted school programs, which provide the best that the New Orleans public school system has to offer. These programs were designed initially to stem white flight. However, a growing number of middle-class blacks are demanding a more equitable share of slots in these special programs. A disproportionately large share of white students is placed in these programs, while blacks, who comprise more than 80 percent of the student population, are often placed on a long waiting list. Low-income black children and poor inner-city schools are too often forgotten altogether in this struggle over scarce resources.

Blacks gained and kept control of city hall when they elected Morial as the city's first black mayor and Barthelemy as its second black mayor. Blacks now wield considerable power on the city council, the school board, and other local elective offices. Black political empowerment, however, has not readily translated into economic power. Some gains were made in the area of minority hiring and contracting with city government, but for the most part, the city's large black underclass remains impoverished, poorly educated, unemployed, unskilled, discriminated against, and largely invisible to the larger community.

3
Atlanta
Mecca of the Southeast

Robert D. Bullard and E. Kiki Thomas

Historical Background

Atlanta was originally the site of an Indian village called Standing Peachtree, which was located at the confluence of Peachtree Creek and the Chattahoochee River.[1] In 1813, a federal militia outpost called Fort Gilmer was established to protect the state from the Creek Indians.[2] Because of the strategic nature of this area, the Georgia state legislature in 1836 authorized a surveyor to locate a site between the Chattahoochee River and the city of Decatur as the terminal point for the Georgia-Tennessee Railroad. With a railroad cut through the mountains of Tennessee, the legislature expected trade links to be opened to the Midwest through connections with the Tennessee, Ohio, and Mississippi rivers. In 1837, the place now called Atlanta was christened Terminus because it was the terminal point for the railroads. In 1843, the name was changed to Marthasville, the name of former Governor Lumpkin's daughter. In 1845, the name was changed to Atlanta, a name associated with the Western and Atlantic railroads.[3]

Atlanta was burned to the ground by Union forces in 1864. By the 1880s, however, city officials were able to promote the city as the "Gateway of the South" because of its increasing importance as a transportation and distribution center. The city reached a population of 75,000 in 1895, the same year it hosted the Cotton States and International Exposition. This exposition celebrated Atlanta's rebirth and its new designation as the "Capital of the New South."[4]

Even though this was a period of rapid industrialization in the United States, Atlanta did not become a great manufacturing center. During the first quarter of the twentieth century, the city's economy became much more diversified than it had been previously. While assuming more distributional functions, Atlanta became a regional city for banking and finance after being selected in 1914 as one of the twelve Federal Reserve Bank cities in the country. Atlanta also became a government center, initially because it attracted industries and professions doing business with the state government. Cultural and educational activities also assumed a large role in the economic and social life of the city. Notably, most of the capital invested in Atlanta was from outside the southeastern region and went into office buildings rather than factories.

Significant commercial and industrial expansion took place in the 1920s. In 1925, the Atlanta Chamber of Commerce invested $1 million in a program called "Forward Metro Atlanta" in order to facilitate the area's development.[5] Atlanta developed further during this period as a transportation center when new hard-surfaced roads brought thousands of vehicles through the city. The city in 1924 leased the land for a municipal airport. As a regional center, the city profited from the accelerated diversity of industry in the Southeast after World War II. It became a center of communications and aviation and began to attract more branch offices of national companies and federal agencies.

The corporate boundaries of Atlanta were precisely established in 1847 by a state law that decreed those limits to be exactly one mile from the state depot in every direction. This made the city a perfect circle. In 1866, the boundaries were expanded to one and one-half miles in every direction. Between 1866 and 1952, the city annexed six incorporated jurisdictions contiguous in Fulton and DeKalb counties. With the implementation of the Atlanta-Fulton County Plan of Improvement, in January 1952, Atlanta's corporate limits were expanded to 83 square miles and by 1980 covered approximately 131 square miles.[6] Most of the city's boundaries are found entirely within Fulton County except for a small segment that extends into Dekalb County. Atlanta has not been involved in any significant annexation of surrounding developments since 1967. Thus, the city's boundaries are somewhat fixed, with little room for expansion. This inability to annex has contributed to uneven growth and development of the area. This growth pattern has important social and economic implications for the mostly black central-city core and the rapidly expanding mostly white suburban ring. Uneven growth between the central city and metropolitan Atlanta has heightened status differences and inequities between blacks and whites. Social and economic isolation of Atlanta's central-city population has become more evident in the 1980s.

Population and Metropolitan Growth

Metropolitan Atlanta covers a fifteen-county area and had a population of more than two million in 1980. Blacks comprised 24.6 percent of the Atlanta SMSA. Metroplitan Atlanta has experienced constant growth since the 1900s. However, growth between 1950 and 1970 accounted for over 57 percent of the population gains made from the turn of the century to 1970. The 1960s were generally considered the boom years of Atlanta. This period was significant because the city began to exert its regional dominance.[7]

The city of Atlanta has also experienced a steady decrease in its share of the metropolitan population since 1960. For example, Atlanta's population made up 42 percent of the SMSA in 1960, 31 percent in 1970, and 21 percent in 1980.[8] The city's population in 1980 was 425,022, of which 282,912, or 66.6 percent, were black. The period 1970–80 saw Atlanta lose over 70,017 individuals, or 14 percent of its total population. In the decade of the 1970s, however, the black share of the city's population increased from 51 percent in 1970 to nearly 67 percent in 1980. Atlanta's black population grew by 12.1 percent in the seventies.

White flight to the suburbs accelerated the process of Atlanta's becoming a predominantly black city. The city has been steadily losing its white population since 1960 (see Table 4.1). During the decade of the 1960s, Atlanta lost over 25 percent of its white population. The city's suburbs, however, gained more than 1.1 million whites and only 170,000 blacks between 1950 and 1980. Black expansion into Atlanta's suburbs occurred largely after 1970. Suburbanization for Atlanta's blacks quite often reflected the segregated housing pattern typical of central-city neighborhoods.

Housing and Residential Pattern

Atlanta's black population in 1970 was found largely in the western and central portions of the city. However, racial transition during the

Table 4.1
Population of Atlanta from 1900 to 1980

Year	Total Population	White	Black	Percent Black
1900	89,872	54,090	35,727	39.7
1910	154,839	102,861	51,902	33.5
1920	200,616	137,785	62,796	31.3
1930	270,366	180,247	90,075	33.3
1940	302,288	197,686	104,533	34.6
1950	331,314	209,898	121,285	36.6
1960	487,455	300,635	186,464	38.2
1970	495,039	240,503	255,041	51.5
1980	425,022	137,878	282,912	66.6

Source: U.S. Bureau of the Census, 1900–1980 *Census of Population and Housing.* Washington, D.C.: U.S. Government Printing Office.

seventies allowed the black population to extend its traditional boundaries into southeastern and southwestern Atlanta. The northern portion of Atlanta remained predominantly white during this transition. Racial transition also occurred in suburban Atlanta. While suburbanization largely meant out-migration of whites, black Atlantans also made the move to the suburbs in the seventies. Blacks in Atlanta's suburbs increased by 200 percent between 1970 and 1980. By 1980, blacks comprised over 14 percent of Atlanta's suburban ring. A number of obstacles have kept blacks out of the suburbs, including low income, housing discrimination, restrictive zoning practices, inadequate public transportation, and fear.[9]

Residential housing patterns in Atlanta remain segregated along racial lines. The 1970s did see some changes in the level of racial segregation. For example, over 92 percent of Atlanta's blacks lived in mostly black neighborhoods in 1970. Ten years later, 86 percent of the city's blacks lived in areas where blacks comprised the majority.[10] Still, only four other cities in the country (Chicago, Philadelphia, Cleveland, and St. Louis) were more segregated than Atlanta in 1980.

Black housing in Atlanta is a story of contrasts. The city, for example, has a number of older and established middle-class neighborhoods, as well as extreme cases of deteriorating low-income neighborhoods. Two-fifths (41.8 percent) of the Atlanta SMSA blacks owned their homes in 1980, compared with nearly two-thirds (61.4 percent) of whites. The number of housing units in the city of Atlanta has been declining in the past decade. For instance, Atlanta's housing units declined by 6 percent between 1972 and 1978. Much of the decrease in the housing stock was a result of demolition from urban renewal and highway construction. Black neighborhoods suffered more from these activities than any other area. On the other hand, housing construction boomed in areas outside the city. For the period 1970–80, the Atlanta SMSA gained over 254,000 new housing units, a 49.2-percent increase. Much of the new housing was built in the white suburban ring.

The quantity of substandard housing in Atlanta actually increased during the 1970s. As late as 1975, approximately 16 percent, or 33,000 units, of Atlanta's housing stock was substandard. By 1980, the number of substandard housing units had increased to 25 percent, or 43,960 units, despite the decline in available units between 1975 and 1980. Thus, one in four housing units in Atlanta remained substandard after the large-scale clearance program in the 1960s and the neighborhood revitalization movement of the 1970s.

More than 900 acres of slum housing were cleared by nine urban renewal projects in Atlanta in the 1960s. In addition, six major redevelopment projects, including the clearance of Buttermilk Bottom, once the city's most notorious slums, were financed with federal funds. The Atlanta Civic Center was constructed on the site of the old Buttermilk Bottom neighborhood. An *Atlanta Constitution* survey found urban renewal and housing code enforcement to be the major culprit in the loss of low-income housing in Atlanta's poor black areas. For example, the twelve census tracts with the worse housing went from 16,000 housing units in 1960 to 9,225 units in 1970. In just a decade, the low-income neighborhoods in the survey lost 41 percent of their housing units.[11]

Atlanta's low-income neighborhoods stand in direct contrast to the growth and development that characterized the metropolitan area. Atlanta's poorest neighborhoods are located in the central and south central sectors of the city. The neighborhoods of Summerhill, Peopletown, Mechanicsville, and Pittsburg, for example, are all located in central and south central Atlanta. The Summerhill and Mechanicsville neighborhoods lost more than 50 percent of their population as a result of the land clearance for the Atlanta Stadium and the highway system (Interstates 75 and 85).

The largest low-income landlord in Atlanta is the Atlanta Housing Authority (AHA), which housed some 52,800 residents, 90 percent of them black, in 17,171 units. Atlanta has the fifth-largest concentration of public housing projects in the country.[12] Included in these figures are 3,284 units where rents are subsidized under the Section 8 program. Nearly 4 percent of the AHA-managed apartments, or some 820 units, were either vacant, undergoing repairs, or simply uninhabitable in 1982. Atlanta's low-income housing projects are often plagued with leaky plumbing, inadequate ventilation, overburdened electrical systems, and peeling paint. For example, the Techwood Homes housing development, the first project operated by AHA, was cited by city housing inspectors for over 10,000 housing code violations in 1981. Atlanta's public housing developments tend to be scattered. Units within the AHA include two-story apartments, small wooden homes, and converted duplexes.

It appears that the Atlanta housing stock that is available to low- and moderate-income families will continue to dwindle in the eighties. Increased pressures can already be felt in near-town neighborhoods where competition for decent and affordable housing has intensified. Metropolitan Atlanta's housing boom of the 1970s benefited a largely white suburban population, at the same time that low- and moderate-income housing was declining in the mostly black central city.

Social and Economic Change

Metropolitan Atlanta has emerged as the commercial, industrial, and financial center of the southeastern United States. It is the center for federal operations in this region, as well as the center of communications, transportation, and distribution. Since its beginning, Atlanta has become a transportation and distribution center because of its strategic location. Today the trucking industry and the interstate highway network, as well as the world's second-busiest passenger airport, help Atlanta maintain its position as a transportation and distribution hub and regional office center. The new midfield terminal at Atlanta's Hartsfield Airport is the largest in the world (2.2 million square feet) and the largest employer in Georgia. In 1981, the airport employed nearly 30,000 persons and had an annual payroll of $892 million.[13]

More than 430 of the Fortune 500 companies have operations in Atlanta. There were seven *Black Enterprise* "Top 100" firms in the metropolitan area in 1986; the Chicago SMSA was the only other area that did as well. Government is a big employer in Atlanta. The city is the capital of Georgia and the seat of Fulton County. Moreover, Atlanta is second only to Washington, D.C., in the number of federal government employees. Federal government hiring policies (for example, civil service and equal opportunity practices) were especially attractive to young black college graduates seeking professional positions. The presence of regional, national, and international corporate headquarters have fostered the development of a large local service sector, including law firms, accounting firms, banks, and insurance companies. There are twenty-nine degree-granting colleges and universities, vocational technical schools, and private business career schools in Atlanta. As a center for medical care, Atlanta has extensive facilities, which include educational and research capabilities.

Atlanta has actively engaged in promoting itself as a national and international trade center. It has more than sixteen foreign banks doing business in the city and thirty-one foreign governments represented by thirteen career consuls and eighteen honorary consuls. Atlanta city government offered financial assistance to promote business expansion and retention as well. The quasi-public Atlanta Economic Development Corporation used federal and private funds to package long-term financing for more than 125 companies, with a total of more than $67 million. A similar function was served by the city's Office of Economic Development. Established in 1982, this office has served as the focal point in city government for economic development.[14]

Much of the efforts to promote development in Atlanta's central business district has been undertaken by Central Atlanta Progress. This organization of downtown business interests was first established in 1941 as the Central Atlanta Improvement Association. John Portman has been a key figure since the sixties in Central Atlanta Progress's effort to transform the downtown area. In 1983, the "Forward Metro Atlanta" marketing campaign was initiated by the Metropolitan Atlanta Council for Economic Development, a body representing the six largest chambers of commerce in the metropolitan area. The $3 million campaign was de-

Mayor Andrew Young, former U.S. congressman and United Nations ambassador, was first elected mayor in 1981 and reelected for a second term in 1985. (Courtesy of the Mayor's Office)

signed to produce 90,000 jobs in the metropolitan area over a three-year period.[15]

Atlanta experienced dramatic growth in downtown office and motel construction in the 1970s. However, the city's net central area employment declined by 3,500 employees between 1970 and 1978. All employment categories experienced growth during this period, with the exception of manufacturing jobs, which declined by 2.3 percent. Despite attempts to bolster the central-city economy, the total labor force in Atlanta declined during the 1970–80 period. While 50 percent of the city's labor force was employed in professional, managerial, technical, clerical, and sales occupations in 1970, over 54 percent of the city's labor force was employed in these occupations in 1980. The city has been losing blue-collar jobs. The city had a net loss of more than 8,000 manufacturing jobs between 1970 and 1978.[16] The largest decrease was in craftsmen, foremen, and operatives occupations.

Metropolitan Atlanta experienced employment gains partly because of the area's location in the Sunbelt and its accessibility to major transportation networks.[17] More than 225,000 jobs were created in the Atlanta metropolitan area in the 1983–86 period. In 1984 alone, there were more than $7 billion in new construction, which resulted in 100,000 new jobs.[18] The bulk of these jobs was concentrated in white-collar occupations, such as wholesale and retail trade, finance, insurance, real estate, and services.[19] Overall, the Atlanta SMSA experienced a 31-percent increase in employment during the seventies.[20]

Atlanta has become a major convention and trade center. It ranked third in the number of conventions hosted annually. In 1982, almost 1.3 million convention delegates visited Atlanta, boosting the city's economy by more than $500 million. Over 75,000 Atlantans were employed in the convention and tourism industry in 1980, with approximately 50 percent unskilled job categories.[21] Atlanta's Visitor and Convention Bureau estimated that more than 8,760 new hotel rooms were constructed in 1985, with approximately one new job for each room. Black workers continue to be concentrated in the low-paying service jobs of the convention industry.

Atlanta has been given a number of names over the years, including the "Jewel of the South," the "City of the 21st Century," "Regional City," and "Black Mecca," just to name a few.[22] Atlanta is not a mecca for thousands of low-income persons who call the city home.[23] The facts do not

Jesse Hill, president of Atlanta Life Insurance Company, is one of Atlanta's leading black civic and business leaders. (Courtesy of Atlanta Life Insurance Company)

Morehouse School of Medicine is a leader in the training of minority doctors and is part of the famous Atlanta University Center. (Courtesy of Morehouse School of Medicine)

support the popular notion that blacks live better in Atlanta than anywhere else.[24] The mystique, however, continues to fuel the black migration stream to the city. Employment prospects for many black Atlantans did not improve significantly in the 1970s. The loss of industrial jobs and the move toward a "white-collar economy" placed a strain on central-city Atlanta in providing employment options for its growing low-income and semiskilled labor pool. A large segment of Atlanta's black population lacked the requisite education or skills for this specialized white-collar economy. Nearly two-thirds (65.2 percent) of whites and two-fifths (43.5 percent) of blacks in the metropolitan area had white-collar occupations in 1980 (see Table 4.2). This problem will likely worsen in future years, since "it is unlikely that the city will create sufficient job opportunities within the city limits."[25] Atlanta's poor, elderly, and unemployed benefited little from the area's growth, as many of the needed services and employment centers shifted to the suburbs.[26]

The line of demarcation between black and white Atlanta is clear. Interstate 20, a major freeway that runs east and west through Atlanta, is the unofficial dividing line that splits the metropolitan area in half. Whites are found largely to the north of I-20 and blacks to the south.

Atlanta Life Insurance Company, the nation's second largest black-owned insurance company. (Courtesy of Atlanta Life Insurance Company)

When one speaks of the rapid job expansion, economic development, and population growth in the Atlanta metropolitan area, it is this mostly white Republican-voting area north of I-20, the "Golden Crescent," where the economic renaissance is concentrated.[27] On the other hand, the core of the metropolitan area is mostly black Democratic-voting central-city Atlanta, where many of its neighborhoods have been passed over by the region's expanding economy.

Both jobs and housing are now concentrated in the suburbs. This phenomenon is taking place not only in Atlanta but reflects a national trend. Nearly two-thirds of all new office space in the United States has been built in the suburbs since 1984, up from one-half in 1980. Suburbanization of home and work has widened the social and economic inequities between metropolitan Atlanta's blacks, who are concentrated in declining central-city neighborhoods, and whites, who are found largely in the prospering suburbs. This problem is exacerbated by housing segregation and inadequate public transportation. The result is a steady whitening of metropolitan's Atlanta work force.

It is not an accident that Gwinnett and Cobb counties, each about 95 percent white and two of the nation's fastest-growing counties, more than fifteen years ago voted against becoming part of MARTA, Atlanta's modern bus-rail system. Only Fulton and DeKalb counties voted to become full partners in MARTA.[28] The vote in the mostly white suburban counties hinged on residents' fear of being "overrun" with blacks from

John Lewis, a longtime civil rights activist, was elected to the U.S. Congress from Atlanta in 1986. (Courtesy of U.S. House of Representatives)

Table 4.2
Civilian Labor Force in the Atlanta SMSA by Race, 1980

All Occupations	Whites (percent)	Blacks (percent)
Managerial and professional	27.8	15.2
Technical, sales, and administrative	37.4	28.3
Service occupations	8.6	22.1
Crafts, operatives, and laborers	25.4	33.6
Farm, forestry, and fishing	0.8	0.8
Total all occupations (number)	757,615	199,601
Total percent	100.0	100.0

Source: U.S. Bureau of the Census, *General Social and Economic Characteristics: Georgia* (Washington, D.C.: U.S. Government Printing Office, 1983).

Atlanta.[29] Getting to the Golden Crescent is not easy without a car. Since many of Atlanta's inner-city residents do not have cars, they are cut off from the region's expanding employment centers. Some black workers (for example, maids, janitors, gardeners, and casual laborers), however, are shuttled in and out of these white suburban counties in an apartheid-type arrangement. The 1985 firebombing of a black family's home in Cobb County and the much-publicized racial incidents in Forsyth County in 1986 reinforced what many blacks knew all along, Jim Crow is alive in metropolitan Atlanta.

Atlanta's black and poor have had extreme difficulty finding permanent employment. These problems were highlighted in a series of articles published in the *Atlanta Constitution*. Black unemployment and underemployment were attributed to a number of factors: (1) many traditional blue-collar or manufacturing jobs are leaving the Atlanta city limits and relocating beyond the public transit lines; (2) many entry-level jobs are on late-night shifts when buses are not in service; (3) the lack of affordable housing for low-income blacks in the counties where many jobs are moving serves as a deterrent; (4) the area's white-collar job market precludes many unskilled and marginally skilled persons from qualifying for new job openings; and (5) racial discrimination severely limits job options and salaries for black workers.[30] The decline in blue-collar jobs in the city of Atlanta and the relocation of new developments to areas that

Table 4.3
Unemployment in the Atlanta SMSA, 1982–86

Year	White	Black	Black Unemployment Rate as Percentage of White Unemployment Rate
1982	4.7	12.3	2.61
1983	4.3	13.3	3.09
1984	3.2	8.6	2.68
1985	3.1	9.9	3.19
1986	2.7	8.4	3.11

Source: U.S. Department of Labor, *Geographic Profile of Employment and Unemployment* (Washington, D.C.: U.S. Government Printing Office, 1981–87).

are inaccessible to public transportation severely limited black Atlantans' job options.

The 1980s have seen black workers in the Atlanta metropolitan area unemployed at a rate from two and a half to three times greater than their white counterparts (see Table 4.3). White unemployment was 4.3 percent in 1983 but was 13.3 percent for blacks, triple the rate for whites. Three years later, both white and black unemployment had dropped, to 2.7 and 8.4 percent, respectively. Again, blacks were more than three times more likely than whites to be unemployed.

Poverty and poor skills will likely place many black families in the endless cycle of inadequate housing conditions, deteriorating neighborhoods, and double-digit unemployment. The national statistics reveal that the poverty rate for all Americans dropped from 22 percent in 1959 to 12.5 percent in 1980. One in four (26 percent) black Atlantan households, compared with one in fifteen (7.2 percent) white households, fell below the poverty line in 1980.[31] Again, black Atlantans were more than three and a half times more likely to be poor than were whites. Low incomes and high unemployment serve as a deterrent for businesses to stay in many poor neighborhoods. Business disinvestment generally follows the out-migration of middle-income residents.

While many of Atlanta's business operations have left the central city, Atlanta's black-owned businesses have remained largely inside the city, serving a black clientele. Some of the city's black-owned firms have also

Table 4.4
Black-Owned Business Firms in Atlanta, 1977 and 1982

Industry Classification	1977 Number	1977 Percent	1982 Number	1982 Percent
Agriculture	—	—	28	0.8
Construction	198	8.8	214	6.1
Manufacturing	24	1.1	24	0.7
Transportation and utilities	212	9.4	190	5.4
Wholesale trade	25	1.1	39	1.1
Retail trade	584	26.0	803	23.0
Finance, insurance, and real estate	163	7.3	216	6.2
Selected services	956	42.6	1,702	48.7
Other industries	82	3.7	280	8.0
Total	2,244	100.0	3,496	100.0

Source: U.S. Bureau of the Census, *1982 Survey of Minority-Owned Business Enterprises: Black.*

shifted to suburban locations following black migration streams. Atlanta is well known for its established black business community. The number of black businesses in the Atlanta metropolitan area has grown over the past several decades. Specifically, the number of black business firms grew from 2,244 in 1977 to 3,496 in 1982. The gross receipts of the city's black-owned firms increased from $129 million in 1977 to $238.5 million in 1982.[32] A distribution of Atlanta's black-owned business firms in 1977 and 1982 is presented in Table 4.4. These data reveal that more than 68.6 percent of Atlanta's black businesses were concentrated in services and retail trade in 1977. Nearly three-fourths (71.7 percent) of the city's black-owned firms were concentrated in these areas in 1982. Retail trade, finance, insurance, and real estate industries led all Atlanta black firms in gross receipts for 1977 and 1982.

Atlanta had four black-owned businesses that made the coveted *Black Enterprise's* "Top 100" list in 1986.[33] The largest black-owned business in Georgia and Atlanta in 1986 was H. J. Russell Construction Company, founded in 1958 by Herman J. Russell. The company was listed by *Black Enterprises* as the third-largest black-owned firm in the United States in 1986, with sales of $118 million. The second-largest black-owned firm in Atlanta was M & M Products Company, which was the thirteenth-largest black business in the United States. This company had sales of $47.2 million in 1986. The third-largest black-owned business in Atlanta was Baracoc-Pontiac, which was the fourteenth-largest black-owned business in the United States, with sales in excess of $44.6 million in 1986. The fourth-largest black-owned firm in Atlanta in 1986 was Robinson Cadillac-Excalibur. This company was the eighteenth-largest black-owned business in the United States; with sales of more than $37.2 million. Of the twenty largest black-owned businesses in the United States, four are located in Atlanta.

Atlanta's Citizens Trust Bank is a landmark in the city's black community. Citizens Trust was the second-largest black-owned bank in the United States in 1986. It was founded in 1921 and "survived the Depression, the 'bank' holiday of the New Deal, and several recessions" and today stands as a "solid financial symbol" of the black Atlanta business community.[34] Atlanta's Citizens Trust Bank employed ninety-two persons and had assets of $97.2 million in 1986. Of the thirty-four black-managed savings and loan associations in the country in 1986, the tenth-largest was Atlanta's Mutual Federal Savings and Loan. It was founded in 1925 and has also survived the hard times that sank so many other black financial institutions. This black savings and loan association had assets of $35.1 million in 1986.[35]

There were thirty-five black-owned insurance companies in the country in 1986. The second-largest black-owned insurance company in the United States is located in Atlanta. Atlanta Life Insurance Company was second only to North Carolina Mutual as the nation's largest black-owned insurance company. The company employed 1,000 workers and had assets of $120.4 million in 1986.[36] Atlanta Life was formed by Alonzo F. Herndon in 1905. The company's chief executive officer, Jesse Hill, Jr., is one of Atlanta's most powerful business leaders. Atlanta Life has made a number of inroads into corporate and white-managed companies. Its progressive and innovative leadership has broadened the base of a company that was founded by a black man born into slavery. Joseph N. Boyce describes the significance of this insurance company in the Atlanta black community as follows:

> The decision to place Atlanta Life's home office at 100 'Sweet Auburn' was both pragmatic and symbolic. While pragmatism dictated that the expanding insurance firm be situated near the city's commerce center, the

building's location symbolizes the renewal of a black business area that is
an integral part of Atlanta Life's history.[37]

Atlanta Life has contributed to economic and community development for black Atlantans who otherwise would have been locked out of
the home-buying market. Specifically, in 1981, this black-owned insurance company provided over $5 million of its assets for real estate mort-
gage loans to black homeowners and small businesses.[38]

Atlanta's "Sweet Auburn Avenue" serves as the center of black business activity in Atlanta, although black entrepreneurs have broadened
their geographic base of operations. Atlanta's black business entrepreneurs provide a wide variety of services to the black community. However, black business owners continue to be underrepresented in the
business arena. Black owners must operate in a market where racism can
determine whether or not a black firm will be successful in getting a con-
tract. The black business community has overcome many of the barriers
in its path. Local colleges and universities continue to produce a steady
stream of young black business entrepreneurs.

School Desegration

Atlanta has a long history of an educated "elite" who have led the
struggle for social change. The city has served as the "black talent academy."[39] Much of the city's black middle class has ties with Atlanta University, founded in 1867 with donations from the American Missionary
Society. This university has been in the forefront in producing black ed-
ucators, scientists, judges, lawmakers, and other leaders. From its meager
beginning in a $350 boxcar, Atlanta University Center (that is, Atlanta
University, Morehouse College, Spelman College, Morris Brown College, Clark College, and Interdenominational Theological Center) has
become the nation's largest consortium of private black colleges. This
consortium has seen an impressive group of scholars pass through its
doors, including W. E. B. Du Bois, John Hope Franklin, Horace Mann
Bond, and Benjamin Mays, just to name a few. The late Martin Luther
King, Jr., civil rights leader and Nobel prize winner, was educated at
Morehouse College.

Black students come from all across the country and around the world to attend college in Atlanta. Many end up making Atlanta their home. The city also attracts a large number of college-educated blacks from other cities. The 1980 statistics on the educational background of Atlanta's metropolitan population revealed that 31 percent of blacks and 29 percent of whites had completed four years of high school; a total of 18 percent of whites and 15 percent of blacks in the Atlanta SMSA had completed one to three years of college; and 25 percent of whites and 15 percent of blacks had completed four or more years of college. [40]

The income gap between blacks and whites in the Atlanta SMSA endures. In 1980, the median income for white families in the Atlanta SMSA was $23,633 and $13,903 for black families. Thus, black families earned only 58.8 percent of the income white families earned in 1980. [41] Recent trends point to a widening of the income gap between blacks, who are found largely in the central city where employment opportunities are dwindling, and whites, who are found in the affluent suburban ring. The average family income in the suburban counties is well over $30,000. [42]

Although the black community continues to lag behind the larger community on a number of economic indicators, Atlanta still serves as a magnet, attracting thousands of individuals seeking their fortunes in the city. New migrants soon discover an Atlanta that is often isolated from the larger metropolitan area. Nowhere is this more apparent than in the public school system. Students in the Atlanta public schools are becoming increasingly isolated, as white flight has shifted the district from 64 percent black in 1970 to 93 percent black in 1985; suburban school districts have remained mostly white. [43] The changing demographics of the school system, however, have allowed blacks to gain control, through the political process, of the school board and the central administration. Black political gains of this type are closely associated with Atlanta's becoming a leader in the New South.

Black Politics

Atlanta has had an active black electorate since the mid-forties. Blacks made up 25 to 30 percent of the city's electorate from 1946 through 1961. [44] As was true in other southern cities, black politics in Atlanta was based on the loose alliance between black ministers and the white business elite. Power, however, rested within the white business leadership.[45] Atlanta's white business elite dominated regional politics through the late 1960s. Beginning in early 1969, the business elite was forced to share its political power with central-city blacks and the growing white suburban jurisdictions.[46] Atlanta in 1969 elected five blacks to its city council. Andrew Young was elected to the U.S. Congress from the city in 1972. One year later, in 1973, Maynard Jackson became the first black mayor of Atlanta.

The 1973 election marked the coming of age of black Atlanta, in that nine of the eighteen city council members were black and five of the nine school board members were black. Jackson carried over 95 percent of the black vote and over 17 percent of the white vote to win almost 60 percent of the votes cast. The incumbent Jackson won the 1976 election by a landslide.[47]

The two-term election of Jackson as mayor of Atlanta was a clear indicator of his political organization. The Jackson administration was confronted with the realities of the white business world and the expectations of the black community. These two groups often had competing interests. Mack Jones, a well-known political scientist from Atlanta University, stated: "The economy is controlled by white interests . . . and black elected officials need the support of these same white elements in order to maintain existing services."[48]

A high priority of the Jackson administration was the inclusion of minority firms in city contracting. Jackson made a number of enemies as a result of his stance on minority participation in city transactions. However, his record on this specific issue is one that clearly points to success. For example, just over 1 percent of the city contracts (that is, $43,759 of the city's $33 million contracts) went to minority firms when Jackson first took office in 1973. By 1983, black business firms accounted for 27 percent of the city contracts, which totaled nearly $44 million.[49] The mandate of minority participation in the new Atlanta airport terminal was another case of Jackson's using the leverage of his office to include minority firms. Jackson held up more than $400 million of airport construction until contractors complied with his minority participation plan. The contractors complied, and the project was completed on time and within the allotted budget.[50]

The 1981 election signaled another move toward black political empowerment. Black Atlantans, for the first time, gained a majority vote on the city council. Andrew Young, former U.S. congressman and ambassador to the United Nations, became the city's second black mayor. Young's election did not take place without controversy and cries of racism. However, the results clearly indicated that blacks were able to wield considerable political influence through their ballots.

The black electorate gained political strength with each election. Black Atlantans in 1984 held more than forty-five elective positions. In addition to the office of mayor, Atlanta had four state senators, nine black state representatives, three black county commissioners, thirteen black city council members, nine black judges, and six black school board representatives.

In 1986, blacks increased their strength to eleven seats on an eighteen-member city council. The same year, they obtained a majority vote on the Fulton County Commission with the election of twenty-nine-year-old Martin Luther King III, son of the slain civil rights leader. John Lewis, a veteran civil rights leader and founder of the Student Nonviolent Coordinating Committee, was elected to the U.S. Congress in 1986.[51] Lewis became the second black from the black majority district to hold this seat. Andrew Young was the first black elected from the Fifth Congressional District in 1972. After Young resigned his congressional seat to become ambassador to the United Nations, Wych Fowler, a white moderate Democrat, was elected to represent the district.

The 1986 Democratic primary pitted a number of well-known blacks against each other for the Fifth Congressional District, a position that became vacant because of Fowler's run for the U.S. Senate. The two most notable included John Lewis and Julian Bond, the charismatic state senator. The crowded field of candidates vying for the seat was narrowed to just two candidates, Bond and Lewis. This election illustrated that Atlanta's black politics and the civil rights movement had matured. The city had two strong black candidates (both men had grown up in the civil rights movement of the sixties) running for the U.S. Congress. The outcome meant that a black person would again represent Atlanta in Washington.

Conclusion

Atlanta over the years has come to be known as a symbol of the New South. The political gains made by Atlanta's black population have not been fully translated into economic gains in the employment and the business development arenas. A sizable segment of Atlanta's black population continues to be ill housed, unemployed, poor, and trapped in deteriorating inner-city neighborhoods with little chance of upward mobility. The out-migration of affluent Atlantans continues to erode the already dwindling tax base. The location of new business developments in the suburbs and outlying areas places extreme pressures on central-city residents seeking employment. The loss of manufacturing jobs and the relocation of newly created white-collar jobs outside the central city has contributed to the whitening of the metropolitan work force.

It appears that the battles that will be fought in Atlanta in the future will center on economics. As a matter of fact, politics and economics may become inseparable areas of contention as resources within the central city diminish. Specifically, jobs, housing, government contracts, education, and other public services will likely become more politicized than they are now. The expectations of many black Atlantans were raised during the massive buildup in the seventies without a corresponding increase in their standard of living. Many other blacks were disappointed when the economic conditions in their areas were not affected by the election and appointment of black officials.

While many of Atlanta's black middle-class residents did benefit from the city's white-collar economy, many low-income, poorly educated residents found few of their needs met during the boom that the Atlanta metropolitan area experienced in the sixties and seventies. What did this mean for Atlanta as a "mecca" for blacks seeking a better life? The economic renaissance has largely been concentrated in the mostly white suburban counties that encircle the city. Many central-city residents are isolated from these employment and housing opportunities because of inadequate transportation and the outright discrimination that occurs in the suburbs.

The reality of life in Atlanta is that the black political advances that were made in the seventies and early eighties are just beginning to pay off in terms of affecting the total Atlanta social and economic structure. Black political empowerment has taken place on an incremental basis. The black presence in the mayor's office, county commission, chamber of commerce, school board, city council and city departments, and planning agencies has made a real difference. However, black leadership in

Atlanta still must face the challenge of moving the city's large underclass into the economic mainstream. The solution to this dilemma seems to be tied to the white business establishment, which still holds the economic purse strings in metropolitan Atlanta.

4
Memphis
Heart of the Mid-South

Sandra Vaughn

Historical Background

Memphis throughout its history has been dependent on the work and efforts of its black population. The first blacks were brought to Memphis (the Fourth Chickasaw Bluff) in the fall of 1795 by the Spaniards.[1] The slaves were brought to build a Spanish fort, which would discourage American settlement and control the Chickasaw Indians. Twenty-three years later, John Overton, General James Winchester, and Andrew Jackson commissioned a survey of the Chickasaw Bluff by William Lawrence. The early town plan followed a rectangular grid of streets but varied from other towns laid out during that time, with its four public squares instead of one central square. The names of the squares—Exchange, Auction, Market, and Court—indicated their intended functions. A public promenade was also laid out along the bluff. This plan showed an early commitment to the assurance of public access to the Mississippi River. General Winchester is attributed with the naming of this city on the Mississippi River for the ancient Egyptian city of Memphis. The town survey resulted in lot sales only to American settlers, which marked the beginning of the small village of Memphis. Memphis was incorporated on December 9, 1826. The land area of the original city was only one-half square mile and had a population of 663 inhabitants.[2] The city grew rapidly, and within thirty years its population was 22,643; blacks comprised one-third of the city's population in 1856.[3]

Early black residents were mainly a part of two freed slave colonies. In 1824, "Free Joe" established a colony, on land deeded to him, several miles outside Memphis.[4] The other colony, in Neosheba, Tennessee (now Ridgeway/Germantown) was established by a Scottish woman, Frances Wright, in 1825. Wright erected a training center on 2,000 acres of land to assist blacks in obtaining formal education and skills.[5] Memphis grew rapidly during the 1800s, largely because of the increased production of cotton in the surrounding countryside. The economic importance of this single agricultural commodity to the region was reflected in the expression "King Cotton."[6] Roads and railway lines were built to make the city a center of commerce for the cotton and farm supplies market. Many sectors of the Memphis economy were dependent on cotton and agribusiness. The early role of Memphis as a regional distribution and processing center for cotton has guided its development to the present.

By 1860, slave trading became a major business in Memphis. There were two slave markets. Memphis, on the eve of the Civil War, was passionately against the elimination of slavery and held strong sentiments against free blacks. Memphis's black population was looked upon with suspicion. Blacks were placed under strict surveillance, education was forbidden them, a night curfew was imposed on them, and they were prohibited from holding night meetings except by permission of the mayor and under police supervision.

Memphis, however, was one of the first southern cities to emancipate its slaves. Blacks in Tennessee were enfranchised in 1867. The newly freed blacks aligned themselves with the Republican Party, and Memphis experienced a "heyday" for blacks in politics. Blacks soon became members of the city council, the school board, and the police force, and many held office in city government. Blacks also played an important role in the day-to-day business life of Memphis. Black labor was sought by the railroads and the levee construction firms. Local factories and trades employed blacks as common laborers and assistants. Blacks also owned small businesses. Black Memphians owned about twenty small service businesses; blacks owned and operated more than 500 drays (hauling carts) and fifty hacks (horses for hire).[7]

Prior to 1879, several outbreaks of yellow fever occurred in Memphis, but little was done to upgrade the unsanitary conditions in the city. Yellow fever reached epidemic proportions in 1879, and government leaders were finally prompted to collect the city's garbage on a regular basis, clean the streets, and build a sewer system. During this time, Memphis lost almost half of its population because of the epidemic and was heavily in debt. The city charter was abolished and the taxing district of Shelby County was created to govern the municipality. Some of the city's privileges were restored in the 1890s. Major sanitary improvements, the discovery of large supplies of pure water, the construction of a bridge spanning the Mississippi River, and other improvements helped make the city a viable entity again.[8]

After the yellow fever epidemic, the city fought to revise its shattered economy. In an effort to regain its footing, Memphis floated a large number of bonds. The first bond was purchased by Robert R. Church, Sr., the South's first black millionaire and the acknowledged "Boss of Beale Street."[9] Church was the patriarch of a family that was to make its mark on Memphis. He built Church's Auditorium on Beale Street in 1900. President Theodore Roosevelt spoke from the stage of the auditorium in 1902. Booker T. Washington gave an address from the same stage in 1913. Adjacent to Church's Auditorium was Church's Park. Both of these landmarks were major focal points for black cultural and social life in Memphis.[10]

Beale Street reached its zenith during the early 1900s. Along Beale Street were real estate and banking offices, dry goods and clothing stores, pawn shops, theaters, saloons and gambling dens, and a host of other small shops. George W. Lee, a black business and political leader, called Beale Street "the Main Street of Negro America" in his book *Beale Street: Where the Blues Began.*[11] Beale Street was the mecca for blacks in the mid-South. On Friday and Saturday nights, blacks came from the surrounding areas to buy groceries, shop, eat, and drink in the black business establishments that lined Beale Street. In its heyday, Beale Street was a very special part of black economic life in Memphis. For example, the Solvent Savings Bank, organized by Robert R. Church, Sr., and the Fraternal Bank and Trust merged in 1926. Solvent Savings Bank was located in the heart of Beale Street.

The city experienced a new wave of migrants in 1900. These new settlers were from the surrounding rural areas. They brought to Memphis a character that resembled that of small rural towns of the Delta: fundamental Protestantism and the idea of white supremacy. There was a "Gone with the Wind" mentality in Memphis, which was reflected in the paternal attitude of the ruling class toward black Memphians. In 1909, Edward H. Crump was elected mayor of Memphis. Crump was from a small Mississippi town and viewed Memphis the same way. In his campaign for mayor, Crump promised to rid the town of "easy riders, pimps, and gamblers." In a song written by W. C. Handy, the "father of the blues," are the following lines:

Table 5.1
Population Characteristics of Memphis, 1900–1980

Year	Total Population	White Number	White Percent	Black Number	Black Percent
1900	102,320	52,380	51.2	49,910	48.8
1910	131,105	78,590	60.0	52,441	40.0
1920	162,351	101,113	62.3	61,181	37.7
1930	253,143	156,535	61.9	96,550	38.1
1940	292,942	171,406	58.5	121,498	41.5
1950	396,000	248,713	62.8	147,141	37.2
1960	497,524	312,799	62.9	184,320	37.0
1970	623,988	379,224	60.8	242,513	38.8
1980	646,356	333,789	51.6	307,702	47.6

Source: U.S. Bureau of the Census, *Census of Population and Housing.*

> Mr. Crump don't 'low no easy riders here
> Mr. Crump don't 'low it—ain't goin' have it here
> We don't care, what Mr. Crump don't 'low
> We gonna bar'l house anyhow
> Mr. Crump can go and catch his-self some air.[12]

Crump did not run off the easy riders. In fact, he was very tolerant of them. He left the mayor's office in 1915 but controlled politics in Memphis until his death in 1954.[13] During Crump's reign, blacks had the right to vote (but only for a Crump candidate). Under Crump the labor force remained divided along racial lines, and labor unions were checked by the Crump machine. Crump suppressed the Klan, ensured that the city was clean, and saw that government was run efficiently—but at a price of freedom and liberty.

Population and Metropolitan Growth

Between 1890 and 1900, the black population of Memphis increased by 21,000, a 60-percent increase. Nearly half (48.8 percent) of Memphis's population in 1900 was black (see Table 5.1). Ten years later, the black share of Memphis's population dropped to 40 percent. Annexation of white areas by the city government and the movement of blacks from the region were major reasons for this decline. Thousands of the city's blacks were attracted to the northern and western industries during World War I.

The Great Depression leveled both blacks and whites economically. Population growth was stagnant for both communities. Birthrates decreased from 19.4 per 1,000 in 1928 to 16 per 1,000 in the 1930s for blacks. The city gained more than 103,000 residents between 1940 and 1950, or a 35-percent increase. The increase occurred largely because of the net in-migration to Memphis and the increase of birthrates for whites and blacks. The birthrate increased more rapidly for blacks than for whites.[14] Memphis continued to experience considerable population growth in the postwar period. The city's population jumped from 497,524 in 1960 to 646,356 in 1980, or a 29.9-percent increase over this period. Blacks also increased their share of the city's population. Blacks comprised 37 percent of Memphis's population in 1960. Two decades later, blacks comprised nearly one-half (47.7 percent) of the city's population.[15]

The 1970–80 period witnessed an 11.9-percent decrease in the city's white population. On the other hand, Memphis's black population increased by more than 26.8 percent in the seventies. Population estimates from the Memphis–Shelby County Health Department indicate that the city's black population exceeded the white population for the first time in 1984.[16] Recent population trends in the mid-eighties point to an increasing black central-city population.

Housing and Residential Pattern

The first urban area of Memphis was composed of a white enclave of merchants and their slaves and rivermen and their families. After the Civil War and the yellow fever epidemics, there were decreases in the white population and increases in the black population. The core of Memphis's central business district and the medical center complex were developed in the early 1900s. These two areas have a long history of white out-migration. By 1940, the area was more than 50 percent black. The residential area near the central business district and the medical center complex have remained predominantly black over the years. Many

blacks settled near downtown Memphis because it was close to employment and was an area where inexpensive housing was available.
Many of Memphis's black neighborhoods have a long and rich history.
The black areas in the city are diverse and present unique case studies of
urban life. For example, South Memphis has some of the city's oldest
black neighborhoods. South Memphis's street boundaries include Crump
Boulevard on the north, Interstate 255 and Bellevue/Elvis Presley Boulevard on the east, McKellar Lake on the west, and Nonconnah Creek,
Interstate 255, and the Illinois Central Railroad on the south. South
Memphis's greatest population growth occurred during the early 1900s.
The 1940 census recorded 64,432 persons living in South Memphis,
more than one-fifth of the Memphis population. There were five blacks
for every four whites in South Memphis in 1940. Between 1940 and
1950, there was a 20-percent gain in population. By 1950, 75,000 people
resided in the area, with the same ratio of blacks to whites as recorded in
1940. Between 1950 and 1970, the area gained 35,000 blacks but lost
approximately 32,000 whites. Blacks made up more than 97 percent of
the South Memphis population in 1970.

The 1980 census showed a decline in the black population in South
Memphis; the area lost about 16 percent of its black population but
gained no whites. A total population of 55,104 blacks lived in the area in
1980. Again, blacks were the overwhelming majority in South Memphis.
Most of the blacks who left South Memphis moved farther south to the
Whitehaven Levi area and the neighborhoods near the Memphis International Airport. The expansion of blacks into neighborhoods to the
south represents an extension of the segregated residential pattern that
typified housing in and near the central business district. South Memphis today is generally a low- and moderate-income area; it has some of
the most densely populated census tracts in Shelby County. The area has
a number of black landmarks, including Booker T. Washington High
School (the first black high school in Memphis, built in 1926);
LeMoyne-Owen College, founded in 1870 as a preparatory school for
blacks, and which in 1930 became a four-year college; and the Martin
Luther King, Jr., park.

North Memphis, on the other hand, is primarily an industrial and low-
to moderate-income residential area. The area is made up of 7,500 acres.
North Memphis, until 1950, was a stable community with a racially
mixed population. There were 57,000 persons living in North Memphis

in 1950, 63,296 in 1960, and about 61,000 in 1970. The area experienced a 3-percent population decline in the 1960–70 period. The greatest population change took place in the seventies and can be attributed largely to white flight from the area. The 1980 census figures show North Memphis to be overwhelmingly black. The area is also well known as the location of the city's oldest black community, the Klondike community. It is also the home of Manassas High School, the second-oldest public school built for blacks in the city. Within the neighborhood, the land area that is adjacent to the Mississippi River is primarily industrial and commerical. The major industries in the North Memphis area include Kraftco, International Harvester, and Firestone Tire and Rubber. However, industrial plant closings, business disinvestments, and out-migration of the better-educated and upwardly mobile residents in the seventies and eighties have left much of North Memphis in a state of severe economic decline. Few public or private efforts have been made to reverse these conditions. Unemployment, underemployment, and poverty rob the community of its vital resources, its people. Those individuals who can afford to escape do, while leaving behind others who are "trapped" in poverty with little hope or chance of escape.

Memphis is both an economically and racially polarized city. Since 1960, the white population has consistently shifted from the central city to the north, south, and east. By contrast, the black population has stayed largely in the northern and southern sections of Memphis, with moderate shifts to the southwestern fringe. The city remains segregated along racial lines. More than 92 percent of the city's blacks lived in black majority neighborhoods in 1970. The 1980 segregation level declined, with 85 percent of the city's blacks living in mostly black residential areas.[17]

For the most part, Memphis's black population continues to live in a crescent-shaped area extending westward from its northern arm along the Wolf River, southward to the Mississippi River, eastward encompassing all of old Memphis, and the Orange Mound area in the south-central part of the city. Black in-migration has been primarily to the older central-core neighborhoods or to the areas next to predominantly black neighborhoods. The seventies witnessed a small number of the more affluent blacks moving into predominantly white areas of the city. However, Memphis and Shelby County's black population continued to be geographically and socially isolated in the seventies and mid-eighties.

The early 1900s saw thousands of blacks leaving Memphis for opportunities in the North. Midwestern cities such as Chicago and Detroit were the final destination for many black Memphians during this migration wave. Blacks continued to be located largely in the central city, where opportunities for home ownership are limited. Home ownership opportunities were greatest in the suburbs where new housing construction was concentrated during the seventies. The Memphis SMSA experienced a 29.8-percent change in housing units between 1970 and 1980. More than 60.3 percent of the housing in the metropolitan area were owner-occupied units. The 1980 census of housing enumerated 129,662 houses owned in Memphis.

Home ownership among blacks increased by a dramatic 64 percent between 1970 and 1980. However, black home ownership still lagged behind that of whites. More than 47.3 percent of Memphis's blacks owned their homes in 1980. Four factors appear to account for the rise in black homeowners: the Fair Housing Act of 1968; rising income; more opportunities for blacks in the job market; and their ability to expand beyond the traditional boundaries of the black central-city neighborhoods.

Social and Economic Changes

Life has never been easy for blacks in the South. The conditions under which many blacks labored did not differ greatly from those under slavery. Black workers were not free, since they did not have the rights and guarantees given to other workers. Black workers were systematically discriminated against, overworked, and underpaid. This exploitation was buttressed by the legal system in the South. Black Memphis was not an exception.

After World War I, the Memphis business community formed the Industrial Welfare Committee. This group studied the labor supply in the city and concluded that "from an industrial viewpoint the Negro labor is one of the best assets of this community."[18] The Memphis community, as a result of the study, was urged to contribute money to improve the working and living conditions of blacks. The Memphis Chamber of Commerce initiated several programs to help foster black business projects and organizations. Memphis's business leaders in 1918 realized the importance of blacks to the city's economic future and tried, though with little success, to reverse the out-migration of blacks to the North.

Memphis had a population of 253,143 in 1930, with its black population numbering 96,550. The city had fallen from fifth to eighth in population among the principal cities in the South and Southeast. The major reason for the city's decline was its lack of job opportunities. The 1930 census showed that 28 percent of Memphis's population were employed in manufacturing, 24 percent in the trades, and 23 percent in domestic or other personal services. The majority of the domestic and personal service jobs were held by blacks, and two-thirds of all farms in Shelby County were operated by blacks, although only 10 percent of the farms were black owned in 1930. The white birthrate dropped from 16 percent to 12.6 percent during this same period. The only major growth in Memphis came from the in-migration of blacks from the rural areas and small towns of Mississippi, Tennessee, and Arkansas. Conditions may have been bad for blacks in Memphis, but they were often worse for many black sharecroppers, tenant farmers, and workers in rural areas.

Economic conditions improved in the city during the forties. War production became a major part of the Memphis economy. For the first time, Memphis became a manufacturing city. Moreover, the decline of cotton and increased farm mechanization in the fifties pushed many off the farm. These changes accelerated the migration of small black and white farmers to Memphis for jobs. As in the past, conservative attitudes toward race relations prevailed. The 1950s, however, saw some important political and social changes occur, which ultimately affected the lives of Memphis's citizens in different ways. The momentous 1954 Supreme Court decision in *Brown v. Board of Education*, declaring that the "separate but equal" doctrine had no place in public education, sent shock waves throughout the nation, particularly in the South. White politicians and citizens were fearful. Many feared that their traditional alignments and customs were about to change. White Memphis hoped that integration could be delayed as long as possible. Black Memphis, on the other hand, saw change taking place far too slowly.

A group of conservative white civic leaders formed an organization called the Citizens for Progress in 1956. This group was against racial integration and was resistant to change. Their slogan was "Keep Memphis Down in Dixie." The Memphis chapter of the NAACP countered the Citizens for Progress group and led the fight for racial equality. The pres-

Civil rights protestors march in front of Memphis city hall during one of the NAACP's "Black Monday" demonstrations organized in 1969 to protest discrimination in Memphis public schools. (Courtesy Ernest C. Withers)

ident of the NAACP, civil rights attorney H. T. Lockard, petitioned the courts in 1955 to desegregate the city's parks, golf courses, and swimming pools. In 1956, the NAACP filed a lawsuit against the Memphis Street Railway Company to desegregate the buses. In 1957, it also petitioned city government to permit blacks to use the public library.

The sixties were a decade of direct action. Blacks waged a frontal assault against institutional racism. They held sit-ins at the downtown lunch counters, Brooks Art Gallery, the Cossitt Library, and other public places. They boycotted department stores, grocery stores, and drug stores. Black Memphis was very much involved in the civil rights movement during the sixties. By the end of 1960, all facilities of the public library and all buses were desegregated, but not without resistance. The sixties were filled with protests, demonstrations, and marches to dramatize the plight of oppressed blacks. The 1968 strike by the Memphis sanitation workers was just one of these protests that drew the attention of national civil rights leaders, including Dr. Martin Luther King, Jr. King was assassinated in Memphis the same year. The strikes, boycotts, demonstrations, and "dream," however, did not end with the killing of King.

Dr. Willie W. Herenton became the first black superintendent of the Memphis City School system in 1979. (Courtesy of Memphis City Schools)

Congressman Harold E. Ford, first elected in 1974, is the only black ever to serve in the U.S. House of Representatives from Tennessee.

Table 5.2
Enrollment in the Memphis City School System by Race, 1970–87

Year	Total Enrollment	Percent White	Percent Black
1970	148,015	48.2	51.8
1971	146,545	46.2	53.8
1972	139,113	42.3	57.7
1973	119,750	32.0	68.0
1974	115,846	29.4	70.6
1975	118,171	29.5	70.5
1976	117,733	28.6	71.4
1977	115,637	27.4	72.6
1978	113,503	26.4	73.6
1979	112,396	25.3	74.7
1980	110,264	24.6	75.4
1981	107,962	23.6	76.4
1982	107,221	23.0	77.0
1983	106,708	23.0	77.0
1984	106,807	22.7	77.3
1985	106,518	22.5	77.5
1986	106,054	22.3	77.7
1987	107,984	21.8	78.2

Source: Memphis City School District, Pupil Research Division (1987).

After many years of struggle, Memphis's public schools were desegregated. However, the district's enrollment has undergone a dramatic change in the process. White flight has left the city schools with a largely black pupil enrollment (see Table 5.2). The racial makeup of the district's students was 48.2 percent white and 51.8 percent black in 1970. A decade later, blacks made up three-fourths and whites one-fourth of the student body. White enrollment in the 1987 school year dropped to just one-fifth of the total district enrollment. Enrollment in suburban school districts has remained largely white. The movement of jobs to the suburbs serves to fuel white flight from the central city. The city and suburban school systems are clear reminders of our two societies, separate and unequal.

Memphis's economic growth during the seventies lagged behind a number of other cities in the South. The city's racial divisiveness and stagnant economy were the main reasons that Memphis was dubbed the "dark spot in the Sunbelt" during the seventies.[19] Major revitalization efforts did occur in the downtown area during the early eighties. Redevelopment activities were encouraged by city and county leaders, and special tax incentives were given to businesses that engaged in revitalization efforts in the once-declining downtown area. The grand reopening of the Peabody Hotel in the fall of 1981 was the largest single influence in the renewed interest and commitment to downtown Memphis. Cotton warehouses and old office buildings were converted to residential and office space, and new office towers were built.

Other major downtown projects included the $62 million Mud Island, a river park linked to central Memphis by monorail, and the Beale Street Historic District, a redevelopment of the once-bustling center of black culture and music in the United States.[20] Beale Street was also surrounded by the black residential areas that were wiped out in the 1960s by urban renewal, often dubbed "black removal." More than $17 million in tax revenue and $5 million of private monies have been expended to develop a three-block entertainment district that would boost the city's tourism. Many of the crumbling buildings that once lined Beale Street (an important part of the area being designated as a landmark) have been demolished, and in their places are nightclubs, restaurants, fast-food outlets, retail shops, and two radio stations (not like the Beale Street of W. C. Handy days). So many buildings have been torn down, with a resulting loss of architectural flavor, and so many street configurations have been changed that the National Park Service in 1986 considered taking the street off its National Register of Historic Places. Many black Memphians also feel that Beale Street has lost a lot of its "soul."

The Cotton Row Historic District and other renovated buildings were reclaimed in the back-to-the-city cycle of the 1980s. Journalist Neal R. Peirce describes other reclamation activities in Memphis:

> [D]espite all the signs of rebirth in downtown Memphis, the most exciting development in town may be the program of a Catholic nun, Sister Elizabeth Bonia, to revive a depressed black neighborhood. Through a mix of

love, imagination and sweat-equity housing, Sister Elizabeth is creating a model, not just for neighborhood survival in hard times, but also for how to give poor people a real stake in their own community.[21]

Major efforts to bring new industry to the Memphis area were begun with promotional materials showing the city's central location in the United States, with the slogan "Memphis, America's Distribution Center." The city's long history as a center for commerce, coupled with the location of such major transportation companies as Federal Express Corporation were major reasons for the distribution center promotion. Tourists and conventioneers have also been targeted by the Memphis Convention and Visitors Bureau. This organization's major theme is "Start Something Great in Memphis."

Memphis's geographic location has proved to be an efficient distribution point for the central United States and international exports, via the Mississippi River, extensive rail and road network, and excellent air transport facilities. Memphis is a center of commerce for the entire mid-South region due to an early goal of civic leaders to make the city a major commercial trade center.[22] Basic industries of the Memphis area are transportation, trade, and services. Manufacturing employment covers a wide spectrum of industrial sectors, including pharmaceuticals, paper products, chemicals, furniture, and automotive parts. Many firms are involved in the processing of food products because of the ready access to agricultural markets.[23]

Memphis often has had to take a backseat to a number of other cities in the region. However, the city occupies a unique status in a number of areas: (1) Memphis is the second-largest inland freight port on the Mississippi River; (2) it is located in the heart of one of the richest agricultural areas of the country; (3) it is the world's largest spot cotton market; (4) it is the second-largest processor of soybeans and third-largest food processor; and (5) it is the headquarters of the 3.6 million members of the Church of God in Christ.[24]

The post–World War II era has seen a tripling in the number of jobs in Memphis. Most of these jobs, however, were in low-wage positions and in the unskilled categories, where a disporportionately large share of black workers are found. The largest employers in the city are government institutions, including public schools. Employment for every sector (except government) experienced healthy increases during the 1983–84 period. Trade and services made up 27.4 percent and 23.2 percent, respectively, of the total employment in the Memphis SMSA. The manufacturing and construction sectors also experienced sizable increases in 1984.[25]

Major employers that have established national or regional headquarters in the Memphis area include Holiday Corporation (formerly Holiday Inns), Federal Express Corporation, Dobbs's House, Guardsmark, Nike, and Merrill-Lynch. The largest manufacturing employers in the Memphis area include Kimberly-Clark, Schering Plough, DuPont, Cleo Wrap, Buckeye Cellulose, Sharp Manufacturing Company, Carrier Air Conditioning, and Dover Corporation.[26] Health services account for a large portion of total Memphis employment. The city has become the center of medical activity in the mid-South and is recognized nationally for its contribution to medical research. Health services account for more than 2,000 jobs.[27] The largest employers are the University of Tennessee Center for the Health Sciences, Baptist Memorial Hospital, and Methodist Hospital. In addition to the University of Tennessee Center for the Health Sciences, there are numerous colleges, universities, and technical schools.

Despite the economic growth that came to the Memphis metropolitan area in the 1980s, blacks still suffered from double-digit unemployment. Black workers were three times more likely than whites to be unemployed for each year during the period 1980–85 (see Table 5.3). The area's black unemployment rate peaked during the 1982 and 1983 recessions, at 17.5 percent and 17.2 percent, respectively. The black jobless rate dropped to 12.1 percent in 1985, still more than 8.5 percentage points higher than the 3.6 percent white jobless rate. Persistent unemployment, poverty, and low incomes have forced many inner-city residents to seek housing elsewhere and have forced many small businesses to close as a result of falling sales.

Memphis's black-owned businesses are concentrated in many of these declining neighborhoods. The city's black business firms, however, clearly point to a period of growth in the 1970s and early 1980s. In 1977, Memphis had more than 1,905 black business firms, with gross receipts of nearly $150 million (see Table 5.4). The bulk of these black firms was concentrated in selective services and retail trade categories. Specifically, there were 812, or 42.6 percent, black firms engaged in service-related fields and 525, or 27.6 percent, black firms engaged in retail trade. Thus,

Table 5.3
Unemployment Rate in the Memphis Metropolitan Area by Race

Year	White	Black	Black Unemployment Rate as Percent of White Unemployment Rate
1980	3.3	11.2	3.39
1981	4.5	14.8	3.22
1982	5.5	17.5	3.18
1983	5.4	17.2	3.18
1984	4.1	13.4	3.26
1985	3.6	12.1	3.36

Source: Tennessee Department of Employment Security, Labor Force Estimates, 1980–86.

more than two-thirds of the black firms fell into these two business categories.[28]

Memphis's black-owned businesses grew by 63.7 percent during this period. The city had 3,119 black-owned firms in 1982. These firms had gross receipts of $140 million in 1982. Black-owned firms continued to be concentrated in the services and retail trade classification in 1982. These two industry categories accounted for 67 percent of Memphis's black-owned business enterprises. Although Memphis's black firms increased their number by 1,214 new businesses between 1977 and 1982, gross receipts for the city's black-owned firms actually dropped by nearly $10 million during this same period.

Memphis has one of the largest black populations of the major cities in the South. However, the city in 1986 had only one firm, Pat Carter Pontiac, to make the Black Enterprise "Top 100 Black Businesses" list. The black automobile dealership, founded in 1981, was the ninety-fifth-largest black-owned business in the United States, with sales totaling $14.5 million in 1985.[30] Memphis does not have a black savings and loan. It does, however, have a black-owned bank, Tri-State Bank, which was the fifteenth-largest black-owned bank in the nation in 1986. The bank, which employed sixty persons, had assets of nearly $45.4 million in

Table 5.4

Black-Owned Business Enterprises in Memphis, 1977 and 1982

Industry Classification	1977		1982	
	Number	Percent	Number	Percent
Agriculture	—	—	38	1.2
Construction	270	14.2	347	11.1
Manufacturing	18	0.9	25	0.8
Transportation and utilities	95	5.0	167	5.4
Wholesale trade	15	0.8	15	0.5
Retail trade	525	27.6	900	28.9
Finance, insurance, and real estate	92	4.8	158	5.0
Selected services	812	42.6	1,192	38.2
Other industries and not classified	78	4.1	277	8.9
Total	1,905	100.0	3,119	100.0

Source: U.S. Bureau of the Census, 1982 Survey of Minority-Owned Business Enterprises: Black.

1985. Memphis's black bank was established in 1945 and continues to be an integral part of the black Memphis community, with its headquarters on Main and Beale streets; it also has branches in South and North Memphis.

Memphis is the home of the fourth-largest black-owned insurance company in the United States, Universal Life Insurance Company. This black insurance company was founded in 1923 and had assets of more than $63.5 million and a staff of 750 persons in 1985. Several other business-oriented groups were organized to assist the Memphis black community in the area of economic development. A local affiliate of the National Business League opened an office in Memphis in 1960. This organization, under the leadership of Leonard Small, served as a catalyst to aid the growth of minority-owned businesses in the area. The major event during this period was the construction of the Metro Shopping Center. This project had the support of a number of influential and established business leaders, including A. Maceo Walker, the president of Memphis's black-owned Tri-State Bank.

Black Politics

Memphis was one of the few southern cities that did not impose rigid restrictions on voting. Tennessee had never required literacy tests as a criterion for voting. The poll tax was abolished in 1953. Even before the Supreme Court decision that outlawed "white primaries," *Smith* v. *Allwright*, Tennessee allowed each county to decide whether blacks would vote in its primaries. Memphis's blacks voted in Democratic primaries as early as 1900.[31] As a matter of fact, Edward H. "Boss" Crump encouraged blacks to vote. The black vote was an important element in his winning elections. In Memphis, the successful candidates traditionally had black support.[32] Crump made his bid for the black vote through black political power brokers who organized and controlled the black electorate of the city.

Robert Church, Jr., son of the city's leading black power broker, was a leading black activist. Church was elected as a delegate to the Republican National Convention in 1912. His influence was felt throughout Memphis's black community, including his power to influence federal political appointments during the 1921–33 era. Church was the political "boss" of the black community and was able to deliver the black vote for the Crump organization. This coalition of Church-Crump lasted until 1928.

Crump, on the other hand, manipulated the white vote as well as the black vote. When Crump died in 1954, his organization disintegrated and a leadership vacuum existed. In 1959, the black leadership mounted a frontal attack. They backed an all-black ticket headed by Russell Sugarmon, who was seeking the office of public works commissioner. The all-black ticket lost. However, the black community had won a symbolic victory by their show of support for black candidates. Memphis had received the message "that from now on the white community would have to recognize their [black] power and deal with them."[33]

City and county government both underwent restructuring during the 1960s and 1970s. There was much discussion on the consolidation of city and county government. Political leaders pushed the need for more efficiency and cost savings through consolidation. Many services were combined, including property assessment functions, planning, libraries, and health departments.[34] Memphis residents voted in a 1966 general referendum to change the form of city government from commission to mayor-council. The new charter provided for a mayor with executive powers and thirteen councilmen with legislative powers. The mayor and councilmen were to be elected for four-year terms. Six councilmen were to hold at-large positions and seven would serve single-member districts. The first officials elected under this new mayor-council structure assumed office in January 1968.

The 1960s saw a number of changes occur in the blacks' struggle for political parity. The power base built by black leaders included the Shelby County Democratic Club, which had developed ward and precinct clubs, the Republicans of Shelby County, and the Volunteer Ticket Organization. The hard work of these pragmatic leaders paid off. Between 1960 and 1964, their efforts brought about the appointment of Odell Horton as assistant U.S. attorney and the election of Russell Sugarmon and A. W. Willis to the state legislature, Jessie Turner to the Constitutional Convention, and H. T. Lockard to the Shelby County Quarterly Court. In 1965, the Volunteer Ticket Organization's candidate for governor, Frank Clement, appointed Ben L. Hooks to the Criminal Court bench.

Two years after the passage of the federal Voting Rights Act of 1965, black candidates were running for mayor and city council. The 1967 campaigns, though not totally successful, launched a direct attack upon political cronyism and bossism. Although A. W. Willis lost the mayor's race, three blacks, Fred Davis, James Netters, and J. O. Patterson, Jr., became members of Memphis's city council in 1968. The number of black elected officeholders in Memphis has increased over the years. Memphis in 1984 had a total of twenty-six black elected officials. The city had one black member in the U.S. House of Representatives, two state senators, four state representatives, four county commissioners, four city council members, eight judges, and three school board members.[35]

Shelby County government was changed by the Restructure Act of 1974 and was approved by the citizens of Shelby County in a 1974 referendum. The former three-member county commission was replaced by the office of county mayor, with full legislative and administrative powers. The eleven-member legislative body became known as the Shelby County Board of Commissioners, formerly the Shelby County Quarterly Court.

Harold Ford in 1974 became the first black from Tennessee to be elected to the U.S. Congress. This was a significant event for black Memphians. Ford defeated three-term congressman Dan Kuykendall by a margin of 574 votes. The Eighth Congressional District of Tennessee, which covers most of the Memphis urban area, was represented for the first time by a black. Harold Ford was reelected in 1984 and 1986, each time by a landslide.

The black population in Memphis has established its voice at the ballot box. Blacks hold a substantial number of important public offices. They have moved into the political decision-making echelons of Memphis–Shelby County. More importantly, they have begun to dismantle the old traditions of white paternalism. Although political gains have been made, a number of problems remain. Journalist Lynn Norment describes these problems:

> Dozens of black leaders emphasize the same critical problems: the polarization of the races in social, economic and employment practices; lack of progressive leadership from City Hall; the lack of a solid industrial base; few economic opportunities for blacks; and progress-halting divisiveness among black leaders.[36]

Among the nation's twenty-five largest cities with voting populations above 30 percent, Memphis in 1987 was the only one that had not elected a black mayor. Blacks represent 47 percent of all registered voters in the city. In city after city, the support of a large number of black voters (typically a 35- to 45-percent black voting population), combined with a small number of white liberals, has meant victory for black mayoral candidates. This combination has not worked in Memphis. It did not work for John Ford, J. O. Patterson, Jr., W. Otis Higgs, or, more recently, Minerva Johnican, a candidate in the 1987 mayoral race. Johnican received less than 1 percent of the white vote. More importantly, less than 40 pecent of the voters in the predominant black precincts voted in the October 1987 city election.

The major barriers to the election of a black mayor in Memphis include the inability of the black leadership to unify behind a strong black candidate, the unwillingness of whites to vote for blacks, the decline in grass-roots political organizations, the nonpartisan nature of the city election, and the neutralizing of race as a political issue.[37] Blacks have consistently gone to the polls and elected white mayors. Black votes are consistently cast in sizable blocs, providing the margin of victory for white candidates. However, when it comes to the black community lining up behind a single black candidate for mayor, the black vote becomes fragmented and splintered. On the other hand, few whites reciprocate by voting for black candidates. The result of the voting patterns of blacks and whites is the perpetuation of the white political power structure at city hall.

Conclusion

It appears that a major issue with which black Memphis must come to grips is how to harness its economic and political resources into a unified force. The city's leadership, black and white, will need to develop strategies to deal with its growing underclass, deteriorating housing, unemployment, and business disinvestment in black and low-income areas. While the downtown redevelopment activities have brought new life into this sector, especially the Beale Street District, there are some questions as to whether the trickle-down process has allowed blacks to benefit from this new growth. Few neighborhood revitalization efforts have been initiated in low- and moderate-income black areas where physical deterioration is unabated.

Memphis, which was considered the "dark spot in the Sunbelt," is beginning to come into its own. It is one of the largest cities in the mid-South. The city's black population is also one of the largest in the Deep South. Memphis's black population has become a sizable economic and political force in the Shelby County and tri-state area (Tennessee, Mississippi, and Arkansas). Unlike many other cities across the country that have large black voter populations, Memphis has been unable to elect a black mayor. Black mayoral candidates have failed in Memphis mainly because of fragmentation within the black community and the unwillingness of whites to vote for black candidates.

Blacks have been able to capture a number of other key political positions. Blacks remain underrepresented in the political and business arena. The challenges that face the black community and the black leadership in Memphis will likely center around how to mobilize the community's resources to move forward in the eighties and beyond. Memphis, like other cities in the South, will likely take on added importance in the years to come.

Memphis continues to be a racially polarized city. However, there are some indications that racial barriers in the city may be diminishing. As blacks gain more economic and political clout, they are likely to exert more influence over the decision-making processes in the Memphis–Shelby County area. The empowered black leadership and community organizations need to develop long-term strategies to combat the persistent problems of employment discrimination, limited educational opportunities, and geographic isolation of the black masses.

5
Birmingham
A Magic City

Ernest Porterfield

Historical Background

Birmingham is located in the north central part of Alabama. Its average altitude is 620 feet, with a range from 58 to 1,200 feet above sea level. The city was officially incorporated in 1871 with a population of 1,200. The Elyton Land Company, recognizing the area's industrial potential, decided that the city to be built near Elyton in Jefferson County would be called Birmingham. In its first twenty years, the population increased to 26,000, and Birmingham was given the nickname "the Magic City," in recognition of its rapid growth.

Coal, iron ore, and the railroads lured a steady stream of migrants to the Birmingham area. Even though the agrarian economy of the Old South had been shattered by the Civil War, coal and ore deposits held promise of a belated industrial revolution, which would transform the devastated plantation economy into a prosperous New South.[1] John T. Milner, chief engineer of the South and North Railroad, was the first to anticipate that fortunes might be made where railroads would eventually cross in the midst of untapped deposits of coal and iron ore. From the crest of Red Mountain, he pinpointed the future intersection of his lines with the east-west lines of the Alabama and Chattanooga Railroad. The area was the creation of profit-minded men willing boldly to take risk.[2]

Birmingham's founders often addressed one another by title of "Colonel." They regarded the mayor's office as their private preserve, named mines and furnaces for their wives (Alice, Hattie, Lady, Mary Pratt), and left their surnames on streets, hotels, hospitals, schools, and suburbs. However, these city fathers were not the ultimate owners of the great iron and steel industry that had been envisioned. The city's great industrial wealth would later shift to outside control. This factor played a crucial role in the development and direction of race relations in the city.

Birmingham's boom began with the discovery that good quality pig iron could be made by combining coking coal with local iron ore. The first reliable supply of coking coal was developed in 1879 by Pratt Coal and Coke Company, owned by "Colonel" Henry F. DeBardeleben, "Colonel" James Withers Sloss, and a mining engineer from New York, Truman H. Aldrich. Eager to reinvigorate its struggling venture, the Elyton Land Company donated prime sites near the railroad juncture to facilitate DeBardeleben and Sloss in the construction of new pig iron furnaces and Kentucky ironmasters in building a rolling mill. The Louisville and Nashville Railroad, under the leadership of Milton Hannibal Smith, took over the ailing South and North Railroad line, infused capital into industrial ventures, and gave freight rate concessions to all. The newly constructed pig iron furnaces, enjoying easy access to coal, iron ore, and railroads, plus an ample supply of cheap black labor, soon produced pig iron at the lowest cost in America; they also undersold pig iron produced in England.[3]

At the end of the Civil War, blacks in Jefferson County gained their freedom, but their lives changed very little. Most continued to farm, sometimes for the men who formerly owned them. However, the size and character of Birmingham's black community changed quickly with the development of the coal and iron industry. Thousands of blacks migrated to the Birmingham area to mine coal and make iron. Most black migrants came from cotton farms in southern Alabama, where they had been kept poor and in debt by a system of sharecropping that allowed them little more freedom than slavery. Black sharecroppers rarely realized a profit from their long days in the field. In fact, their only real freedom was to leave the farm, which thousands did when they heard blacks could earn wages that were paid in cash and on a regular basis in Birmingham.

The move to Birmingham represented a great change to people accustomed to the simple life of an isolated cotton farm. The new arrivals usually found that their work had more drudgery than excitement. Many were coal miners, working at a dirty and dangerous occupation. Black workers were generally confined to the most menial and lowest-paying jobs in the mills. In fact, most workers understood which were "white" jobs and which were "black" jobs. Many blacks, especially women, worked as domestic servants. Black men frequently were yardmen and chauffeurs for affluent whites. Although these jobs were low-paying, they usually offered more security than the industrial jobs, which were subject to long layoffs during strikes and economic recessions.

Despite the hard work, low pay, and racial discrimination that blacks experienced, life in Birmingham was generally an improvement over what they had known on the farm. They had more money, a diverse social life, more freedom from white domination, and better access to education for their children. Most blacks lived in areas that were generally, but not strictly, segregated. New arrivals often moved into a "company house," a three- or four-room frame house that was owned by a coal or steel company. Usually identical in structure, company houses stood in rows, and several rows made up a company "village." Blacks and whites were segregated by rows of houses, which often stood back to back. Thus, company villages respected segregation in principle, but in reality they did not keep the two races very far apart.

By 1900, most of Birmingham's small iron companies had been forced to merge into three absentee-owned corporations: Sloss-Sheffield Steel and Iron Company, Republic Iron and Steel Company, and Woodward Iron Company. But Tennessee Coal Iron and Railroad Company was by far Alabama's largest and most powerful, owning thirteen furnaces, all fed from its own mines, and a princely domain of 400,000 acres of coal and iron lands. Of its 210,000 shares of stock in 1900, only 660 were held by Alabamians, and only one person from Birmingham served on its seventeen-member board of directors.[4]

Although Birmingham was recognized as the industrial capital of the New South, its coming of age had been marred by fierce strife between labor and management. For example, its labor force was a volatile mix of social hostilities and economic rivalries: poor whites, former slaves, and recent emigrants from the British Isles, Italy, and southern Europe, all competing for jobs. To complicate matters further, unions competed against nonunion labor, and free miners against convict laborers.

The use of state and county convicts as cheap labor for industry had grown out of a truce between planter interests of the Black Belt and new industrialists. Agrarian leaders, suspecting that Birmingham's jobs would lure tenants and sharecroppers from the cotton fields, initially fought the boomtown and viewed the New South as a phrase of "Yankee invention." The mineral region, underrepresented in the legislature after its population grew, complained that the planters in the Black Belt, ruling over powerless black majorities, had more than their share of legislative seats and influence. Convict leasing, thus, was profitable to industry, and it helped to keep taxes low.[5] The leasing of convicts to private industry did not end until the first administration of Governor Bibb Graves. Graves was elected in 1926 as a neo-Populist candidate.

Convicts who survived their sentences in the mines usually remained in the area, adding to the unsavory reputation of "Bad Birmingham." Since the 1880s, Birmingham had been widely recognized as the most crime-ridden city for its size in the nation. For example, the number of arrests each year between 1888 and 1908 was roughly equivalent to one-third of its total population. However, this statistic was misleading. Birmingham's police jurisdiction actually extended beyond the city limits to mining districts, such as Beer Mash, Buzzard's Roost, Scratch Ankle, and Hole-in-the-Wall. The rowdyism of such areas was reflected in the city's crime rate.[6] Moreover, Jefferson County paid its law enforcement officials a fee for each person arrested or sentenced, thereby rewarding zealotry in apprehending offenders suspected of gambling and other minor offenses.

Birmingham in the twenties still had not achieved its potential. It was still the "great workshop town" rather than a cosmopolitan area of the South. It was more akin to Tulsa and Oklahoma City than to its mature neighbors such as New Orleans, Atlanta, or Nashville. The overwhelming majority of its people were working-class, economically insecure, and racially polarized. Still strongly influenced by their rural origins and a lingering tradition of frontier individualism, many white laborers held strong antiunion views. Many valued the right to work more highly than union loyalty in times of strikes. Blacks, on the other hand, were pawns of the fee system and convict leasing. They were economically as well as politically impotent. The city's blacks remained in economic bondage.[7]

At the outbreak of World War II, Birmingham's economy moved into high gear. Throughout the 1940s, Birmingham's steel industry remained a strong part of the economy. The once-magic city gradually slipped into economic stagnation in the postwar years.[8] Despite an abundance of empty war plants, no major industry had chosen to locate in the Birmingham area during this period. Schools and other public services were inadequately funded because of the low property tax structure. The root of the problem, many civic promoters insisted, was absentee ownership of the city's major industries.[9]

Critics complained that U.S. Steel, although directly employing 40,000 Birmingham workers and indirectly responsible for thousands of other jobs, treated Birmingham like a southern stepchild so as to protect its financial holdings in the East. It was also suspected that the company had actively blocked other industries from entering the city, which might have created competition for labor and caused Birmingham's low wage structure to rise. Those concerned with city financing complained that the steel giant deliberately placed its mills and offices outside the tax limits of Birmingham and fought a move to absorb these municipalities or unincorporated areas into the growing central city.[10]

Birmingham's population continued to grow despite the economic upheavals of the forties and fifties. Though much of the "magic" had disappeared, it remained the premier industrial city in the South and the largest city in Alabama.

Population and Metropolitan Growth

Since its incorporation in 1871, Birmingham had experienced a steady population growth each decade until 1960. The decline that began in 1960 continued through 1980 (see Table 6.1). The Birmingham SMSA consists of 3,358 miles and includes four counties: Jefferson, St. Clair, Walker, and Shelby. The Birmingham SMSA had a population of 832,387 in 1980.[11] Birmingham ranked seventh among the largest southeastern metropolitan areas. It represented 22 percent of Alabama's total population and ranked forty-sixth in population among the nation's top 300 metropolitan areas. While population in the city of Birmingham declined in the seventies, the population in Jefferson County actually increased from 644,991 in 1970 to 671,197 in 1980. Birmingham represented 46.7 percent of the Jefferson County population in 1970, compared with 42.4 percent in 1980. Population increases registered in Jefferson County, however, were much smaller than those found in the other counties that made up the Birmingham SMSA. For example, Jefferson County's population grew by 4 percent between 1970 and 1980. The population increases registered by the other counties included 74.3 percent for Shelby County, 47.4 percent for St. Clair County, and 22.1 percent for Walker County.

One of the most significant demographic changes during the 1960–80

Table 6.1
Population of Birmingham, 1870–1980

Year	Population	Percent Increase/Decrease
1870	1,200	—
1880	3,086	157.2
1890	26,178	748.3
1900	38,415	46.7
1919	132,685	254.4
1920	178,806	25.8
1930	259,678	31.1
1940	267,583	3.0
1950	326,037	17.9
1960	340,887	4.4
1970	300,910	−11.7
1980	284,388	−5.5

Source: U.S. Bureau of the Census, *Census of Population and Housing.*

period was in racial composition. Two important changes occurred between 1960 and 1970. First, Birmingham experienced an 11.7 percent decline in its population from 340,887 to 300,910. Second, while both white and black population declined, the proportion of blacks increased as a part of the total population. From 1960 to 1970, the white population decreased by 15.4 percent, compared with a 6.5-percent decrease in the black population. From 1970 to 1980, the white population decreased by 28 percent, while the black population increased by 20 percent.[12] Much of this decrease can be explained by the exodus of the white population to the suburbs. The racial composition of the city from 1900 to 1980 is shown in Table 6.2.

Housing and Residential Pattern

Until the 1960s, the largest single concentration of blacks in Birmingham was Southside, an area immediately south of the city's central business district. Before the urban renewal program of the mid-sixties, shotgun row houses covered much of the area. Domestics, foundry workers, and a sprinkling of teachers occupied the houses. Black-owned cafés,

Table 6.2
Racial Composition of Birmingham, 1900–1980

Year	Population	White		Black	
		Number	Percent	Number	Percent
1900	38,415	21,832	56.9	16,575	43.1
1910	132,685	80,369	60.6	52,305	39.4
1920	178,806	108,550	60.7	70,230	39.3
1930	259,678	160,551	61.8	99,077	38.2
1940	267,593	158,622	59.3	108,938	40.7
1950	326,037	195,922	60.1	130,025	39.1
1960	340,887	205,620	60.3	135,113	39.7
1970	300,910	173,911	58.0	126,388	42.0
1980	284,388	124,711	43.9	158,217	55.6

Source: U.S. Bureau of the Census, *Census of Population and Housing.*

shops, and service-oriented businesses served an all-black clientele and could be found operating on almost every other corner. Southside residents bought most of their food at corner groceries run by Italians and Lebanese but rarely by blacks. Small Baptist churches were sprinkled liberally throughout the neighborhood. Some of these churches still hold services today, albeit with smaller congregations. Southside was so large and densely populated that its residents recognized subsections of the neighborhood. For instance, Beer Mash was the name assigned to the area between Third Avenue South and Twenty-sixth Street.

Several large, predominantly white neighborhoods in Birmingham have had distinct black sections, which were sometimes considered, especially by their own residents, as separate neighborhoods. For example, Tuxedo Junction in Ensley, Collegeville in North Birmingham, Zion City in Woodlawn, and Kingston in East Birmingham all were black enclaves in mostly white neighborhoods. Each was bordered on at least one side by white residential areas. Despite the close proximity of the races in these neighborhoods, relatively little racial conflict surfaced before the 1940s.

Several of Birmingham's black neighborhoods have had a long history as middle-class areas. Enon Ridge, which now lies just northwest of Interstates 59 and 65 in the downtown area, became a fashionable place to live for the city's black professionals in the 1890s. Shortly after the turn of the century, the neighborhood of Smithfield, an area just north of Legion Field, was developed. This neighborhood attracted black teachers and the growing number of black professionals. In the 1940s, South Titusville, near Elmwood Cemetery, began to attract upwardly mobile working-class blacks, many of them from Southside, who could afford to own their homes.

Residential segregation along racial lines was the dominant housing pattern in Birmingham. The city in the 1950s was the "largest and most rigid bastion of segregation."[13] Birmingham was the "Johannesburg of the South." Racial segregation in housing, however, did show some signs of waning during the 1970–80 period. For example, more than 92 percent of the city's blacks lived in mostly black areas in 1970, and 85 percent lived in similar areas in 1980.[14] Blacks in Birmingham, on the other hand, were more likely to own their homes, compared with blacks nationally. Nearly 53 percent of the city's blacks owned their homes in 1980, while 44 percent of blacks nationally owned their homes. More than two-thirds (67.7 percent) of the whites in the Birmingham area owned their homes in 1980.[15]

The demand for low- and moderate-income housing in Birmingham far exceeded the supply during the seventies and the mid-eighties. The Birmingham Housing Authority provided 9,047 families with housing assistance in 1987. A breakdown of the various housing assistance programs operated by the Birmingham Housing Authority in 1987 is presented in Table 6.3. The city's conventional public housing program continued to be the single largest government-assisted housing for low-income residents; some 6,800 units were provided in this program. The remainder of low-income government housing is provided under the Section 8 rental assistance program.

While blacks composed more than one-half of the city's population in 1980, more than three-fourths of the city's substandard housing was concentrated in black neighborhoods. Efforts by the city to solve the housing problem of low-income residents have achieved mixed results. The city's black neighborhoods over the years have lost a substantial share of their low- and moderate-income housing stock as a result of fires, demolition, and abandonment. Replacement housing for the city's large low-income population has been slow to materialize. There is clearly a need for more

Table 6.3
Housing Assistance Programs Provided to Birmingham's
Low-Income Households, 1987

Programs	Number of Families Receiving Assistance
Existing Section 8	1,564
Section 8 moderate rehabilitation	423
Section 8 voucher program	260
Public housing units	6,800
Total	9,047

Source: Housing Authority of the City of Birmingham (1987).

housing subsidies and rental assistance to the residents who cannot afford
standard housing.

Female-headed households made up approximately 30 percent of the
total housing needs of low-income families in 1980. Some special housing problems encountered by female-headed households were addressed
by the city's Housing Rebate and Deferred Payment programs. Of a total
of 2,265 rebates and grants made to low-income persons, 1,651, or 73
percent, were made to female household heads. Of these 1,651 recipients,
80 percent were elderly and handicapped. The large percentage of elderly
and handicapped women points to the fact that traditional sources of
mortgage assistance did not meet their needs.

Low-income housing programs are in trouble in Birmingham and in
most other cities. Costs to build and subsidize new units have gone sky-
high. Rental assistance and housing subsidies for low-income households
are shrinking. Few family units have been built under the Reagan administration. Units for the elderly have fared little better. Housing programs have been a prime target on the chopping block because they
committed billions of dollars nationwide for rent subsidies in fifteen- to
forty-year contracts with private owners. The rents were often higher
than those for similar units for unsubsidized tenants, although utilities
were included. Low and moderate-income households in Birmingham
will face increasing problems in obtaining decent and affordable housing
in the future. These conditions were especially acute for the more than
25,000 city households who in 1986 lived in substandard housing.[16]

Social and Economic Change

In addition to poor housing conditions, Birmingham's black community has had to face the obstacles of discrimination and rigid segregation.
The city in the 1950s and 1960s was the nation's most thoroughly segregated city.[17] Life in Birmingham has always been shaped by its rigid
apartheid-type racial policies. Theaters, restaurants, hotels, and ceme-
teries were separated on the basis of race. Elevators, water fountains, and
restrooms were marked "white" or "colored," and the financially hard-
pressed city struggled to maintain two sets (separate and unequal) of
schools, libraries, parks, and hospitals.

Although Memphis, Nashville, Atlanta, and Mobile each had a sprinkling of black policemen, not a single black served on Birmingham's police force in the 1950s. Not one black doctor practiced in the "white"
hospitals nor belonged to the Jefferson County Medical Society. Only in
the areas of voting, wage scales, and social welfare, all fostered by federal
initiatives from Washington, had Birmingham's blacks made progress
since the start of the twentieth century.

An attempt to launch a Birmingham chapter of the National Urban
League failed in 1949 when white business and civic leaders withdrew
their financial support. A chapter of the Urban League had been organized in Atlanta as early as 1919 and was supported by that city's Community Chest. Birmingham was not so fortunate. The sole avenue for
dialogue between the blacks and whites, an interracial committee within
the Community Chest agency, was disbanded by agency leaders in 1955
after whites threatened to boycott the entire fund-raising campaign.
Thus, Birmingham entered the era of racial revolution, the mid- and
late-fifties, without a single channel of communication through which
whites and blacks might negotiate.

Some of Birmingham's more moderate leaders adopted a posture of re-
sisting change by legal stratagems (for example, "freedom of choice" laws
for schools). But in general, the city's image during the fifties and sixties
was increasingly darkened by beatings, bombings, protest demonstrations, and arrests. After it was ordered to integrate recreational facilities,
Birmingham city government closed more than sixty-eight parks, thirty-
eight playgrounds, six swimming pools, and four golf courses. The Birmingham Bar Association debated whether to urge compliance with the

law. After many hours of deliberations, they finally voted to take no position on the matter.[18]

Observing that the power structure refused to seek change openly, the Young Men's Business Club, a maverick group of young professionals and businessmen, took the initiative in changing Birmingham's form of government from a commission to a mayor-council. This movement was spearheaded by two young attorneys, Erskine Smith and David Vann, both of whom had Birmingham roots that went back for almost a century. Implicit in the proposed change was the hope of creating a better racial climate by replacing Eugene "Bull" Connor and his fellow commissioners with more tractable leaders of city government. Connor warned his followers that Vann, who had once served as a law clerk to Supreme Court Justice Hugo Black, had been sent by Black "to brainwash us."[19] Birmingham citizens, nevertheless, voted to adopt the mayor-council system.

This action was a major turning point for Birmingham, even though its immediate result was chaos at city hall. Albert Boutwell, chosen for his moderate stance on civil rights, defeated Connor for mayor in April 1963, but "Bull" and his fellow commissioners contested the mayor-council election. For six weeks in the spring of 1963, while Birmingham was in the grip of its most intense racial crisis, no one was clearly in charge of city government. Awaiting a decision by the Alabama Supreme Court, both groups of officials claimed the right to govern until the court confirmed the election of Boutwell and the council.

Although the majority of Birmingham's whites had indicated a willingness to make some racial accommodations, Dr. Martin Luther King, Jr., decided to proceed with a massive display of nonviolent resistance by Birmingham's young blacks. On May 3, 1963, Connor ordered the use of fire hoses and police dogs against the demonstrators. This action, pictured in countless newspapers and on millions of television screens, evoked a national storm of outrage and resulted in a summit meeting between local leaders and Birmingham's white power elite, with the federal government acting as an intermediary. A settlement was reached within a week. Birmingham's white leadership abandoned its hard line, and the downtown area was desegregated, better jobs were promised to blacks, and all demonstrators were released from jail.[20] Despite the concession, the worst incident of racial turmoil in Birmingham occurred on Sunday

Richard Arrington, Jr., Mayor of Birmingham, first elected in 1979. (Courtesy of the Mayor's office)

Freedom Manor, a senior citizens' complex, is the latest addition of the Housing Authority Birmingham District housing program to the Historical Fourth Avenue District of downtown Birmingham. Many civil right activities took place in this area during the sixties. (Courtesy Housing Authority of the Birmingham District)

morning, September 15, 1963, when a bomb exploded in the Sixteenth Street Church. The explosion killed four young black girls, Cynthia Wesley, Addie Mae Collins, Carole Robertson, and Denise McNair.

Birmingham's leadership faltered in its race relations during a time when archrival Atlanta was proclaiming itself "too busy to hate" and when moderate reform was taking place peaceably in Charleston,

The inscription below (as it is typed here) is on the large white base of the statue of Dr. Martin Luther King, Jr., which is located in Kelly Ingram Park, on 5th and 6th Avenues and 16th and 17th Streets North, Birmingham, Alabama.

Dr. Martin Luther King, Jr.

Born	Assassinated
Jan. 15, 1929	Apr. 4, 1968

". . . Yes, if you want to say that I was a drum major, say that I was a drum major for justice: say that I was a drum major for peace. . . . "

His dream liberated Birmingham from itself and began a new day of love, mutual respect and cooperation.

This statue of Dr. Martin Luther King, Jr., erected by citizens of Birmingham, is an indication of their esteem for him and an appreciation of his sacrificial service to mankind.

Unveiled: Jan. 20, 1986
Carlo Roppa, Sculptor

Mobile, Nashville, and Memphis. Each of these other southern cities had a longer history to develop a leadership that was imbued with a sense of responsibility for the conduct of community affairs. Charleston was founded in the seventeenth century, Mobile and Nashville in the eighteenth century, and Memphis and Atlanta were founded well before the Civil War. In early Birmingham, however, social prestige came almost entirely from economic success. In short, the individuals with the most economic power in Birmingham also enjoyed the highest social status.[21]

Black Birmingham in the 1980s suffers from many of the problems that plagued it in the 1960s. For example, the income gap between its black and white citizens endures. The 1980 census reported a median white family income of $19,550, compared with $11,425 for a black family. In short, black households in the city earned just 58 percent of what their white counterparts earned. Black families are also four and a half times more likely to be in poverty than are whites in the city; 6 percent of the city's white families and 28 percent of Birmingham's black families fell below the poverty level in 1980.

Blacks have had difficulty finding employment in the private sector as well as in government. The hiring practices of Birmingham city government is indicative of how much discrimination was part of the structure. The city in 1966, for example, had only nine black classified employees out of a total of 1,698. Most unclassified workers who held menial janitorial or groundskeeper jobs, however, were black. Almost a decade later, in 1975, the city still had only 155 blacks among its 2,233 classified workers. The police and fire departments were among the most resistant to change. The city got its first black police officer in 1966. In the following decade, blacks comprised just 5 percent of the police force. The figures for the fire department were no better. In 1976, eight years after the first black fire fighter had been hired, only 2.1 percent of the fire department personnel was black.

In an attempt to dismantle the dual hiring policies, the Birmingham NAACP in early 1974 filed a lawsuit challenging the city's and Jefferson County's employment practices. The U.S. Justice Department joined the plaintiffs in the lawsuit a year later. In January 1981, a federal district judge in Birmingham found that various hiring policies in the police and fire departments did discriminate against blacks. The ruling was upheld on appeal, and a second trial addressing other personnel board policies began in 1979. By fall, the various parties in the lawsuit had launched

Table 6.4
Full-Time Employee Profile by Race for the City of Birmingham,
1987

Occupations	Total	White		Black	
		Number	Percent	Number	Percent
Administrative	72	54	2.5	17	1.2
Professional	484	343	16.2	137	9.4
Technical	321	237	11.2	84	5.7
Protective services	1,038	786	37.1	251	17.2
Paraprofessional	107	53	2.5	52	3.6
Office/clerical	399	192	9.1	206	14.1
Skilled crafts	210	152	7.2	57	3.9
Service/maintenance	958	301	14.2	655	44.9
Total[a]	3,589	2,118	59.0	1,459	40.7

Source: City of Birmingham, *Affirmative Action Report* (December 1987).

[a]The total percent does not equal one hundred because twelve workers of "other" races are included in the total number of employees and accounted for 0.3 percent of the city work force.

serious negotiations to work out a settlement. A consent decree that mandated increased hiring of women and minorities was entered into in August 1981. By 1987, blacks made up one-third (32.4 percent) of the police force and one-fifth (19.1 percent) of the fire fighters.[22]

The composition of the city's work force has also shown some dramatic improvements since the 1981 consent decree. Blacks represented nearly 41 percent of the 3,589 classified city employees in 1987. Black workers, however, continued to be concentrated largely in low-paying, low-skill, menial-type positions. Some 45 percent of the city's black employees worked in service/maintenance job categories, compared with only 14 percent of their white counterparts. Nearly 30 percent of the white city employees held managerial and professional positions, while only 16 percent of black workers held such positions in 1987 (see Table 6.4).

Most of the major department heads and high-ranking positions at city hall are still held by whites. The black department heads in 1987 included the city attorney, the director of streets and sanitation,[23] and the director of housing. The city has survived both economic and racial trauma. The towering smokestacks and massive rail yards of Birmingham, once considered the industrial capital, the "Pittsburgh of the South," are largely idle and now serve only as reminders of a past economic era.[24] Economic recessions in the early eighties saw the city's industrial base further eroded by the loss of blue-collar jobs. Birmingham is a classic example of an industrial-based economy struggling to survive in a postindustrial era. The loss of more than 30,000 iron- and steel-related jobs has been difficult to replace. The city has, however, made some inroads in diversifying its economy, attracting new industries, and expanding opportunities for black workers and black business entrepreneurs.

The economic climate in which Birmingham's black businesses have had to operate has shown some improvement over the years. Discrimination kept many blacks from attempting business enterprises. The Jim Crow system (though it was not designed for that purpose) actually helped some black business owners. Black businesses often had a "captive" black clientele. For example, W. R. Pettiford and his partners enjoyed modest success for a number of years around the turn of the century in the Alabama Penny Savings Bank, largely because they loaned money to blacks when white-owned banks would not. Most black businesses provided a personal service to other blacks. A case in point is Charles M. Harris, who founded the Davenport and Harris Funeral Home in 1899. He also started the Protective Burial Association in 1923. Under his plan, a family of seven could get complete burial coverage for thirty-five cents a week. The burial association evolved into the Protective Industrial Life Insurance Company of Alabama, which in 1982 was the thirteenth-largest black insurance company in the United States. The company had assets of more than $7.8 million.[25]

Dr. A. G. Gaston is probably the premier black business entrepreneur in the United States. He followed a pattern of business development similar to that of Harris but took it a step further. Beginning with the Smith and Gaston Funeral Homes in 1923, he first added the Booker T. Washington Insurance Company. This black insurance company ranked eighth among the nation's black-owned insurance firms, with assets of $22 million in 1982. Gaston later added a business college, drugstore, hotel, radio station, and a savings and loan association to his business holdings. He founded Citizens Federal Savings and Loan Association in

Table 6.5
Distribution of Black-Owned Birmingham Businesses, 1977 and 1982

Business Classification	1977		1982	
	Number	Percent	Number	Percent
Agricultural	—	—	60	1.0
Construction	60	8.3	57	5.0
Manufacturing	7	1.0	7	0.6
Transportation and utilities	32	4.4	36	3.1
Wholesale trade	12	1.7	20	1.7
Retail trade	192	26.6	270	23.6
Finance, insurance, and real estate	23	3.2	42	3.7
Selected services	363	50.4	617	53.9
Other industries and not classified	32	4.4	85	7.4
Total	721	100.0	1,145	100.0

Source: U.S. Bureau of the Census, *1982 Survey of Minority-Owned Business Enterprises: Black.*

1957. Birmingham's black-owned savings and loan had assets of more than $40 million and was the nation's eighth-largest black savings and loan in 1982.

Bradford Industrial Insurance Company, Birmingham's other black insurance company, was founded in 1932. It was the nation's twenty-sixth-largest black insurance company, with assets of $2 million in 1982. The total assets of Birmingham's black insurance companies increased from $23 million in 1977 to more than $33 million in 1982, or a 43-percent increase.

Birmingham has never had one of its firms to make the *Black Enterprise* "Top 100" list, as have such rival cities as Atlanta and Charlotte. The number of black-owned firms in the city has been expanding over the years. In 1977, Birmingham had 721 black-owned business enterprises, with gross receipts of $39.2 million. By 1982, the number of black-owned business enterprises had grown to 1,145 (see Table 6.5), with gross receipts more than $47.1 million. Birmingham's black-owned firms experienced a growth rate (number of firms) of more than 59 percent between 1977 and 1982. However, the gross receipts of these firms grew by only 20 percent during this same period. More than three-fourths of the city's black businesses were concentrated in services and retail trade.[26]

Black Birmingham is still underrepresented in the business arena as owners and managers. Few blacks serve on corporate boards and decision-making bodies. Black Birmingham continues to be a consumer-oriented community that has yet to realize its full economic power and potential. Black consumer dollars simply flow out of the black community. The economic gains made by blacks in the city during the 1970s and 1980s are far from impressive. Blacks in Birmingham, on the other hand, have made substantial strides in the political arena.

Black Politics

No achievement was more important than the gaining of the right to vote. Four years after the passage of the historic Voting Rights Act of 1965, attorney Arthur Shores, a black, was elected to the city council, and blacks would subsequently win other public offices. Birmingham's city council included among its nine members two blacks and two women in 1971. By 1976, the most segregated city in the nation was moving toward integration. Almost as if it had always been this way, blacks shared schools, parks, libraries, restaurants, and hotels. Blacks also moved into management-level positions in city government and private industry.

The 1970s saw a continued maturation in the city's black community. Perhaps the strongest indicator of Birmingham's progress was the election of Dr. Richard Arrington, a black educator and a longtime city council member, as mayor in late 1979. The election of Arrington as Birmingham's first black mayor was accompanied by the usual high expectations of blacks and the heightened anxieties of the white business establishment. Arrington has built a strong political organization through the Jefferson County Citizens Coalition, a group he helped start. This organization's slate of candidates routinely wins local elections.

In 1985, Birmingham got its first black majority on the city council. While the Arrington administration has had some problems awarding minority firms contracts with the city (for example, state law prohibits minority business ordinances, which are popular in many other states), it has increased the presence of blacks in nearly all city departments.[27] Overall, Arrington has cultivated a productive relationship with the Birmingham business community. Construction continues in the downtown

area. Birmingham did not collapse into chaos when a black man took
charge of city government, as many whites had feared. The contributions
of the city's first black mayor to Birmingham's improved race relations are
summarized by journalist Margaret Edds:

> Many people have contributed to Birmingham's improved racial climate,
> but none more than Richard Arrington. To the hardedged, brittle climate
> of the 1960s, he brought a competence and quiet dignity that disarmed
> those who said no black man was capable of running Alabama's largest
> city. His even-tempered, nonthreatening style and academic background
> were perhaps the perfect antidotes to the hysteria that had so captivated
> earlier generations. A new Birmingham, less wedded to a brutal past than
> to an optimistic future.[28]

The 1980s have also seen Birmingham's blacks expand their political
influence and power base. In addition to the mayor, Birmingham had two
black state senators, six state representatives, four city council members,
and five constables who held office in 1984.[29] By 1987, six of the nine city
council seats and two of the five county commission seats were held by
blacks. These changes that occurred in the political arena are impressive
by any standard. They are especially impressive milestones given the history of race relations in Birmingham. Blacks in Birmingham and Jefferson County, however, continue to be underrepresented in elective offices
and on appointed commissions and decision-making boards.

Although blacks have held membership on the school board for more
than two decades, the city did not get a black school superintendent until
the beginning of the 1984–85 school year. The city's public schools have
become a political battleground. The quality of programs has suffered
over the years as a result of white flight, dwindling enrollment, and ero-
sion of the city's tax base. Birmingham's public school system is mostly
black and poor. In 1987, blacks made up more than three-fourths of the
46,523 students enrolled in the public schools.[30] Blacks made up just 47
percent in 1960. Housing segregation and the concentration of blacks in
the central city and whites in the suburbs further complicate the tasks of
school desegregation and guaranteeing all students equal access to quality education.

Conclusion

It seems that Birmingham, "the Magic City," has come a long way in terms of its image as one of the toughest cities in the South if one happened to be black. While white racism continues to persist in nearly every institution in the city, many of the conflicts and overt hostilities have declined to a large degree. The federal courts and civil rights legislation outlawed segregation more than two decades ago. However, black and white Birmingham residents live in two separate and unequal worlds. Housing and residential areas largely reflect the pattern established under Jim Crow. Blacks are concentrated in the central city, while whites are found largely in the suburbs. The city has been losing population and jobs to the growing suburban counties. White flight has left Birmingham's public schools with an overwhelming black student population. A growing number of middle-income blacks are also quitting the public schools, leaving behind a large concentration of poor students who have few middle-income role models.

Birmingham was tagged "Johannesburg of the South" in the sixties. The city now has a black mayor. Blacks comprise a majority on the city council. They hold seats on the county commission, state legislature, and other public offices. Blacks hold numerous administrative posts in city government. The gains that have been made over the past several decades have not eliminated the underrepresentation of blacks in elective offices. The political gains, however, represent the first steps in bringing about a degree of parity between blacks and whites.

Few barriers that would make the black community economically independent have fallen in the area of economic and business development. Redlining, inner-city disinvestment, housing discrimination, and limited employment opportunities persist as problems in Birmingham as well as the nation as a whole. Black unemployment has remained high throughout the 1970–87 period. The city's black neighborhoods have been ravaged by periodic economic recessions. Unemployment among blacks, and particularly among black youth, endured at epidemic proportions in the seventies and early eighties, and the future of many low-income black youth seems bleak. Birmingham's ghetto areas are in a state of deep depression and have been that way for years. Change has come slowly in Birmingham. However, the bottom line is that the city and its residents are moving in the direction to accommodate change.

6
Blacks in Tampa

Robert A. Catlin

Historical Background

After the defeat of Seminole chief Osceola in 1842,[1] slaveholders moved into Florida and Hillsborough County and started dairy, citrus, and winter vegetable farms.[2] Hundreds of blacks moved from South Georgia and North Florida to Tampa after the Civil War seeking work, only to meet strong resistance from the newly reestablished white government.[3]

Conditions improved somewhat for blacks during the 1880s, as Tampa broadened its economic base to include rail lines, the cigar industry, phosphate refinement, and a port. Buoyed by this growth, the black population of Tampa grew from less than 800 in 1865 to 1,601 in 1890 and 4,382 in 1900. Much of this growth was the result of the large group of Afro-Cubans who moved to Tampa with their white Cuban counterparts during the 1890s to work in cigar factories. In Cuba, the two groups interacted without rigid racial segregation. However, upon coming to the United States, the white Cubans soon found out that in order to be more "American" they would have to dissociate themselves from their darker brothers. According to Joan Steffey:

> On arriving in the United States, the Afro-Cuban was forced to adjust himself to an even more strict color line which dictated separation. Black Cubans encountered the discrimination not only of custom but of the State. In civic functions Americans in the city of Tampa could accept white Cubans but not "niggers." Even among their countrymen there is evidence that Afro-Cubans were forced to develop and maintain separate social functions although they worked closely with their white countrymen in the cigar factories.[4]

142

This phenomenon caused the Afro-Cubans to separate themselves from Afro-Americans, and integration of the two groups did not take place until after World War II. This separation fragmented black Tampa for years, and the residual effects remain today. The original black community for both Afro-Americans and Afro-Cubans was an area just east of Ybor City known as "the Scrub."[5] Originally, the Scrub consisted of small garden plots; but as the black population of Tampa expanded, the area became a tightly compacted ghetto. While smaller black communities developed in West Tampa, Port Tampa, and the rural areas of Seffner and Plant City, the Scrub became Tampa's major black concentration, housing more than 3,000 people by 1910, almost half of Tampa's total black population. It remained the major center of black Tampa until the late 1950s and early 1960s, when urban renewal and highway construction leveled the area and dispersed its residents.

A real boon to the economy of black Tampa was the organization of the International Longshoremen's Union Local 1402 by black stevedores in the port of Tampa in 1935. Led by James Lavelle, this union met with bitter resistance on the part of whites, and many key black organizers were fired.[6] However, after a spirited court battle under the leadership of Perry Harvey, Sr., the legitimacy of the union was upheld, and wages for black longshoremen rose almost to the level enjoyed by whites.[7] With the coming of World War II, the port of Tampa became the nation's largest, employing thousands of well-paid blacks who, to this day, form the backbone of Tampa's black economy.

Population and Metropolitan Growth

The Tampa–St. Petersburg SMSA is located on the gulf coast of central Florida and includes Hillsborough, Pinellas, and Pasco counties. The metropolitan area experienced tremendous growth in the 1970–80 period, with a population increase of more than 43 percent. The Tampa–St. Petersburg area had more than 1.5 million persons in 1980, or a net gain of more than 480,000 persons since 1970.[8] The Tampa–St. Petersburg metropolitan area was one of the nation's ten fastest-growing areas in 1980 (see Table 7.1).

The black population in the Tampa area also increased in the 1970–80 period. For example, the number of blacks in the metropolitan area in-

Table 7.1
Population in Tampa–St. Petersburg SMSA, 1960–80

Year	Total Population	Black	Percent Black
1960	809,238	92,651	11.4
1970	1,088,549	113,194	10.4
1980	1,569,134	145,688	9.3

Source: U.S. Bureau of the Census, *City and Metropolitan Area Data Book 1982*.

creased from 92,651 in 1960 to over 145,688 in 1980. The black share of the metropolitan population, however, actually shrank during this same period. Blacks comprised 11.4 percent of the metropolitan population in 1960, 10.4 percent in 1970, and 9.3 percent in 1980. The bulk of the black population resided in the central cities of Tampa and St. Petersburg. The city of Tampa, for example, had a population of 271,423, of which 63,835, or 23.5 percent, were black. St. Petersburg's 41,000 blacks, on the other hand, made up 17.2 percent of the city's 271,523 population in 1980. Blacks comprised 4 percent of the population that resided outside the central cities.[9]

Despite the growth that the Tampa area experienced in the seventies, its black community did not fare so well. For example, blacks were four times as likely to be below the poverty level as whites. Tampa's 35.1 percent black poverty rate was surpassed only by the poverty rates of blacks in New Orleans and Milwaukee. Black families in the Tampa area were nearly four times as likely to be headed by females, compared with their white counterparts. Blacks were less likely to be college graduates and were more likely to be unemployed than whites. Black Tampans earned only 62 percent of the income earned by white Tampans in 1980 (see Table 7.2).

Nearly one-half (49.9 percent) of Tampa's blacks owned their homes in 1980. The average mortgage payment for black Tampans was lower than that paid by blacks in the Houston, Atlanta, or Dallas–Ft. Worth metropolitan areas. The median mortgage payment in black Tampa was $237 in 1980, compared with $301 in Houston, $348 in Atlanta, and $245 in the Dallas–Ft. Worth area. Black Tampans must still solve the problem of overcrowding, aging housing stock in the central city, and general physical deterioration of older inner-city neighborhoods. Rising

Table 7.2
Selected Characteristics of the Tampa–St. Petersburg
SMSA by Race, 1980

Characteristic	White	Black
Percent female-headed households	10.9	42.4
Percent below poverty	9.4	35.1
Percent college graduates	13.6	7.0
Percent unemployed	4.5	8.5
Percent homeowners	73.6	49.9
Median family income	$17,005	$10,504

Source: U.S. Bureau of the Census, *Provisional Estimates of Social, Economic and Housing Characteristics* (Washington, D.C.: U.S. Government Printing Office, 1982).

costs in the seventies and eighties precluded many blacks from the home ownership market. Limited income also complicated the process of leasing housing in the rental sector.

Housing and Residential Pattern

Residential segregation remains a problem in Tampa. By 1980, more than one-half of all blacks in the city lived in neighborhoods that were at least 75 percent black. Until World War II, black Tampans lived in a typical southern urban spatial pattern: numerous small communities interspersed with white neighborhoods. In the old Scrub neighborhood of Ybor City and in West Tampa, blacks and Cubans lived on adjacent blocks or even mixed within the same block. However, after World War II, this began to change. The postwar housing boom in the 1950–54 period found almost 100,000 whites moving into the suburbs just north of Tampa. This area was quickly annexed by the city in an attempt to increase the percentage of whites in Tampa and keep down the longtime political influence of the Latins and the new influence of black voters.[10] Black neighborhoods expanded to fill the void left by departing whites, and several small enclaves consolidated, so that by 1960, there were only two major black neighborhoods: East Tampa, which included Belmont Heights, Ybor City, College Hill, and Jackson Heights; and West Tampa,

Table 7.3
Population in Tampa and Hillsborough County, 1970–80

	1970	1980
Tampa		
Total population	277,767	271,523
Black population	64,720	63,835
Percent black	19.7	23.5
Suburban Hillsborough County		
Total population	212,498	375,437
Black population	11,928	22,629
Percent black	5.6	6.0
Total—Hillsborough County		
Total population	490,265	646,960
Black population	66,648	86,464
Percent black	13.6	13.4

Source: U.S. Bureau of the Census, *Census of Population and Housing.*

which included the old black neighborhood on Tampa's west side and the black portion of Hyde Park.

Blacks represented 13.6 percent of Hillsborough County's population in 1970. In the city of Tampa, there were 54,720 blacks, comprising 19.7 percent of the population, while in the suburban areas the figures were 11,928, or 5.6 percent, respectively (see Table 7.3). Of the seventy-four census tracts in Tampa, almost half had less than 1 percent black residents. In the suburbs, more than half of the forty tracts had less than 1 percent black occupancy. More than sixteen of seventy-four Tampa census tracts had 50 percent or higher black occupancy, while only three of the forty suburban tracts had more than 50 percent black residents.

Some startling changes had developed in Tampa by 1980. The number of Tampa census tracts with less than 1 percent black residents shrank from thirty-five to ten, while those with 1 to 5 percent black populations rose from seven to twenty-four. Those with 5 to 25 percent black populations rose from eleven in 1970 to eighteen in 1980, while those with 50 percent or more blacks grew slightly from sixteen in 1970 to nineteen in 1980. The black population in Tampa rose by more than 9,000 residents to comprise 27 percent of the city's total population. The city's total pop-

Table 7.4
Percent Black in Tampa Census Tracts, 1970–80

| Percent Black | Number of Census Tracts | | | |
| | 1970 | | 1980 | |
	Number	Percent	Number	Percent
0–1	35	47.3	10	13.5
1–5	7	9.5	24	32.4
5–25	11	14.9	18	24.3
25–50	5	6.7	3	4.1
50–75	6	8.1	9	12.2
75+	10	13.5	10	13.5
Total census tracts	74	100.0	74	100.0

Source: U.S. Bureau of the Census, *Census of Population and Housing.*

ulation at the same time dropped from 277,767 to 271,523 (see Tables 7.4 and 7.5).

Changes in suburban Hillsborough County were just as dramatic. The number of tracts with less than 1 percent black populations dropped from twenty-two in 1970 to ten in 1980, while those ranging from 1 to 5 per-

Table 7.5
Percent Black in Suburban Hillsborough County
Census Tracts, 1970–80

| Percent Black | 1970 | | 1980 | |
	Number of Tracts	Percent	Number of Tracts	Percent
0–1	22	55.0	10	25.0
1–5	8	20.0	16	40.0
5–25	7	17.5	10	25.0
25–50	0	0.0	2	5.0
50–75	2	5.0	1	2.5
75+	1	2.5	1	2.5
Totals	40	100.0	40	100.0

Source: U.S. Bureau of the Census, *Census of Population and Housing.*

cent doubled from eight to sixteen; ten of the forty tracts had black populations in the 5 to 25 percent range, while only two had 50 percent or more black residents. The black population doubled in the suburban areas from 11,928 in 1970 to 22,629 in 1980, more than keeping up with the total percentage increase of just over 75 percent. The percentage of blacks in suburban Hillsborough County increased from 5.6 percent in 1970 to 6 percent in 1980 and occurred in a widely dispersed manner, rather than simply in the expansion of the existing black community. The black population in Tampa increased during the 1970s period, while the city was experiencing a slight overall decrease.

The degree of segregation was lower in 1980 than ten years earlier. A number of factors contributed to the reduction of residential segregation between 1970 and 1980, including (1) the declining significance of territoriality, or "turf," due to in-migration dynamics; (2) new construction as the primary component of suburban growth; (3) the transfer of managerial and technical personnel from "Frost Belt" areas; (4) initiatives by the U.S. Armed Forces; (5) the Hillsborough County public school desegregation decision of 1970; (6) the presence of highly identifiable role models in the suburbs; and (7) the lack of well-established middle-class neighborhoods in either Tampa or suburban Hillsborough County.

Northern central cities in general had periods of major growth during 1900–1940 and varying degrees of decline in World War II. Northern suburbs had their largest growth during the late forties, fifties, and early sixties, reaching stability before 1970. On the other hand, southern cities such as Tampa grew mainly during the 1950s and 1960s, with its suburban growth beginning in the sixties and continuing through the seventies. Tampa's central city and suburban neighborhoods are newer and less resistant to change, compared with many northern neighborhoods, since territoriality is much less established. Moreover, Tampa was settled by migrants from the North and Midwest as well as other areas of the Deep South. Regardless of past prejudices, these new residents upon arrival were more inclined to "live and let live."

While Tampa was substantially developed by the early 1960s, growth in suburban Hillsborough County has been a fairly recent phenomenon. Suburban Hillsborough County's population grew from 125,000 in 1960 to 275,000 in 1980 and 350,000 by 1987. The area was a prime location for new single-family home construction and planned subdivisions. The vast majority of blacks who moved to suburban Hillsborough County during the seventies and early eighties purchased new housing at the same time as their white neighbors.

During the 1970s, several major American corporations transferred thousands of executive-level personnel into Tampa, including a large number of blacks. For example, in 1979 and 1980, IBM transferred 1,500 technicians and programmers from White Plains and Armonk, New York, to Tampa, and about 8 percent of these workers were black. Westinghouse transferred more than 1,000 employees to Tampa in the late 1970s, and about 10 percent of those were black. The transfers came at a time when open housing was rigorously enforced and when sales prices and interest rates were attractive enough for blacks to settle in new suburban housing or comfortable dwellings in previously all-white areas of Tampa.

Tampa is home to MacDill Air Force Base, a major installation that is staffed by more than 5,000 military and 10,000 civilian personnel. Until 1968, the Air Force followed the prevailing custom of allowing the posting of segregated real estate listings for off-base housing. However, in 1969, the practice was strictly forbidden, and realtors and apartment owners who discriminated on the basis of race were prohibited from advertising or securing payments channeled through service personnel in the form of quarters allowances. This policy contributed to the gradual integration of the Interbay area of Tampa.

All of Florida's school districts are by law coterminous with county boundaries. When the U.S. District Court ordered the Hillsborough County school district to desegregate in 1971, no school could have less than 10 percent black enrollment or more than 30 percent black enrollment. Since the desegregation order applied countywide (city and suburbs), white flight was avoided. Whites had no place to run, since private schools were already filled to capacity. The countywide order apparently encouraged housing integration.

The National Football League placed a new franchise in Tampa in 1976. Since the team's beginning, more than one-half of the players have been black. These players bought homes in the suburbs, and their purchases were well publicized. This gave other black Tampans, both native residents and newcomers, the green light to seek housing in integrated surroundings.

The aforementioned factors might best be described as "pull" factors that drew people to a particular area. In the case of Tampa, many upwardly mobile blacks were "pushed" into integrated housing by the lack of suitable alternatives. Tampa and suburban Hillsborough County never developed prestigious, upper-middle-class black communities, such as Los Angeles's Baldwin Hills, Houston's Chasewood or MacGregor, Dallas's Oak Cliff, or Washington, D.C.'s "Goldcoast." In those cities, black middle-class families could purchase homes with the comfortable knowledge that their home appreciation would be as good or better than in similar all-white or integrated neighborhoods.

Social and Economic Change

The immediate postwar years found black Tampans turning to the political process as a means of improving conditions in housing, education, employment, recreation, and health care. With the outlawing of the white primary in the U.S. Supreme Court decision *Smith v. Allwright*, blacks began to vote in large numbers, despite a series of minor nuisances put in the way to discourage registration, such as disguising the registration office, closing the office without notice, and rude treatment by registration officials.[11] By 1950, there were 7,587 blacks registered to vote, out of a total electorate of just over 40,000.[12]

Tampa, like many of its counterparts, experienced urban unrest in the sixties. On June 11, 1967, following the fatal shooting of a black burglary suspect by a white police officer, rioting broke out in the Central Avenue district, with the resultant destruction of more than a dozen white- and black-owned businesses. The Kerner Commission in commenting on this riot stated:

> Although officials prided themselves on supposedly good race relations and relative acceptance by whites of integration of schools and facilities, Negroes, composing almost 20 percent of the population, had had no one of their own race to represent them in positions of policy or power, nor to appeal to for redress of grievances.
>
> There was no Negro on the city council; none on the school board; none in the fire department; none of high rank on the police force. Six of every 10 houses inhabited by Negroes were unsound. Many were shacks with broken window panes, gas leaks, and rat holes in the walls. Rents averaged $50 to $60 a month. Such recreational facilities as did exist lacked equipment and supervisors.[13]

Although minor concessions were made after the riots—a few blacks were appointed to top-level jobs, such as assistant city attorney, antipoverty program administrator, and mayor's assistant—little has changed in Tampa's black community over the last two decades. Even though the countywide school system was integrated in 1971 and housing segregation declined during the 1970s, there were no blacks on the city council, county commission, or state legislative delegation until 1972. The number of black-owned businesses in 1982 was proportionately less than the figure reported in 1927. Blacks are still plagued by inadequate housing, poor education, job discrimination, and police brutality, conditions that contributed to sporadic outbreaks of urban unrest in the eighties. While Tampa did not experience the overt racism of lynchings, mob violence, or fierce resistance to community expansion that had been faced by cities such as Atlanta, Birmingham, Memphis, or Montgomery, overall social and economic conditions for blacks were worse than in those cities.

A number of federal programs have been tried in Tampa over the years with mixed results. Urban renewal projects, for example, were initiated in the late 1950s. One project involved the clearing of old warehouses and junkyards in a section adjacent to the downtown area. Little relocation was included, and the project was judged a success because taxes paid in 1970 were twelve times higher than those paid in 1955, before the project started. Another project involved clearance of the Scrub, Tampa's first major black settlement, between 1955 and 1968. Nearly 5,000 families were relocated, almost all of whom were black or Latin. By 1976, only 1,254 units of new housing had been constructed on the cleared land, and except for the local community college, there were no takers for the other parcels.[14] Although only one housing unit was built for every four destroyed, all of the new dwellings were for low- and moderate-income families, a rarity in the history of urban renewal.

After the 1967 riot and the scathing description of economic conditions in Tampa's black community by the Kerner Commission, Tampa leaders, headed by Mayor Dick Greco, undertook a major effort to upgrade conditions in black Tampa, focusing on housing renovation and social programs rather than wholesale clearance. Tampa's application for the Model Cities program was approved in 1968, and a new governmental agency, the Metropolitan Development Agency (MDA), was created to administer that program and related categorical grants, such as Urban Renewal, the Neighborhood Development program, rehabilita-

The Reverend A. Leon Lowry was the first black to be elected to Hillsborough County School Board in 1977 and the first to be elected to public office in the history of Tampa. (Courtesy of the *Florida Sentinel Bulletin*)

James T. Hargrett made history when he was elected to the Florida State Legislature from Tampa in 1982. (Courtesy of the *Florida Sentinel Bulletin*)

tion loans, and CETA. The agency was the first major Tampa city agency to hire a substantial number of blacks in professional jobs. Among the many blacks recruited by MDA was Alton White, a bright and energetic young man who was to become MDA's executive director in 1972. White later ran for mayor, finishing a strong third in the 1975 election. He served as special assistant to the mayor before being appointed in 1979 as director of the Tampa Housing Authority in 1979, where he served until 1984.

The Model Cities program was confined mainly to Tampa's black community and a few low-income white neighborhoods. Between 1970 and 1975, nearly $12 million was expended. More than 2,000 homes were renovated, and 900 dilapidated units on individual lots were torn down and replaced by new single-family or duplex housing. A new multipurpose service center was built in West Tampa, and more than $3.2 million was spent on social service projects. Other improvements included street paving, refurbishing of playgrounds, and street lighting. The major improvements were the creation of Riverfront Park, a $5.5 million complex and picnic grounds adjacent to the North Boulevard Homes public housing project, and 1,648 units of moderate-income housing in 1972–74 under the Section 236 program.[15]

After William Poe was elected mayor in 1975, he dismantled Tampa's MDA, transferring its functions to mainline city departments. While this was done in the spirit of "efficiency," the real reason seemed to be that MDA was becoming too powerful and too much of a threat to the downtown power elite who wished to see urban redevelopment focused on the central business district, rather than poor and black neighborhoods. The city's Community Development Block Grant program in 1975 consolidated the former categorical programs administrated by MDA. The entire city of Tampa, rather than just the city's "poverty pockets," was eligible for funds. By the mid-seventies, the euphoria of President Johnson's "Great Society" had worn off, to be replaced by a white backlash and a feeling that blacks had received more than enough federal funds for community and economic development activities. Since 1978, Community Development Block Grant and Urban Development Action Grant monies have been mainly targeted to downtown development and to moderate-income neighborhoods mostly outside of the black community.

The need for additional low-cost housing in Tampa far exceeds the supply. The city, in 1982, had 5,024 units of conventional public housing in thirteen major projects, ten of which were for families and three for the elderly. The total occupancy was 21,000, of which 90 percent were black. However, in family housing, blacks comprised 96 percent of the total, while in the units for the elderly, whites were in a slight majority (53 percent). Several small scattered-site family projects were recently constructed in all-white neighborhoods with surprisingly little opposition from established residents. There were also 900 Section 8 units scattered throughout the city. Over 2,000 families and individuals remain on the public housing authority waiting list.

The Tampa Housing Authority has experienced the same problems as those in other cities, namely, aging physical plant, increasing maintenance, and public safety costs. Residents are less able to pay than they were a few years earlier due to high unemployment, cutbacks in social service programs, and reduced federal support in operating subsidies. The local housing authority operated a variety of social service and recreation programs during the 1970s. These programs were terminated along with their staffs in 1982. The housing authority, as late as 1980, operated a sound jobs program that served more than 5,000 teenagers. The youth jobs program was cut to only 2,000 jobs for the summer of 1982 and 500 by 1987. Low-income youths in public housing have few employment options since the public programs have been scaled down, and unemployment has become a way of life for the majority of these youths, most of whom will reach adulthood without ever having held a steady job. Unemployment has reached an acute stage, especially for inner-city black areas where businesses have closed their doors or moved out of the neighborhood altogether.

Tampa had 185 black-owned businesses in 1927.[16] The city had only four black physicians, five black dentists, and only one black lawyer. The next five decades saw Tampa's black-owned businesses grow to more than 480 firms with total gross receipts of $15.7 million in 1977.[17] The period 1977–82 also witnessed an increase in the total number of black-owned businesses in the city. Tampa had 606 black-owned business enterprises in 1982, with gross receipts of some $20.2 million.[18] Tampa's black-owned firms increased their number by 26 percent and their gross receipts by 28 percent between 1977 and 1982. Black-owned businesses grew in every industry classification during the 1977–82 period, except for construction and finance, insurance, and real estate classifications

Table 7.6
Distribution of Tampa's Black-Owned Businesses, 1977 and 1982

Industry Classification	1977		1982	
	Number	Percent	Number	Percent
Agricultural services	—	—	14	2.3
Construction	41	8.5	35	5.8
Manufacturing	6	1.3	8	1.3
Transportation and utilities	47	9.8	56	9.2
Wholesale trade	2	0.4	4	0.7
Retail trade	128	26.7	143	23.6
Finance, insurance, and real estate	26	5.4	24	4.0
Selected services	190	39.6	279	46.0
Other industries and not classified	40	8.3	43	7.1
Total	480	100.0	606	100.0

Source: U.S. of the Census, *1982 Survey of Minority-Owned Business Enterprises: Black.*

(see Table 7.6). Tampa had forty-one black-owned construction companies in 1977 and thirty-five in 1982. The number of finance, insurance, and real estate firms owned by blacks in the city decreased from twenty-six in 1977 to twenty-four in 1982. Overall, Tampa's black-owned business firms were concentrated in the services and retail trade classifications.

No Tampa business has ever made the *Black Enterprise* "Top 100" list. However, the two most prominent black firms in the city are the Central Life Insurance Company and Community Federal Savings and Loan Association. Central Life was founded in 1922. It had a staff of 120 persons and assets of $7.7 million in 1985.[19] Tampa's lone black-owned insurance company was the fifteenth-largest black insurance company in the United States. Central Life's headquarters occupies a modern five-story structure located in West Tampa on an old urban renewal site.

Community Federal Savings and Loan Association is one of the two black savings and loan in Florida. The other one is Washington Shores Federal Savings and Loan in Orlando. Tampa's black-owned savings and loan was founded in 1967. It was ranked as the nation's seventeenth-largest black savings and loan in 1982, with assets of $23.4 million.[20] Community Federal is located in a modern office building in Tampa's old Scrub district. While some blacks have made the move to the suburbs, Tampa's black-owned firms are found largely in the city's segregated black neighborhoods.

School Desegregation

Integration of the Hillsborough County public schools began in the early 1960s, although by 1967, only 5 percent of black children attended classes with whites. By the late 1960s, pressure began to be placed on Florida's local officials by the federal government, which threatened a cut-off of funds. Finally, in 1971, the federal courts ordered the complete de-segregation of county schools after voluntary compliance measures, such as pairing, freedom of choice, and mandated pupil assignments, failed to produce any visible results.[21]

The federal order was monumental in scope. Because blacks comprised 20 percent of the student body, school officials were instructed to maintain an "approximate" 80 percent white/20 percent black pupil ratio in each school. However, blacks paid an extremely heavy price for integration. Under a complex formula, black children were bused for all but two of their twelve years of schooling, while whites had to put up with the inconvenience of busing for only two years.[22] All of the elementary schools in black neighborhoods were eventually closed, and the two black senior high schools, Blake and Middleton, were downgraded to junior high status.

The downgrading of Blake and Middleton high schools was strongly opposed by Tampa's black community. For more than twenty-five years, the two schools had been fierce and proud rivals, athletically and scho-lastically. Both had strong athletic programs, especially in football. During the period of 1946–71, these schools produced more than 200 college scholarship winners and a number of professional football players, including Israel Lang, Carlton Oates, Earl Edwards, Lloyd Mumpford, and Ted Washington. Although less than one-half of all tenth graders eventually graduated, and of that group only about 15 percent went on to college, Blake and Middleton gradually built a solid group of alumni, which included physicians, teachers, businessmen, attorneys, ministers, and others who in later years became the core of Tampa's present black middle class.

After a decade and a half since the initial court order, neither blacks nor whites are satisfied. A 1982 survey by the *Tampa Tribune* found that 51 percent of whites still preferred segregated schools.[23] Blacks were concerned that a large share of the district's new schools were built in rapidly growing suburban areas, while their children had to be bused longer and longer distances.[24] In addition, the number of black administrators had declined as a result of school desegregation efforts. For example, there were fewer black principals in 1985 than in 1970.

Until the opening of the University of South Florida in 1960, the only institution of higher education was the privately owned and operated University of Tampa, a small undergraduate-oriented school, which up to that time never had more than 1,500 students. Blacks were not allowed to enroll as undergraduates until 1966, although some black teachers began to take graduate-level courses in the late 1950s. The University of Tampa, in 1982, had only fifty blacks among its 2,000-member student body and none on the eighty-seven member full-time faculty.

The University of South Florida, located on Tampa's northern fringe about ten miles from the black community, opened to an all-white student body in 1960. The first black enrolled one year later. Blacks did not start to attend the university in substantial numbers until the early 1970s. Blacks in 1987 accounted for only 4.1 percent of the 24,000 undergraduate students, although blacks comprised more than 20 percent of the high school graduates in the university's sixteen-county service area. Graduate-level enrollment figures were even worse. In 1987, only 3 percent of the 3,000 graduate and professional school students were black. Given the availability pool, the black/white faculty ratio was a little better. In 1987, there were thirty-six black faculty members out of a total faculty of 1,128. Only one black held the rank of full professor, and a majority of the other black faculty members had not been tenured by 1987.

The lack of a predominantly black university in Tampa and historically poor representation in the student bodies at the University of Tampa and the University of South Florida are factors that have deeply hurt black Tampa. Only 7 percent of black adults in the Tampa–St. Petersburg SMSA had college degrees in 1980. Tampa has experienced a serious black "brain drain." Students in years past had to leave the city in order to attend college, and few returned. Even in the 1980s, more college-educated black youngsters leave the city than return, but the city has begun to attract blacks with college educations as a result of the expanding local economy.

Black Politics

A massive drive was mounted in the forties to register black Tampans. By 1950, blacks represented nearly one-fifth of the registered voters in Tampa.[25] The white power structure responded to this drive by changing the form of government from a city council elected from wards to a council elected at large. Blacks, however, were not elected to public office in the city until the mid-seventies. Tampa's first black elected official was the Reverend Leon Lowry, Sr., pastor of Beulah Baptist Church. Lowry was elected to the school board in 1976. County court judge Perry A. Little was first appointed by Governor Reuben Askew in 1977 and was elected without opposition in 1978. The 1980s saw the first blacks elected to the Tampa City Council, the Hillsborough County Commission, the state legislature, and the county circuit court. Tampa in 1988 had seven black elected officials: James Hargrett, Jr., state representative for District 63; Reubin Padgett, Jr., county commission member, District 4; Perry Harvey, Jr., city council member, District 3; Thomas Skinner, circuit court judge; Perry A. Little and Charles L. Wilson, Jr., county court judges; and A. Leon Lowry, Sr., school board member for Hillsborough County.[26]

The reason for the paucity of black elected officials is due mainly to one factor: the at-large election system. While black candidates have unsuccessfully run for office in the past, black participation in Tampa politics in past years consisted mostly of individuals and organized groups supporting liberal white or Hispanic candidates. While most black-supported candidates were elected, the resultant benefits to the black community in the form of public services and government jobs were minimal. Less than 3 percent of the professional-level jobs with the city of Tampa and Hillsborough County governments were held by blacks in 1987. In 1987, there were only forty-eight black police officers out of a force of 612, with no black holding a rank above major. By the city's own admission, the vast majority of Community Development Black Grant funds were targeted to moderate-income, predominantly white areas, rather than low-income black neighborhoods.[27] Although the at-large system governing all local governmental jurisdiction was changed to mixed-district and at-large systems for the Tampa City Council and Hillsborough County Commission in 1984, it will be years before residual benefits to the black community are evident.

Conclusion

The data seem to point to the fact that black Tampa was largely left out of the boom of the seventies and early eighties. Its black community historically was divided by the contrasting heritages of its Afro-Cuban and Afro-American ancestors and was victimized by white racism. The 1980s reveal that black Tampa is economically worse off than many of its sister communities in the South. Although housing is less expensive and more integrated than in a number of other southern cities, the vast majority of black Tampans cannot find or afford decent, safe, and sanitary housing. Black family life has been devastated, with more than four of every ten households headed by a female. Blacks in Tampa are underrepresented in the business and political arena. Incremental change has taken place over the past decade or so. However, black Tampans need to develop strategies that will accelerate the pace of economic and political empowerment.

The principal reason for this phenomenon is that, in Tampa, blacks were systematically excluded from the political process by at-large representation. The state legislature went to single-member districts in 1982, and the city and county adopted a mixed system of single-member and at-large districts in 1984, producing the first black state representative, city councilmen, and county commissioners in Tampa's history. However, Tampa is still far behind cities such as Atlanta, New Orleans, Houston, and Birmingham in political inclusion. In recent years, social scientists have noted that black political power produces tangible results for the black community, not only in jobs and contracts for middle-class individuals and firms, but in sending a strong signal to the private sector to be more equitable as well.[28] Other reasons for black Tampa's plight could be the loss of community identity, caused mainly by the closing of traditionally black elementary and high schools, a phenomenon not experienced elsewhere.

Conclusion
Problems and Prospects

Robert D. Bullard

The South beginning in the mid-seventies was associated with the land of opportunity for blacks. The seventies saw the South become a leader in the creation of nonagricultural jobs. Increased economic opportunities attracted migrants from the postindustrial economy of the North. The South was able to stem the massive out-migration of its black citizens. Some 53 percent of the nation's blacks lived in the South in 1980, a percentage unchanged since 1970.[1] Black migration patterns were reversed in the mid-seventies, when more than 195,000 blacks moved to the South than left during the 1975–80 period. This pattern continued through the mid-eighties, when more than 87,000 blacks moved into the region than left during the 1980–85 period.[2] The North was no longer considered the promised land.

In 1980, blacks comprised the majority population in Atlanta (66.6 percent), Birmingham (55.6 percent), and New Orleans (55.3 percent); blacks comprised just under one-half (47.6 percent) of Memphis's population in 1980. The black population in large metropolitan areas in the South exploded during the seventies. The 1970–80 period, for example, saw the black population in the Atlanta and Houston SMSAs grow by 43.5 and 35.5 percent, respectively. Houston's central-city black population numbered over 440,000 in 1980, a population larger than the entire city of Atlanta.

The "Go South" and "Stay South" themes became potent messages in the black communities across the nation. Blacks were searching for the "New South," a region that was prominently displayed in booster campaigns of emerging southern cities. The South attracted both the skilled and the unskilled, educated and uneducated, as well as low-income and middle-income blacks who sought to make their fortune in the city. Southern cities in the seventies attracted more poor residents than they

161

lost. The inner core of many southern cities closely resembled that of their northern ghetto counterparts. Jobs were moving to the suburbs at the time that blacks were increasing their share of the central cities.

The economic picture for black workers in the South has been one of persistent and chronic unemployment. The black unemployment rate has remained more than two times that for whites in the region. Moreover, the 1970s ended with black unemployment figures in double digits in eight of the twelve southern states. By 1980, double-digit black unemployment was the established trend through the mid-eighties in all twelve southern states (see Table 8.1). The recessions of the early 1980s exacted an especially heavy economic toll on the black work force. The 1983 annual average black unemployment rate, for example, was a high of 26.5 percent in Alabama, 24 percent in Mississippi, 23.9 percent in Arkansas, and 23.1 percent in Tennessee. There was very little for black communities in these economically depressed states to cheer about, since nearly a quarter of their work force was unemployed. The evidence of a New South was not compelling when one considers the fact that blacks in Arkansas, Mississippi, and Tennessee were three times more likely to be unemployed when compared to their white counterparts.

Economic conditions in 1984 saw some improvement in the region, as exhibited by declining unemployment. On the other hand, black unemployment figures (which had shown a downward trend) continued to be significantly higher than that of whites. Economic recession in the oil patch locked many Texas and Louisiana residents out of the job market and caused revenue shortfalls in state financing. Texas, which had long been thought to be "recession proof," struggled with ways to balance its budget. The 1983 black unemployment rate averaged more than 17.9 percent in Texas and 19.3 percent in Louisiana.[3]

Economic problems brought on by falling oil prices did not disappear in the mid-eighties. The gap between black and white unemployment rates actually widened over the years. The 1985 unemployment figures were 14.2 percent for blacks in Texas and 19.9 percent for blacks in Louisiana. Revenue losses from the oil industry spelled doom for many black workers, businesses, and homeowners. Moreover, this depressionlike condition destabilized many middle-income black neighborhoods and exacerbated existing social problems (crime, physical decline, abandonment, disinvestment, school closures, etc.) in many low-income black neighborhoods.

Table 8.1
Annual Average Unemployment Rate in Twelve Southern States for Selected Years

State	1979		1980		1983		1984		1985	
	White	Black	White	Black	White	Black	White	Black	White	Black
Alabama	5.4	13.0	6.6	15.6	9.7	26.5	7.3	23.1	6.9	16.9
Arkansas	4.4	17.3	6.5	14.9	7.7	23.9	6.6	24.9	5.5	25.6
Florida	4.9	10.9	5.1	10.0	7.1	16.5	4.8	14.0	4.9	11.8
Georgia	3.7	11.1	4.8	13.1	5.3	14.5	4.2	11.3	4.3	12.5
Kentucky	5.3	9.6	7.7	14.4	11.0	21.5	8.7	17.8	8.7	19.5
Louisiana	4.5	12.8	4.8	12.2	9.0	19.3	7.6	16.5	8.1	19.9
Mississippi	3.7	10.5	4.8	14.0	7.9	24.0	7.0	20.0	6.7	17.8
North Carolina	3.7	8.9	5.1	12.1	6.0	18.9	4.5	14.9	4.2	10.1
South Carolina	4.4	6.9	4.9	11.9	7.6	15.0	5.3	11.2	4.2	13.9
Tennessee	4.6	12.8	5.7	15.8	9.2	23.1	6.6	21.0	6.9	15.4
Texas	3.7	8.5	4.5	11.1	6.7	17.9	5.0	13.4	6.0	14.2
Virginia	3.4	11.1	3.8	11.1	4.5	14.0	3.8	11.1	4.2	11.6

Source: U.S. Department of Labor, *Geographic Profile of Employment and Unemployment* (Washington, D.C.: U.S. Government Printing Office, 1979, 1980, 1983, 1984, 1985).

The national unemployment rate in 1985 was 6.2 percent for whites and 15.7 percent for blacks. Black unemployment in the Southern census region averaged 14 percent, compared with 12 percent in the Northeast, 22.2 percent in the Midwest, and 13 percent in the West.[4] Youth unemployment (sixteen- to nineteen-year-olds) continued to be a national problem. This problem was more acute for black teenagers, more than 40.6 percent of whom were unemployed in 1985. Employment prospects for black teenagers during the mid-eighties were slightly better in the South than in the Midwest and West and about the same in the Northeast. Still, more than 37.8 percent of the black teenagers in the South were unemployed in 1985.

The city's role as an economic "launching pad" for upwardly mobile blacks was diminished by the disinvestment process taking place in central cities and the relocation of new industries to distant suburbs. The social climate of the South was drastically changed by the civil rights movement, a movement concentrated mainly in southern cities. The region's major cities became the centers of economic and political change and rising black expectations. Blacks were drawn to the region's large central cities. From Atlanta to Memphis, blacks were struggling to get a piece of the American Dream and reap some of the benefits of the emerging New South. The struggle of blacks in Birmingham during the sixties, "the Johannesburg of the South," is legendary. The expectations of black citizens were similar in Houston, Tampa, and Memphis. Blacks in city after city wanted and expected what all Americans wanted and expected, an opportunity to fulfill their dreams.

There can be little doubt that the opportunity structures in these southern cities did change in the seventies and mid-eighties. However, many social, economic, and political barriers have gone unabated. Ownership of property, land, and private businesses remains a central part of the American Dream of success, a dream that has eluded millions of blacks. The American society places a great deal of emphasis on private initiative and the aquisition of material wealth. The distribution of wealth and power can be viewed as a by-product of this process. Blacks in the South, and the United States in general, however, have been historically underrepresented in the area of ownership (land, housing, and businesses). This underrepresentation has been a result of many factors, including institutional barriers and changing demographic patterns. The massive movement of blacks from the rural South, for example, accelerated the decline of black land ownership. The rural-urban migration stream, and especially the movement into large central cities outside the South, also limited the opportunities for black home ownership. It is ironic that southern blacks are losing their land at such an alarming rate at the same time that they are making economic and political inroads.[5]

Increased housing construction, combined with government subsidized mortgages, rapidly changed the housing picture in the South. More than one-half (51.1 percent) of blacks in the region owned their homes in 1983, compared with nearly three-fourths (71.4 percent) of whites.[6] Black home ownership varied within the region. Of the six southern SMSAs studied, black home ownership rates were highest in Birmingham (52.9 percent) and Tampa–St. Petersburg (49.9 percent) and lowest in New Orleans (35.2 percent). Black home ownership rates stood at 47.2 percent in Memphis, 47.2 percent in Houston, and 41.8 percent in Atlanta.

Black housing in the South continues to be of lower value than that of other housing in the region. Black homes often have more deficiencies than their white counterparts. In 1980, the South was the only region that showed a marked difference between black and white housing quality. Housing inadequacy has been increasing in the nation's large urban areas. This is partly a result of housing construction priorities and targeted development in the suburbs and areas outside the central cities. Recent national trends point to a dwindling supply of low- and moderate-income housing stock.[7] The South has not escaped this national trend. While competition for single-family housing is fierce, the spirit of ownership continues to dominate the thinking of southern blacks. Among blacks in the region, the common saying "This house may not be a palace, but it's mine" continues to keep alive the dream of ownership.

The bulk of the single-family homes built in southern cities was constructed in the suburbs. Construction priorities of developers increased housing opportunities primarily for whites, higher-income households, and former homeowners who had accumulated capital to finance down payments.[8] Black suburbanization has often meant successive spillover from black neighborhoods or an extension of the segregated housing pattern typical of the central city. Many of the problems that have been associated with life in the central city (for example, crime, crowding, and physical decline) have become problems that more and more suburban blacks face in their daily lives.[9]

Residential segregation, discriminatory real estate practices, and unfair lending insitutions have severely limited housing opportunities available to blacks.[10] Residential segregation decreased between 1970 and 1980 in major urban centers. However, blacks and whites continue to live largely in separate communities. Atlanta was the most racially segregated large southern city, with more than 86 percent of its blacks living in mostly black areas in 1980. New Orleans, on the other hand, was the least segregated large southern city in 1980, with 76 percent of its black population living in mostly white areas.[11] White flight to the suburbs has left schools in big cities with a largely minority student population. Blacks made up more than 92 percent of the students enrolled in the Atlanta public schools in 1986. In other city school systems, blacks represented 84 percent of the pupil enrollment in New Orleans, 82 percent in Birmingham, and 78 percent in Memphis. Black and Hispanic students made up more than 81 percent of the total enrollment in the Houston school district in 1986.

Housing discrimination, residential segregation, and a host of institutional barriers complicate school desegregation efforts, contribute to the decline of central cities, and limit blacks' access to employment opportunities, which are rapidly shifting to the suburbs. Housing barriers that restrict black residential options to central cities artificially limit black upward mobility, wealth accumulation, and investment through home ownership.

The high black unemployment rate in southern cities is a reflection of the changing job market in postindustrial America, which is characterized by "a capital-intensive restructuring of the industrial and manufacturing sector and a phenomenal growth of service industry."[12] It is also a reflection of central city/suburban housing and business location patterns. The postindustrial job market in urban areas often calls for levels of education and skills beyond that of many inner-city blacks.[13]

A growing black underclass is trapped in declining central cities, where few opportunities are available to reach job centers located in the suburbs. Public transit is often inadequate or nonexistent. This dilemma is probably epitomized in metropolitan Atlanta where MARTA, the city's modern bus-rail system, is cut off from the job-rich suburban counties of the area's "Golden Crescent" (that is, Gwinnett and Cobb counties). The decision by the mostly white suburban counties not to become a partner in MARTA and the decisions by industries to locate in these counties have contributed to whites' gaining a greater share of the Atlanta metropolitan area work force. The economic renaissance that has fueled the Atlanta success story has benefited the mostly white suburban counties that surround the mostly black city of Atlanta.

Double-digit unemployment rates ravaged many black communities in the mid-eighties. In 1986, for example, black unemployment was 19.3 percent in Memphis, 19.2 in Houston, 16.8 in New Orleans, and 11.6 percent in Tampa–St. Petersburg. The same year, whites had a 4.9 percent unemployment rate in Memphis, a 8.9 percent rate in Houston, a 8.5 percent rate in New Orleans, and a 5 percent unemployment rate in Tampa–St, Petersburg.[14] Rising unemployment and poverty have undermined the stability of black family and community life. Extreme poverty existed amid palm trees in Tampa and New Orleans and in the shadow of the steel-and-glass high-rise office towers in Atlanta and Houston. More than one-third of black families in New Orleans, Tampa–St. Petersburg, and Memphis fell below the poverty line in 1980; more than one-fourth of the blacks in Atlanta and Birmingham were below the government poverty threshold in 1980; and one-fifth of all black Houstonians lived in poverty in 1980. Black poverty coexisted amid the rising New South. The New South for many residents translated into heightened status differences and a widened economic gap between the skilled and unskilled.

The black-white income gap was part of the Old South and persisted in the New South.[15] Houston and Atlanta had two of the most affluent black communities in 1980. Still, black families in metropolitan Houston earned just 61 percent of the income earned by whites in the area. Black families in metropolitan Atlanta, on the other hand, earned 59 percent of the income earned by white families. The income gap will likely continue as long as blacks are concentrated in low-wage service occupations. Blacks in the six study cities were two and one-half times more likely to be employed in service occupations than their white counterparts (see Table 8.2).

Black workers were more highly concentrated in blue-collar jobs than were whites. Conversely, blacks were less likely to be found in white-collar occupations. The largest concentration of blacks in white-collar occupations was found in the Atlanta and Houston metropolitan areas. A little over two-fifths (43.5 percent) of metropolitan Atlanta's blacks and two-thirds (65.2 percent) of whites held white-collar occupations in 1980. Two-fifths (41.7 percent) of the blacks in metropolitan Houston

Table 8.2
Distribution of Blacks and Whites in the Labor Force, 1980

| | Occupational Distribution (percent) | | | | | |
| | White Collar | | Blue Collar | | Service | |
SMSA	White	Black	White	Black	White	Black
Houston	63.3	41.7	28.3	35.7	7.6	20.5
New Orleans	63.8	38.1	26.3	34.9	9.2	26.1
Atlanta	65.2	43.5	25.4	33.6	8.6	22.1
Memphis	64.7	35.0	28.6	39.8	8.7	23.7
Birmingham	60.8	34.9	30.5	39.7	7.7	24.8
Tampa–St. Petersburg	58.0	34.9	27.1	34.9	12.9	27.1

Source: U.S. Bureau of the Census, General Social and Economic Characteristics (Washington, D.C.: U.S. Government Printing Office, 1983).

and nearly two-thirds (65.2 percent) of the whites worked in white-collar jobs.

The economic recessions of the early eighties pushed many low-income black neighborhoods further down the economic pecking order, while destabilizing long-standing middle-class black neighborhoods and businesses. Hard times in the oil patch in Texas and Louisiana, for example, left a trail of business foreclosures and for-sale signs in once-stable black communities along the Gulf Coast from Houston to New Orleans. Many black businesses in the urban South grew despite the recurring recessions. The majority of black-owned businesses is located in the southern United States, where the majority of the nation's black population is also found. The South in 1982 accounted for more then 50 percent of the nation's black-owned business enterprises and 45 percent of their business receipts.[16] Black businesses in the South grossed nearly $5.6 billion in 1982.

Black business operations continue to be concentrated in southern cities that have large black populations (see Table 8.3). Houston had by far the largest number of black-owned business enterprises, with 10,019 firms in 1982. Houston's black businesses grossed $283.7 million in 1982. The gross receipts of Atlanta's 3,493 black-owned business enterprises totaled $238.5 million in 1982. Atlanta's black business community, though

Table 8.3
Distribution of Black-Owned Businesses in Selected Cities, 1982

City	Number of Firms 1982	Gross Receipts 1982 ($\times$ $1,000)	Number in "Top 100" 1986	Black Population in 1980
Houston	10,019	283.7	1	440,346
New Orleans	3,563	112.7	0	308,149
Atlanta	3,493	238.5	6	282,911
Memphis	3,119	139.9	1	307,702
Birmingham	1,145	47.1	0	158,224
Tampa	606	20.2	0	63,835

Source: U.S.Bureau of the Census, *1982 Survey of Minority-Owned Enterprises: Black*; U.S. Bureau of the Census, *Provisional Estimates of Social, Economic and Housing Characteristics*; Black Enterprise, "Top 100 Black Businesses," *Black Enterprise* 16 (June 1986).

much smaller in number, is one of the most widely known and firmly established in the nation. There were six Atlanta area firms on the *Black Enterprise*'s "Top 100" list in 1986.[17] Chicago was the only other city that could match that statistic.

Black owned businesses account for a relatively small part of the United States' gross national product (GNP). Black business firms' receipts totaled 0.46 percent of the GNP in 1972 but was down to 0.39 percent in 1985.[18] Economist Andrew Brimmer predicts that blacks will likely expand their share of the total national receipts in the eighties but will lose in other areas. Brimmer notes, for example, that receipts from black businesses equaled 13.5 percent of the total black income in 1969 and only 8.9 percent in 1980. If current trends continue, the black share may drop to 7 percent by 1990.[19]

A substantial share of the resources within the black community is still owned by outsiders. Black business owners play an important role in the economic stability of the black community. Black financial institutions contribute to the building of a solid economic base within areas that have been systematically redlined by white institutions. Black banks, savings and loans, mortgage companies, and insurance firms enable the black community to expand its home and business ownership base.[20] Atlanta, for example, is home of the nation's second-largest black

Table 8.4
Black-Owned Financial Institutions in the Study Cities

City	Black-Owned Bank	Black-Owned Savings and Loan	Black-Owned Insurance Company
Houston	—	Standard Savings	—
New Orleans	Liberty Bank	United Federal	Gertrude Geddes Willis
			National Service
			Industrial
			Majestic Life
			Rhodes Life
Atlanta	Citizen Trust	Mutual Federal	Atlanta Life
Memphis	Tri-State	—	Universal Life
Birmingham	—	Citizen Federal	Booker T. Washington
			Protective Industrial
			American Trust Life
Tampa	—	Community Federal	Central Life

Source: Black Enterprise, "Top 100 Black Enterprises," *Black Enterprise* 16 (June 1986).

bank (Citizen Trust) and second-largest black insurance company (Atlanta Life). The other southern cities included in this study also have an array of black-owned financial institutions (see Table 8.4). These financial institutions provide leadership that has an economic base.

The eighties have seen economics and politics become critical areas of concern in the black community. As the nation experiences an era of scarcities, everyone has had to learn to live with less. Many cities have had to grapple with ways of coping with dwindling local revenue and federal financial support and rising municipal service costs. Close monitoring by citizen watch groups needs to be undertaken to evaluate how the dwindling public monies are spent. Special efforts need to be undertaken by black elected officials to see that funds designated for blighted inner-city areas are not diverted toward "downtown" projects and "yuppie playgrounds." The problem of inadequate housing, declining neighborhoods, underrepresentation of blacks in the business arena, and the absence of a coherent economic master plan are major obstacles to black economic independence and political empowerment.

Blacks have made substantial gains toward political empowerment with the passage of the 1965 Voting Rights Act. There were 1,469 black elected officials in 1970; 4,912 in 1980; 5,654 in 1984; and 6,681 in 1987.[21] There were twenty-three blacks in the U. S. Congress in 1987. This number represented only 5.3 percent of the 435 members of the House of Representatives. Blacks made up 12 percent of the nation's population and nearly 20 percent of the South's population in 1980. However, in 1987, only four blacks from the Deep South were serving in congress (Harold Ford of Memphis, Mickey Leland of Houston, John Lewis of Atlanta, and Michael Espy of Yazoo City, Mississippi). Espy in 1986 became the first black elected to the U. S. Congress from Mississippi since Reconstruction.

Black population gains in the South have the potential for exerting a strong influence on the electoral process in the region. Reapportionment plans that were developed from the 1980 census have meant more black political representation in municipal, county, state, and federal elective offices. A little more than one-half, or 53 percent, of the nation's blacks live in the South. However, nearly 62 percent of the black elected officials were found in the South in 1984.[22] The North Central region had 20 percent of the black elected officials; the Northeast, 12.2 percent; and the West, 5.9 percent of the black elected officials.

The 1980s have seen the southern states and their major cities emerge as political battlegrounds for the black vote. A number of large southern cities had black mayors in 1987, including Atlanta, New Orleans, Charlotte, Richmond, Birmingham, and Little Rock. After repeated attempts, Memphis has failed to elect a black mayor in a city that is one-half black. Memphis continues to be racially polarized and its black community severely fragmented. Overall, voter education and registration drives, along with intensified "get-out-and-vote" campaigns have been a boon to black political office seekers in large cities and urban areas that have substantial black voting-age populations. In 1984, Atlanta led all southern cities with forty-three black elected officials, followed by Houston, with twenty-nine black officeholders.[23] There were twenty-six black elected officials in Memphis; New Orleans had twenty; Birmingham had eighteen; and Tampa had four black elected officials in 1984. Despite the efforts at the local level, blacks remain underreprented as political officeholders.

There are clear indications that the "sleeping giant," the black electorate in the South, is awakening. Blacks are also gradually moving into decision-making offices on local school boards and in superintendent positions that have the potential of shaping future educational policies. For example, Atlanta, New Orleans, Memphis, and Birmingham all had black school superintendents in 1987. The degree to which the black electorate is mobilized to change the status quo in education is often related to the black community's political clout. Black communities that have strong political organizations generally have had more success in getting their candidates elected (or appointed) to key policy-making positions, when compared with black communities that have weak political organizations.

The struggle to control large urban school districts in the South has become the new civil rights battleground in the eighties. Battles often revolve around issues such as the underrepresentation of blacks in administrative positions, minority teacher hiring, teacher experience in poor and affluent schools, and the quality of educational programs in inner-city schools.[24] Urban school boards have become polarized along racial and class lines. A number of factors have contributed to this polarization: teacher discontent, teacher assignment, teacher hiring and termination, school closings, pupil transfers, and pupil assignment to magnet, talented/gifted, and special education programs.

A new form of school segregation appears to be emerging in large urban school districts. A disproportionately large share of low-income black students attend schools apart from whites but also apart from their middle-income black counterparts. The battle over magnet schools and the limited slots in the talented and gifted programs most often is between middle-income blacks and whites who have remained in the public schools. Low-income black youths more often than not end up in overcrowded, poorly equipped, and inadequately staffed inner-city schools.

Finally, the expanding economy of the South during the seventies heightened status dilemmas and social inequities between blacks and whites. Economic recessions in the eighties have eroded many of the gains made in the seventies. A large segment of the black South, many rural and central-city blacks, received few, if any benefits from the rediscovery of the New South. Social, economic, and political progress passed over thousands of black households. Moreover, the favorable business climate, which was so often cited for the southern region's popularity in the 1970's, often translated into low wages, poverty, and powerless black workers. To many blacks, the New South was nothing more than an extension of the Old South with only minor modifications.

Resistance to black economic and political parity with the larger society has not disappeared. Black southerners still encounter obstacles in registering to vote and in actually voting. Black voters still must face at-large elections, distant polling places, gerrymandered districts, annexations, acts and threats of intimidation, economic blackmail, and similar practices designed to dilute their voting strength.[25] Black housing choices and ownership opportunities are limited because of institutional barriers. The issues surrounding school desegregation have not all been resolved. Black workers continue to be denied jobs and promotions because of their race. Discrimination has taken on a more sophisticated face, which makes it easy to practice but difficult to prove. Black residents in the South still have many hurdles to overcome. Until blacks, a group that makes up one-fifth of the region's population, share more fully in the resources of the South, there will not be a New South.

Notes

■■■■■■■■■■■■

Introduction: The Lure of the New South

1. U.S. Department of Housing and Urban Development, *Report of the President's Commission for a National Agenda for the Eighties* (Washington, D.C.: U.S. Government Printing Office, 1980), 165–69; also John D. Kasarda, "The Implications of Contemporary Distribution Trends for National Urban Policy," *Social Science Quarterly* 61 (December 1980): 373–400; Richard M. Bernard and Bradley R. Rice, eds., *Sunbelt Cities: Politics and Growth since World War II* (Austin: University of Texas Press, 1983), 1–30.

2. See John Kasarda, Michael D. Irvin, and Holly L. Hughes, "The South Is Still Rising," *American Demographics* 8 (June 1986): 34.

3. Ibid.

4. David C. Perry and Alfred J. Watkins, eds., *The Rise of the Sunbelt Cities* (Beverly Hills: Sage, 1977), 77; Kasarda, "Implications of Contemporary Distribution Trends," 373–400; John D. Kasarda, "Caught in the Web of Change," *Society* 21 (1983): 41–47; William J. Wilson, *The Truly Disadvantaged: The Inner City, the Underclass, and Public Policy* (Chicago: University of Chicago Press, 1987), 180–81.

5. National Urban Coalition, *The Situation in Urban America: A Spring 1982 Report* (Washington, D.C.: National Urban Coalition, 1982), 46; Robert D. Bullard, "The Black Family: Housing Alternatives in the '80s," *Journal of Black Studies* 14 (March 1984): 341–51.

6. Chet Fuller, "I Hear Them Call It the New South," *Black Enterprise* 12 (November 1981): 41.

7. Ibid., 41–44.

8. U.S. Bureau of the Census, *State and Metropolitan Area Data Book 1982* (Washington, D.C.: U.S. Government Printing Office, 1982), ixxx.

9. William C. Matney and Dwight L. Johnson, *America's Black Population: A Statistical View, 1970–1982* (Washington, D.C.: U.S. Government Printing Office, 1983), 1.

174

10. Ibid., 1–2.

11. Isaac Robinson, "Blacks Move Back to the South," *American Demographics* 8 (June 1986): 40–43.

12. Ibid., 43.

13. Kasarda et al., "The South Is Still Rising," 33.

14. George E. Hall, "A Statistical Portrait of Black Americans," adapted remarks from a speech, U.S. Bureau of the Census (1981).

15. Gurney Breckenfeld, "Refilling the Metropolitan Doughnut," in *The Rise of the Sunbelt Cities*, ed. Perry and Watkins, 238.

16. Ibid.

17. U.S. Commission on Civil Rights, *The Federal Fair Housing Enforcement Efforts* (Washington, D.C.: Government Printing Office, 1979), 230; National Urban Coalition, *The Situation in Urban America*, 1–2; Robert D. Bullard, "Persistent Barriers in Housing Black Americans," *Journal of Applied Social Sciences* 7 (Fall–Winter 1983): 19–31; Franklin James, Betty I. Cumming, and Eileen A. Tynan, *Urban Minorities in the Sunbelt* (New Brunswick, NJ: Rutgers University Center for Policy Research, 1984).

18. U.S. Department of Housing and Urban Development, *Report of the President's Commission for a National Agenda*, 18.

19. U.S. Bureau of the Census, *State and Metropolitan Area Data Book 1982*, xxx.

20. See U.S. Bureau of the Census, *The Social and Economic Status of the Black Population in the United States: An Historical View, 1790–1978* (Washington, D.C.: U.S. Government Printing Office, 1979), 136; also Matney and Johnson, *America's Black Population*, 23.

21. Phillip L. Clay, "Housing and Neighborhoods," in *The State of Black America 1981*, ed., National Urban League (New York: National Urban League, 1981), 87–118. For an in-depth discussion of this topic, see Jamshid A. Momeni, ed., *Race, Ethnicity, and Minority Housing in the United States* (Westport, CT: Greenwood Press, 1986).

22. Matney and Johnson, *America's Black Population*, 20–23.

23. Ibid., 20.

24. U.S. Bureau of the Census, *The Social and Economic Status of the Black Population*, 136–38.

25. See U.S. Bureau of the Census, *The President's National Urban Policy Report: 1980* (Washington, D.C.: U.S. Government Printing Office, 1980), 140; Wilhelmina A. Leigh, "Changing Trends in Housing," in *The State of Black America 1980*, ed. National Urban League, 149–97; and Sue S. Marshall, "The Community Development Block Grant Program and Unmet Needs," *The Urban League Review* 5 (Summer 1981): 27–34.

26. Robert D. Bullard and Odessa L. Pierce, "Black Housing in a Southern Metropolis: Competition for Housing in a Shrinking Market," *The Black*

Scholar 11 (November–December 1979): 60–67; Robert D. Bullard and Donald L. Tryman, "Competition for Decent Housing: A Focus on Housing Discrimination in a Sunbelt City," *The Journal of Ethnic Studies* 7 (Winter 1980): 51–63; G.L. Houseman, "Access of Minorities to Suburbs," *The Urban Social Change Review* 14 (1981): 11–20.

27. For a detailed discussion of the plight of the black underclass, see Robert D. Bullard, *Invisible Houston: The Black Experience in Boom and Bust* (College Station: Texas A&M University Press, 1987).

28. David R. Goldfield, *Promised Land: The South since 1945* (Arlington Heights, IL: Harlan Davidson, 1987), 216–18.

Chapter 1. Blacks in Heavenly Houston

1. Kenneth Wheeler, *To Wear a City's Crown: The Beginning of Urban Growth in Texas, 1836–1865* (Cambridge: Harvard University Press, 1968), 2.

2. O. F. Allen, *The City of Houston from Wilderness to Wonder* (Temple, TX: O. F. Allen, 1936), 1.

3. Wheeler, *To Wear a City's Crown*, 109.

4. Don E. Carleton and Thomas H. Kreneck, *Houston Back When We Started* (Houston: Houston City Magazine, 1979), 7.

5. Erna Smith, "Fourth Ward Mobilizing to Preserve Heritage," *The Houston Post* (March 9, 1980).

6. Houston City Planning Department, *Houston Year 2000* (Houston: City of Houston, 1980), II-3.

7. *The Informer*, June 14, 1919.

8. Helen Sanders, "Antioch Baptist Church," *Black Focus* (December–January 1977): 6–8.

9. Henry Allen Bullock, *Pathways to the Houston Negro Market* (Ann Arbor: J. N. Edwards, 1957), 62–63.

10. Henry Allen Bullock, *Profile of the Houston Negro Business Enterprises: A Survey and Directory of Their Attitudes* (Houston: Houston Negro Chamber of Commerce, 1962), 16.

11. U.S. Bureau of the Census, *State and Metropolitan Area Data Book 1982*, 100.

12. See Bullard and Pierce, "Black Housing in a Southern Metropolis," 60–67; Barry Kaplan, "Houston: The Golden Buckle of the Sunbelt," in *Sunbelt Cities*, ed. Bernard and Rice, 196–212.

13. David G. McComb, *Houston the Bayou City* (Austin: University of Texas Press, 1968), 157.

14. *Report of the City Planning Commission* (Houston: City of Houston, 1929), 25.

15. See Karl Taeuber and Alma F. Taeuber, *Negros in Cities: Residential Segregation and Neighborhood Change* (Chicago: Aldine Publishing, 1965); also Karl Taeuber, "Racial Residential Segregation, 28 Cities, 1970–1980," Center for Demography and Ecology Working Paper No. 83-12, University of Wisconsin–Madison (March 1983), 3.

16. See Kathryn Nelson, *Recent Suburbanization of Blacks: How Much, Who and Where?* (Washington, D.C.: U.S. Department of Housing and Urban Development, 1979), 5; and Larry Long and Diana DeAre, "The Suburbanization of Blacks," *American Demographics* 3 (September 1981): 20.

17. Bullard, "The Black Family: Housing Alternatives in the '80s," 341–51.

18. See Houston Community Development Division, "Survey of the Riceville Area of Activity" (December 3, 1980), 3; and Ginger H. Hester, "Bordersville: Catching Up to the 20th Century," *Playsure Magazine* (January 1980): 20; *Houston Post*, December 13, 1981.

19. National Urban Coalition, *Displacement, City Neighborhoods in Transition* (Washington, D.C.: National Urban Coalition, 1978), 5–8.

20. Elizabeth Austin, "Nearer to Town Than Thee," *Houston City Magazine* 3 (June 1979): 43.

21. Houston City Planning Department, *Housing Analysis: Low and Moderate Income Areas* (Houston: City of Houston, 1978), 113.

22. Bullock, *Pathways to the Houston Negro Market*, 61.

23. See Richard West, "Only the Strong Survive," *The Texas Monthly* 7 (February 1979): 94–105.

24. Bullard, *Invisible Houston*, 55.

25. Ibid., 54–59; Bullard and Tryman, "Competition for Decent Housing," 51–63.

26. Houston City Planning Department, *Houston Year 2000*, 18.

27. Housing Authority of the City of Houston, *Annual Report of the Housing Authority of the City of Houston* (Houston: HACH, 1984), 3.

28. See U.S. Government of Labor, "Autumn 1981 Urban Family Budgets" (Autumn 1981); and Houston Chamber of Commerce, "Houston Facts 81: Current Facts Concerning the Nation's Fifth Largest City" (Houston: Houston Chamber of Commerce, 1981).

29. U.S. Bureau of the Census, *Advanced Estimates of Social, Economic and Housing Characteristics: Texas* (Washington, D.C.: U.S. Government Printing Office, 1983), 145.

30. Bullard, *Invisible Houston*, 81–83.

31. Houston Job Training Partnership Council, *Annual Report Program for 1985* (Houston: HJTPC, 1985), 23.

32. U.S. Bureau of the Census, *State and Metropolitan Area Data Book: 1982*, 124.

33. U.S. Department of Labor, *Geographic Profile of Employment and Unemployment* (Washington, D.C.: U.S. Government Printing Office, 1983 and 1984).

34. Bullard, *Invisible Houston*, 78.

35. U.S. Bureau of the Census, *1982 Survey of Minority-Owned Business Enterprises: Black* (Washington, D.C.: U.S. Government Printing Office, 1982), 87.

36. Black Enterprise, "Top 100 Black Businesses," *Black Enterprise* 13 (June 1983): 109–10.

37. Ibid., 79.

38. William E. Terry, *Origin and Development of Texas Southern University* (Houston: D. Armstrong, 1968), 12–27.

39. See Michael L. Gillette, "Heman Marion Sweatt: Civil Rights Plaintiff," in *Black Leaders: Texans for Their Times*, ed. Alwyn Barr and Robert A. Calvert (Austin: Texas State Historical Association, 1981), 157–90.

40. Ibid., 181.

41. See Houston Area Urban League, *Quality Education and Minority Educational Opportunity* (Houston: Houston Area Urban League, 1978), 1–2.

42. Gary Orfield, *School Desegregation Patterns in the States, Large Cities and Metropolitan Areas 1968–1980* (Washington, D.C.: Joint Center for Political Studies, 1983), 31.

43. Houston Area Urban League, *Quality Education and Minority Educational Opportunity*, 33–35; also Kenneth Jackson, "Toward Quality Education: The Case of HISD," Texas Southern University Report Series (Houston, June 1983), 23.

44. *Houston Chronicle*, October 21, 1983.

45. *Houston Post*, May 23, 1985.

46. *Houston Chronicle*, September 16, 1983.

47. *Houston Post*, September 23, 1983; *Houston Chronicle*, September 16, 1983.

48. See Donald S. Strong, "The Rise of Negro Voting in Texas," *American Political Science Review* 42 (1948): 513.

49. Harris County Council of Organizations, *Profile of the Houston Negro Community* (Houston: HCCO, 1966), 41–43.

50. See Thomas E. Cavanaugh, "The Reagan Referendum: The Black Vote in the 1982 Election," paper presented at the Annual Meeting of the Midwest Political Science Association, Chicago (April 20–23, 1983), 1–3.

51. Albert K. Kernig and Susan Welch, *Black Representation and Urban Policy* (Chicago: University of Chicago Press, 1980), 472.

Chapter 2. New Orleans: A City That Care Forgot

1. P. F. Lewis, *New Orleans: The Making of an Urban Landscape* (Cambridge, MA: Ballinger, 1976), 32.

2. John S. Kendall, "New Orleans' Peculiar Institution," *The Louisiana Historical Quarterly* 23 (1940): 868.

3. John W. Blassingame, *Black New Orleans: 1860–1880* (Chicago: University of Chicago Press, 1973), 9.

4. James E. Winston, "The Free Negro in New Orleans, 1803–1860," *The Louisiana Historical Quarterly* 21 (1938): 1075.

5. Lewis, *New Orleans*, 37.

6. Daphne Spain, "Race Relations and Residential Segregation in New Orleans: Two Centuries of Paradox," *Annals of the American Academy of Political and Social Science* 441 (January 1979): 85.

7. Lewis, *New Orleans*, 40.

8. Spain, "Race Relations and Residential Segregation in New Orleans," 87.

9. Lewis, *New Orleans*, 44.

10. Ibid., 45.

11. Ralph Thayer, *The Evolution of Housing Policy in New Orleans* (New Orleans: Institute for Governmental Studies, Loyola University, 1978).

12. Ibid., 25.

13. Ibid., 27.

14. Lewis, *New Orleans*, 62.

15. Harlan Gilmore, "The Old New Orleans and the New: A Case for Ecology," *American Sociological Review* 9 (1944): 393.

16. Lewis, *New Orleans*, 98.

17. U.S. Bureau of the Census, *New Orleans, Louisiana, Minority Percentages Ranges by Census Tract* (Washington, D.C.: U.S. Government Printing Office, 1980).

18. Fair Housing Office of New Orleans, "The New Orleans Fair Housing 1981 Properties," 1.

19. *New Orleans Times Picayune*, November 4, 1981, sec. 6, p. 3.

20. Lewis, *New Orleans*, 99.

21. Thayer, *The Evolution of Housing Policy*, 53.

22. Lewis, *New Orleans*, 99.

23. Thayer, *The Evolution of Housing Policy*, 62.

24. Ibid., 58.

25. Lewis, *New Orleans*, 99.

26. Report of the Housing Authority of New Orleans, City of New Orleans, January 1, 1981, p. 1.

27. Department of Housing and Urban Development, Community Block Grant Application, City of New Orleans, October 1, 1979–September 30, 1980.

28. A report by the city of New Orleans, *The Dynamics of Growth: Three Years of Progress*, 1978–81.

29. See Arnold R. Hirsch, "New Orleans: Sunbelt in the Swamp," in *Sunbelt Cities*, ed. Bernard and Rice, 100; "A Sunbelt City Plays Catch-Up," *Business Week*, March 6, 1978, pp. 69–70.

30. Hirsch, "New Orleans," 101.

31. Ibid., 109.

32. Interviews with Lea McDere and Jerome Lambo, Office of Economic Development, New Orleans, December 4, 1981.

33. City of New Orleans, Office of Economic Development, Small and Minority Business Set-Aside Program, 1981.

34. City of New Orleans, Office of Economic Development, "Minority Business Enterprise New Notes," June 1981.

35. U.S. Bureau of the Census, *Provisional Estimates of Social, Economic and Housing Characteristic* (Washington, D.C.: U.S. Government Printing Office, 1982), 65.

36. Ibid., 44; Louisiana Department of Labor, "Unemployment Projections," 1982.

37. U.S. Bureau of the Census, *1982 Survey of Minority-Owned Business Enterprises: Black*.

38. William G. McCall, *Louisiana's Official Resistance to Desegregation* (Nashville: Vanderbilt University, 1964), 9.

39. Ibid., 10.

40. Roger A. Fischer, "The Post-Civil War Segregation Struggle," in *The Past as Prelude: New Orleans 1718–1968*, ed. Hodding Carter (New Orleans: Pelican Publishing House, 1968), 300.

41. Ibid., 134.

42. See David Coughlin Marshall, "The Higher Education of Negroes in the State of Louisiana," Doctoral Dissertation Series Nos. 17 and 447 (1956), 157.

43. See fifth annual report of the Consent Decree Monitoring Committee, State of Louisiana, *Implementation of the Consent Decree* (Civil Action No. 80–3300, 1985), 2–9.

44. Ibid., 3.

45. See Morton Inger, *Politics and Reality in an American City: The New Orleans School Crisis of 1960* (Chicago: Aldine Publishing, 1968), 9–50.

46. Monte Piliawsky and Paul J. Stekler, "The Evolution of Black Politics in New Orleans" (unpublished paper, 1986), 8.

47. Ibid.

48. Ibid., 10.

49. Ibid., 15.

50. Gary Bovlind, "Power Brokers: Black Political Organizations—The Growing Vital Force in Local Government," *New Orleans* 20 (October 1985): 49.

51. Piliawsky and Stekler, "The Evolution of Black Politics in New Orleans," 19.

52. Alvin J. Schexnider, "Political Mobilization in the South: The Election of a Black Mayor in New Orleans," in *The New Black Politics: The Search for Political Power*, ed. Michael B. Preston, Lenneal J. Henderson, Jr., and Paul Puryear (New York: Longman, 1982), 228.

53. Piliawsky and Stekler, "The Evolution of Black Politics in New Orleans," 20.

54. Joint Center for Political Studies, *Black Elected Officials: A National Roster 1984* (New York: UNIPUB, 1984), 165–81.

55. Allan Katz, "Both Camps Playing Record to the Hilt," *New Orleans Times Picayune*, October 13, 1985, p. A-10.

56. Monte Piliawsky, "The Impact of Black Mayors on the Black Community: The Case of New Orleans' Ernest Morial," *The Review of Black Political Economy* 13 (Spring 1985): 15–16.

57. Allan Katz, "No More Mr. Nice Guy," *New Orleans Times Picayune*, February 14, 1982, sec. 1, p. 23.

58. Ibid., 48.

59. Piliawsky, "The Impact of Black Mayors," 7.

Chapter 3. Atlanta: Mecca of the Southeast

1. Metropolitan Planning Commission, *Up Ahead: A Metropolitan Land Use Plan for Metropolitan Atlanta* (Atlanta: Metropolitan Planning Commission, 1952), 12.

2. Susan H. Smith, *How, When and Where Atlanta* (Atlanta: Maramac Publishing, 1982), 18–25.

3. See Metropolitan Planning Commission, *Up Ahead*, 16; Franklin Garrett, *Atlanta and Environs* (Athens: University of Georgia Press, 1969); U.S. Department of Housing and Urban Development, *The Land Use and Urban Development Impacts of Beltways Case Studies* (Washington, D.C.: U.S. Government Printing Office, 1980), A-2; and Bradley R. Rice, "Atlanta: If Dixie Were Atlanta," in *Sunbelt Cities*, ed. Bernard and Rice, 31–57.

4. Rice, "Atlanta: If Dixie Were Atlanta," 31.

5. Metropolitan Planning Commission, *Up Ahead*, 17.

6. See U.S. Bureau of Census, *State and Metropolitan Area Data Book 1982*, 361.

7. Fulton County Department of Planning, *Comprehensive Plan Summary Report* (March 1978), 7.

8. U.S. Bureau of the Census, *State and Metropolitan Area Data Book 1982*, 361.

9. Rice, "Atlanta: If Dixie Were Atlanta," 53.

10. Taeuber, "Racial Residential Segregation, 28 Cities, 1970–1980," table 1.

11. *Atlanta Constitution*, "Black and Poor in Atlanta," October 21, 1981.

12. Nathan McCall, "Atlanta: City of the Next Generation," *Black Enterprise* 17 (May 1987): 56.

13. Rice, "Atlanta: If Dixie Were Atlanta," 40.

14. City of Atlanta, *Comprehensive Development Plan: 1984–1988* (Atlanta: Bureau of Planning, 1983), 14.

15. Ibid., 31.

16. City of Atlanta, *Comprehensive Development Plan*, 5.

17. Research Atlanta, *Decade of Decision* (Atlanta: Research Atlanta, 1980), 6.

18. Art Harris, "Too Busy to Hate," *Esquire* 103 (June 1985): 129.

19. McCall, "Atlanta: City of the Next Generation," 58.

20. U.S. Department of Housing and Urban Development, *The Land Use and Urban Development*, A-2.

21. City of Atlanta, *Comprehensive Development Plan*, 6.

22. McCall, "Atlanta: City of the Next Generation," 58.

23. Margaret Edds, *Free at Last: What Really Happened When Civil Rights Came to Southern Politics* (Bethesda, MD: Adler and Adler, 1987), 55.

24. See Charles Jaret, "Is Atlanta a 'Black Mecca?' Black Migration and Living Conditions in the Urban South," paper presented at the annual meeting of the Southern Sociological Society in Charlotte, North Carolina, April 10–13, 1985.

25. Research Atlanta, *City Council Task Force on Economic Development* (Atlanta: Research Atlanta, 1980), 88.

26. Research Atlanta, *Decade of Decision*, 10.

27. David Beers and Diana Hembree, "The New Atlanta: A Tale of Two Cities," *The Nation* 244 (March 21, 1987): 359.

28. Rice, "Atlanta: If Dixie Were Atlanta," 53.

29. Edds, *Free at Last*, 75.

30. *Atlanta Journal* and *Atlanta Constitution*, "Black and Poor in America," October 18, 1981.

31. U.S. Bureau of the Census, *Provisional Estimates of Social, Economic and Housing Characteristics*, 60.

32. U.S. Bureau of the Census, *1982 Survey of Minority-Owned Business Enterprises: Black*, 75.

33. Black Enterprise, "The Top 100 Black Businesses," *Black Enterprise* 16 (June 1986): 105.

34. Phil Petrie, "Dividends of Experience," *Black Enterprise* 12 (June 1982): 137.

35. Black Enterprise, "Black Savings and Loan Associations," *Black Enterprise* 16 (June 1986): 163.

36. Black Enterprise, "Black Insurance Companies," *Black Enterprise* 16 (June 1986): 179–79.

37. Joseph N. Boyce, "The King of Sweet Auburn Avenue," *Black Enterprise* 2 (June 1982): 137.

38. Ibid.

39. McCall, "Atlanta: City of the Next Generation," 56.

40. U.S. Bureau of the Census, *Provisional Estimates of Social, Economic and Housing Characteristics*, 60.

41. Ibid.

42. Edds, *Free at Last*, 358.

43. Ibid., 55; McCall, "Atlanta: City of the Next Generation," 58.

44. See Clarence A. Bacote, "The Negro in Atlanta Politics," *Phylon* 16 (Winter 1955): 335–50; Jake Walker, "Negro Voting in Atlanta: 1951–1961," *Phylon* 24 (Winter 1963): 379–87; Mack H. Jones, "Black Political Empowerment in Atlanta: Myth and Reality," *Annals of the Academy of Political and Social Sciences* 439 (September 1978): 90–117.

45. Harris, "Too Busy to Hate," 130.

46. See Floyd Hunter, *Community Power Structure: A Study of Decision Makers* (Chapel Hill: University of North Carolina Press, 1953); Floyd Hunter, *Community Power Succession: Atlanta's Policy-Makers Revisited* (Chapel Hill: University of North Carolina Press, 1980).

47. Jones, "Black Political Empowerment in Atlanta," 109.

48. Ibid.

49. McCall, "Atlanta: City of the Next Generation," 58.

50. Rice, "Atlanta: If Dixie Were Atlanta," 52.

51. McCall, "Atlanta: The City of the Next Generation," 56.

Chapter 4. Memphis: Heart of the Mid-South

1. James Roper, *The Founding of Memphis 1818–1820* (Memphis: Memphis Sesquicentennial, 1970), 23.

2. Charles W. Crawford, *Yesterday's Memphis* (Miami: E. A. Seeman Publishing, 1976), 17.

3. Ibid., 18.

4. George W. Lee, *Beale Street: Where the Blues Began* (New York: R. O. Ballou, 1934), 15.

5. Ibid., 16.

6. Robert A. Sigafoos, *Cotton Row to Beale Street* (Memphis: Memphis State University Press, 1979), 31.

7. Alrutheus A. Taylor, *The Negro in Tennessee* (Spartanburg, SC: The Reprint Company, 1974), 155.

8. See Annette E. Church and Roberta Church, *Robert R. Church, Sr.: Memphis' First Black Capitalist* (Memphis: Memphis Sesquicentennial, 1969), 17; also Clark Porteous, "A Short History of Memphis," in *Know Your Government* (Memphis: Memphis City Council, 1986), 29–30.

9. Church and Church, *Robert R. Church, Sr.*, 17.

10. Ibid., 27.

11. Lee, *Beale Street*, 13.

12. W. C. Handy, ed., *A Treasury of Blues* (New York: C. Boni, 1949), 18.

13. For a discussion of the Crump years, see William Miller, *Mr. Crump of Memphis* (Baton Rouge: Louisiana State University Press, 1964).

14. Memphis–Shelby County Health Department, "Birth Rates in Shelby County, 1935–1945" (1946).

15. U.S. Bureau of the Census, *State and Metropolitan Area Data Book 1982*, 401.

16. Memphis–Shelby County Health Department, *The 1984 Vital Statistics Report, Memphis–Shelby County, Tennessee* (Memphis, June 1985), 1.

17. Taeuber, "Racial Residential Segregation, 28 Cities, 1970–1980," 3.

18. David M. Tucker, "Black Pride and Negro Business in the 1920s: George Washington Lee of Memphis," *Business History Review* 43, no. 4 (1969): 437.

19. See Neal R. Peirce, "Memphis Proves Value of Working Together," *Houston Post*, May 24, 1982.

20. Center City Commission, *Annual Report* (1984).

21. Peirce, "Memphis Proves Value of Working Together."

22. Center for Business and Economic Research, Metropolitan Area Economic Report (Nashville: Tennessee State Planning Office, University of Tennessee at Knoxville, 1981), 98.

23. Memphis–Shelby County Office of Planning and Development, *Labor Profile, Memphis MSA* (Memphis: Planning and Development, 1985), 4.

24. See Lynn Norment, "Memphis," *Ebony* 37 (June 1982): 121.

25. Memphis–Shelby County Office for Planning and Development, *Labor Profile, Memphis MSA*, 4.

26. Ibid., 1–2.

27. Ibid., 2.

28. U.S. Bureau of the Census, *1977 Survey of Minority-Owned Business Enterprises: Black* (Washington, D.C.: U.S. Government Printing Office, 1979), 152.

29. U.S. Bureau of the Census, *1982 Survey of Minority-Owned Business Enterprises: Black*, 86.

30. Black Enterprise, "The Top 100 Black Businesses," *Black Enterprise* 16 (June 1986): 113.

31. Margaret Price, *The Negro Voter in the South* (Atlanta: Southern Regional Council, 1957), 31.

32. See David M. Tucker, *Memphis since Crump* (Knoxville: The University of Tennessee Press, 1980), 17.

33. Jack R. Vander Silk, ed., *Black Conflict with White America* (Columbus, OH: Charles E. Merrill Publishing, 1970), 97.

34. Sigafoos, *Cotton Row to Beale Street*, 332.

35. Norment, "Memphis," 121.

36. Joint Center for Political Studies, *Black Elected Officials: A National Roster 1984* (New York: UNIPUB, 1984), 339–46.

37. Anthony Cooke, "Memphis Runs against Trend to Elect Black," *The Commercial Appeal*, October 25, 1987, p. A-1.

Chapter 5. Birmingham: A Magic City

1. Ethel Armes, *The Story of Coal and Iron in Alabama* (Birmingham: Book-Keepers Press, 1972), 110.

2. Ibid., 219.

3. Ibid., 271.

4. See Malcolm C. McMillan, *The Land Called Alabama* (Austin: Stek-Vaughn, 1968), 260.

5. Frank L. Owsley, John C. Stewart, and Gordon T. Chappell, *Know Alabama: An Elementary History* (Northport, AL: Colonial Press, 1965), 197.

6. Armes, *The Story of Coal and Iron*, 515.

7. Carl V. Harris, "Economic Power and Politics: A Study of Birmingham, Alabama, 1890–1920" (Ph.D. dissertation, University of Wisconsin, 1970), 465–80.

8. Irving Beiman, "Birmingham: Steel Giant with a Glass Jaw," in *Our Fair City*, ed. Robert S. Allen (New York: Vanguard Press, 1941), 99–102.

9. Ibid.

10. Virginia Van der Veer Hamilton, *Alabama: A Bicentennial History* (New York: W. W. Norton, 1977), 147.

11. U.S. Bureau of the Census, *State and Metropolitan Area Data Book 1982*, 25.

12. Center for Urban Affairs, *Birmingham, Alabama: A Housing Study* (Birmingham: University of Alabama at Birmingham, 1977), 12–15.

13. Hamilton, *Alabama*, 139.

14. Taeuber, "Racial Residential Segregation, 28 Cities, 1970–1980" 3; Jerry W. Fly and George R. Reinhart, "Racial Segregation during the 1970s: The Case of Birmingham," *Social Forces* 58 (June 1980): 1255–62.

15. U.S. Bureau of the Census, *State and Metropolitan Area Data Book 1982*, 35.

16. The Housing Authority of the Birmingham District, *Annual Report* (Birmingham: City of Birmingham, 1987), 1.

17. Stephen Oates, *Let the Trumpet: The Life of Martin Luther King, Jr.* (New York: Harper and Row, 1982), 210; Hamilton, *Alabama*, 139.

18. Edward S. LaMonte, "Politics and Welfare in Birmingham 1900–1974" (Ph.D dissertation, University of Chicago, 1976), 226–42.

19. Ibid., 226–42.

20. Ibid., 142.

21. Harris, "Economic Power and Politics," 69–70.

22. City of Birmingham, *Affirmative Action Report: Full-Time Employee Profile* (Birmingham, December 1987), 18.

23. Edds, *Free at Last*, 102.

24. Ibid., 109.

25. Black Enterprise, "Black Insurance Companies," *Black Enterprise* 12 (June 1982): 176–77.

26. U.S. Bureau of the Census, *1982 Survey of Minority-Owned Business Enterprises: Black*, 69.

27. Edds, *Free at Last*, 102; City of Birmingham, *Affirmative Action Report*, 18.

28. Edds, *Free at Last*, 121–22.

29. Joint Center for Political Studies, *Black Elected Officials*, 23–26.

30. Birmingham Board of Education, *Enrollment Data* (Birmingham, 1987).

Chapter 6. Blacks in Tampa

1. Kenneth W. Porter, "Florida Slaves and the Free Negroes in the Seminole War 1835–1842," in *Promises to Keep*, ed. Bruce A. Glasund and Allen M. Smith (Chicago: Rand McNally, 1972), 119.

2. Julia Floyd Smith, *Slavery and Plantation Growth in Antebellum Florida* (Gainsville: The University of Florida Press, 1914), 17.

3. Karl H. Grismer, *Tampa: A History of the City of Tampa and the Tampa Bay Region of Florida* (St. Petersburg: St. Petersburg Printing Company, 1950), 75–77.

4. Joan Marie Steffey, "The Cuban Immigrants of Tampa, Florida 1886–1889" (unpublished master's thesis, University of South Florida, 1975), 47.

5. Ibid., 49–50.

6. Hillsborough County Museum, *Black Tampa: The Roots of a People*, black history project (Tampa, 1979), 10.

7. Ibid., 14.

8. U.S. Bureau of the Census, *State and Metropolitan Area Data Book 1982*, 288.

9. Ibid., 436.

10. Charles J. Parrish, "Minority Politics in a Southern City: Tampa, Florida 1950–1960" (unpublished master's thesis, University of Florida, 1960), 13–15.

11. Ibid., 11.

12. Ibid., 12.

13. National Advisory Commission on Civil Disorders, *Report of the National Advisory Commission on Civil Disoders* (New York: Bantam Books, 1968), 43–44.

14. See Thomas Sherberger, "Ybor City: The Legacy of Urban Renewal," *Tampa Tribune*, May 21, 1980.

15. Metropolitan Development Agency. *Annual Report Tampa* (July 1975), 1–18.

16. Arthur Raper, J. H. McGrew, and B. E. Mays, *A Study of Negro Life in Tampa* (Tampa: Tampa Urban League, 1927), 49.

17. U.S. Bureau of the Census, *1977 Survey of Black-Owned Business Enterprises: Black*, 150.

18. U.S. Bureau of the Census, *1982 Survey of Minority-Owned Business Enterprises: Black*, 74.

19. Black Enterprise, "Black Insurance Companies," *Black Enterprise* 16 (June 1986): 178–79.

20. Black Enterprise, "Black Savings and Loans," *Black Enterprise* 16 (June 1986): 163.

21. Edward Williams, "Full Scale Integration Ordered in County Schools," *Tampa Tribune*, May 26, 1971.

22. Under the integration order, blacks were to be bused to white schools from kindergarten through grade five, junior high (grades eight and nine), and senior high, while whites were to be bused to the sixth- and seventh-grade "centers," which were converted black elementary and junior high schools and located in black neighborhoods. Some whites were bused to junior high schools in black areas.

23. Edward Kaiser, "School Attitudes Survey Finds Mixed Results," *Tampa Tribune*, April 11, 1982.

24. Sherry Howard, "Black Leaders Are Concerned about Desegregation's Impact," *Tampa Tribune*, May 18, 1979.

25. Parrish, "Minority Politics in a Southern City," 11.

26. Joint Center for Political Studies, *Black Elected Officials*, 99–105.

27. City of Tampa, *Annual Performance Report*, Community Development Block Grant Program, CD Years I–IV, 1975–81.

28. See Peter K. Eisinger, "Black Mayors and the Politics of Racial Economic Advancement," in *Readings in Urban Politics Past, Present, and Future*, ed. Harlan Hahn and Charles H. Levine (New York: Longman, 1984), 249–60.

Conclusion: Problems and Prospects

1. Matney and Johnson, *America's Black Population*, 1.

2. Ibid., 1–2; Robinson, "Blacks Move Back to the South," 40–43.

3. U.S. Department of Labor, *Geographical Profile of Employment and Unemployment* (Washington, D.C.: U.S. Government Printing Office, 1986), 10–20.

4. Ibid., 3–9.

5. Robert S. Browne, *Only Six Million Acres: The Decline of Black-Owned Land in the Rural South* (New York: Black Economic Research Center, 1973), 3.

6. James W. Hughes and George Sternlieb, *The Dynamics of America's Housing* (New Brunswick, NJ: Rutgers University Center for Urban Policy Research, 1987), 112.

7. See Robert D. Bullard, "Blacks and the American Dream of Housing," in *Race, Ethnicity, and Minority Housing*, ed. Momeni, 53–68.

8. Franklin D. Wilson, *Residential Consumption, Economic Opportunity, and Race* (New York: Academic Press, 1979), 74–79; R. W. Lake, "Racial Transition and Black Home Ownership in American Suburbs," *Annals of the American Academy of Political and Social Sciences* 441 (January 1979): 142–56; Bullard, "The Black Family," 341–51.

9. Joint Center for Political Studies, *Blacks on the Move: A Decade of Demographic Change* (Washington, D.C.: Joint Center for Political Studies, 1982), 62.

10. Joe T. Darden, "Accessibility to Housing: Differential Residential Segregation for Blacks, Hispanics, American Indians, and Asians," in *Race, Ethnicity, and Minority Housing*, ed. Momeni, 109–26.

11. Karl Taeuber, "Racial Residential Segregation, 28 Cities, 1970–1980," 3.

12. William J. Wilson, *The Truly Disadvantaged*, 180–81. See also Bruce Williams, *Black Workers in an Industrial Suburb* (New Brunswick, NJ: Rutgers University Press, 1987), chap. 5.

13. Kasarda, "Caught in the Web of Change," 41–47; William J. Wilson, "The Black Underclass," *Wilson Quarterly* 8 (Spring 1984): 88–99.

14. U.S. Department of Labor, *Geographic Profile of Employment and Unemployment, 1986* (Washington, D.C.: U.S. Government Printing Office, 1987), 88–106.

15. See Bullard, *Invisible Houston*, 79–80.

16. U.S. Bureau of the Census, *1982 Survey of Minority-Owned Business Enterprises: Black*, 16.

17. Black Enterprise, "Top 100 Black Businesses," *Black Enterprise* 16 (June 1986): 105–13.

18. E. R. Bourdon, et al., "Economic Prospects for Blacks in the 1980s," *Congressional Research Service Report*, no. 81-26FE (December 18, 1981), 34.

19. Andrew F. Brimmer, "Blacks in Business in the 1980s: More Salaried Managers Than Owners," *Black Enterprise* 12 (July 1982): 30.

20. Robert S. Browne, "Institution Building for Urban Revitalization," *The Review of Black Political Economy* 10 (Fall 1979): 38.

21. Joint Center for Political Studies, *Black Elected Officials*, 9; John Britton, "Twenty Years of Black Political Progress," Fifth National Policy Institute, Washington D.C., January 20–23, 1988, pp. 9–10.

22. Joint Center for Political Studies, *Black Elected Officials*, 2.

23. Ibid., 349–57.

24. Bullard, *Invisible Houston*, 126–33.

25. For a thorough discussion of the issues surrounding black voting, see Chandler Davidson, ed., *Minority Vote Dilution* (Washington, D.C.: Howard University Press, 1984).

Select Bibliography

Allen, Robert S., ed, *Our Fair City*. New York: Vanguard Press, 1941.

Armes, Ethel. *The Story of Coal and Iron in Alabama*. Birmingham: Book-Keepers Press, 1972.

Bacote, Clarence A. "The Negro in Atlanta Politics." *Phylon* 16 (Winter 1955): 335–50.

Barr, Alwyn. and Robert A. Calvert, eds. *Black Leaders: Texans for Their Times*. Austin: Texas State Historical Association, 1981.

Beers, David, and Diana Hembree. "The New Atlanta: A Tale of Two Cities." *The Nation* 244 (March 21, 1987): 347, 357–60.

Beiman, Irving. "Birmingham: Steel Giant with a Glass Jaw." In *Our Fair City*, ed. Robert S. Allen. New York: Vanguard Press, 1941.

Bernard, Richard M., and Bradley R. Rice, eds. *Sunbelt Cities: Politics and Growth since World War II*. Austin: University of Texas Press, 1983.

Blassingame, John W. *Black New Orleans: 1860–1880*. Chicago: University of Chicago Press, 1973.

Breckenfeld, Gurney. "Refilling the Metropolitan Doughnut." In *The Rise of the Sunbelt Cities*, ed. David C. Perry and Alfred J. Watkins. Beverly Hills: Sage, 1977.

Browne, Robert S. *Only Six Million Acres: The Decline of Black-Owned Land in the Rural South*. New York: Black Economic Research Center, 1973.

Bullard, Robert D. "Blacks and the American Dream of Housing." In *Race, Ethnicity, and Minority Housing in the United States*, ed. Jamshid A. Momeni. Westport, CT: Greenwood Press, 1986.

———. "The Black Family: Housing Alternatives in the '80s." *Journal of Black Studies* 14 (March 1984): 341–51.

———. *Invisible Houston: The Black Experience in Boom and Bust*. College Station: Texas A&M University Press, 1987.

———. "Persistent Barriers in Housing Black Americans." *Journal of Applied Social Sciences* 7 (Fall–Winter 1983): 19–31.

Bullard, Robert D., and Odessa L. Pierce. "Black Housing in a Southern Metropolis: Competition for Housing in a Shrinking Market." *The Black Scholar* 11 (November–December 1979): 60–69.

Bullard, Robert D., and Donald L. Tryman, "Competition for Decent Housing: A Focus on Housing Discrimination in a Sunbelt City." *The Journal of Ethnic Studies* 7 (Winter 1980): 51–63.

Bullock, Henry Allen. *Pathways to the Houston Negro Market.* Ann Arbor: J. N. Edwards, 1957.

Carter, Hodding, ed. *The Past as Prelude: New Orleans 1718–1968.* New Orleans: Pelican Publishing House, 1968.

Church, Annette E., and Roberta Church. *Robert R. Church, Sr.: Memphis' First Black Capitalist.* Memphis: Memphis Sesquicentennial, 1969.

Crawford, Charles W. *Yesterday's Memphis.* Miami: E. A. Seeman Publishing, 1976.

Darden, Joe T. "Accessibility to Housing: Differential Residential Segregation for Blacks, Hispanics, American Indians, and Asians." In *Race, Ethnicity, and Minority Housing in the United States*, ed. Jamshid A. Momeni. Westport, CT: Greenwood Press, 1986.

Davidson, Chandler, ed. *Biracial Politics: Conflict and Coalition in the Biracial South.* Baton Rouge: Louisiana State University Press, 1972.

———. *Minority Vote Dilution.* Washington, D.C.: Howard University Press, 1984.

Edds, Margaret. *Free at Last: What Really Happened When Civil Rights Came to Southern Politics.* Bethesda, MD: Adler and Adler, 1987.

Eisinger, Peter K. "Black Mayors and the Politics of Racial Economic Advancement." In *Reading in Urban Politics Past, Present, and Future*, ed. Harlan Hahn and Charles H. Levine. New York: Longman, 1984.

Fuller, Chet. "I Hear Them Call It the New South." *Black Enterprise* 12 (November 1981): 41–44.

Garrett, Franklin. *Atlanta and Environs.* Athens: University of Georgia Press, 1969.

Gillette, Michael L. "Heman Marion Sweatt: Civil Rights Plaintiff." In *Black Leaders: Texans for Their Times*, ed. Alwyn Barr and Robert A. Calvert. Austin: Texas State Historical Association, 1981.

Glasund, Bruce A., and Allen M. Smith, eds. *Promises to Keep.* Chicago: Rand McNally, 1972.

Goldfield, David R. *Promised Land: The South since 1945.* Arlington Heights, IL: Harlan Davidson, 1987.

Grismer, Karl H. *Tampa: A History of the City of Tampa and the Tampa Bay Region of Florida.* St. Petersburg: St. Petersburg Printing Company, 1950.

Hamilton, Virginia Van der Veer. *Alabama: A Bicentennial History.* New York: W. W. Norton, 1977.

Hahn, Harlan, and Charles H. Levine, eds. *Readings in Urban Politics Past, Present, and Future.* New York: Longman, 1984.

Harris, Art. "Too Busy to Hate." *Esquire* 103 (June 1985): 129–33.

Hirsch, Arnold R. "New Orleans: Sunbelt in the Swamp." In *Sunbelt Cities: Politics and Growth since World War II,* ed. Richard M. Bernard and Bradley R. Rice. Austin: University of Texas Press, 1983.

Houseman, G. L. "Access of Minorities to Suburbs." *The Urban Social Change Review* 14 (1981): 11–20.

Houston City Planning Department. *Houston Year 2000.* Houston: City of Houston, 1980.

Hughes, James W., and George Sternlieb. *The Dynamics of America's Housing.* New Brunswick, NJ: Rutgers University Center for Urban Policy Research, 1987.

Hunter, Floyd. *Community Power Structure: A Study of Decision Makers.* Chapel Hill: University of North Carolina Press, 1953.

———. *Community Power Succession: Atlanta's Policy-Makers Revisited.* Chapel Hill: University of North Carolina Press, 1980.

Inger, Morton. *Politics and Reality in an American City: The New Orleans School Crisis of 1960.* Chicago: Aldine Publishing, 1968.

James, Franklin, Betty I. Cumming, and Eileen A. Tynan. *Minorities in the Sunbelt.* New Brunswick: NJ: Rutgers University Center for Policy Research, 1984.

Jaret, Charles. "Is Atlanta a 'Black Mecca?' Black Migration and Living Conditions in the Urban South." Paper presented at the annual meeting of the Southern Sociological Society in Charlotte, North Carolina, April 10–13, 1985.

Joint Center for Political Studies. *Blacks on the Move: A Decade of Demographic Change.* Washington, D.C.: Joint Center for Political Studies, 1982.

———. *Black Elected Officials: A National Roster 1984.* New York: UNIPUB, 1984.

Jones, Mack H. "Black Political Empowerment in Atlanta: Myth and Reality." *Annals of the Academy of Political and Social Sciences* 439 (September 1978): 90–117.

Kaplan, Barry. "Houston: The Golden Buckle of the Sunbelt." In *Sunbelt Cities: Politics and Growth since World War II,* ed. Richard M. Bernard and Bradley R. Rice. Austin: University of Texas Press, 1983.

Karnig, Albert K., and Susan Welch. *Black Representation and Urban Policy.* Chicago: University of Chicago Press, 1980.

Kasarda, John D. "The Implications of Contemporary Distribution Trends for National Urban Policy." *Social Science Quarterly* 61 (December 1980): 373–400.

———. "Caught in the Web of Change." *Society* 21 (1983): 41–47.

Kasarda, John D., Michael D. Irvin, and Holly J. Hughes. "The South Is Still Rising." *American Demographics* 8 (June 1986): 32–40.

Lake, R. W. "Racial Transition and Black Home Ownership in Amercan Suburbs." *Annals of the American Academy of Political and Social Sciences* 441 (January 1979): 142–56.

Lee, George W. *Beale Street: Where the Blues Began.* New York: R. O. Ballou, 1934.

Lewis, P. F. *New Orleans: The Making of an Urban Landscape.* Cambridge, MA: Ballinger, 1976.

Long, Larry, and Diana DeAre. "The Suburbanization of Blacks." *American Demographics* 3 (September 1981): 16–22.

Marshall, Sue A. "The Community Development Block Grant Program and Unmet Needs." *The Urban League Review* 5 (Summer 1981): 27–34.

Matney, William C., and Dwight L. Johnson, *America'a Black Population: A Statistical View, 1970–1982.* Washington, D.C.: U.S. Government Printing Office, 1983.

McCall, Nathan. "Atlanta: City of the Next Generation," *Black Enterprise* 17 (May 1987): 56–58.

McCall, William G. *Louisiana's Official Resistance to Desegregation.* Nashville: Vanderbilt University, 1964.

McComb, David G. *Houston the Bayou City.* Austin: University of Texas Press, 1968.

———. *Houston: A History.* Austin: University of Texas Press, 1981.

McMillan, Malcolm C. *The Land Called Alabama.* Austin: Stek-Vaughn, 1968.

Miller, William. *Mr. Crump of Memphis.* Baton Rouge: Louisiana State University Press, 1964.

Momeni, Jamshid A., ed. *Race, Ethnicity, and Minority Housing in the United States.* Westport, CT: Greenwood Press, 1986.

National Advisory Commission on Civil Disorders. *Report of the National Advisory Commission on Civil Disorders.* New York: Bantam Books, 1968.

National Urban Coalition. *The Situation in Urban America: A Spring 1982 Report.* Washington, D.C.: National Urban Coalition, 1982.

National Urban League. *The State of Black America 1981.* New York: National Urban League, 1981.

Nelson, Kathryn. *Recent Suburbanization of Blacks: How Much, Who and Where?* Washington, D.C.: U.S. Department of Housing and Urban Development, 1979.

Orfield, Gary. *School Desegregation Patterns in the States, Large Cities and Metropolitan Areas 1968–1980.* Washington, D.C.: Joint Center for Political Studies, 1983.

Perry, David C., and Alfred J. Watkins, eds. *The Rise of the Sunbelt Cities.* Beverly Hills: Sage, 1977.

Piliawsky, Monte. "The Impact of Black Mayors on the Black Community: The Case of New Orleans' Ernest Morial." *The Review of Black Political Economy* 13 (Spring 1985): 5–23,

Porter, Kenneth W. "Florida Slaves and the Free Negroes in the Seminole War 1835–1842." In *Promises to Keep*, ed. Bruce A. Glasund and Allen M. Smith. Chicago: Rand McNally, 1972.

Preston, Michael B., Lenneal J. Henderson, Jr., and Paul Puryear, eds. *The New Black Politics: The Search for Political Power.* New York: Longman, 1982.

Price, Margaret. *The Negro Voter in the South.* Atlanta: Southern Regional Council, 1957.

Rice, Bradley R. "Atlanta: If Dixie Were Atlanta." In *Sunbelt Cities: Politics and Growth since World War II*, ed. Richard M. Bernard and Bradley R. Rice. Austin: University of Texas Press, 1983.

Robinson, Isaac. 'Blacks Move Back to the South." *American Demographics* 8 (June 1986): 40–43.

Sale, Kirkpatrick. *Power Shift: The Rise of the Southern Rim and Its Challenge to the Eastern Establishment.* New York: Random House, 1975.

Schexnider, Alvin, J. "Political Mobilization in the South: The Election of a Black Mayor in New Orleans." In *The New Black Politics: The Search for Political Power*, ed. Michael B. Preston, Lenneal J. Henderson, Jr., and Paul Puryear. New York: Longman, 1982.

Sigafoos, Robert A. *Cotton Row to Beale Street.* Memphis: Memphis State University Press, 1979.

Smith, Julia Floyd, *Slavery and Plantation Growth in Antebellum Florida.* Gainesville: The University of Florida Press, 1914.

Smith, Susan H. *How, When and Where Atlanta.* Atlanta: Maramac Publishing, 1982.

Taylor, Alrutheus A. *The Negro in Tennessee.* Spartanburg, SC: The Reprint Company, 1974.

Taeuber, Karl. "Racial Residential Segregation, 1980." In *A Decent Home*, ed. Citizen Commission on Civil Rights. Washington, D.C.: Center for National Policy Review, 1983.

———. "Racial Residential Segregation, 28 Cities, 1970–1980," Center for Demography and Ecology Working Paper No. 83–12. University of Wisconsin-Madison, March 1983.

Taeuber, Karl, and Alma F. Taeuber. *Negroes in Cities: Residential Segregation and Neighborhood Change.* Chicago: Aldine Publishing, 1965.

Terry, William, E. *Origin and Development of Texas Southern University.* Houston: D. Armstrong, 1968.

Tucker, David M. *Memphis since Crump.* Knoxville: The University of Tennessee Press, 1980.

U.S. Bureau of the Census. *Advanced Estimates of Social, Economic and Housing Characteristics: Texas*, Washington, D.C.: U.S. Government Printing Office, 1982.

———. *Census of Population and Housing*. Washington, D.C.: U.S. Government Printing Office, 1900–1980.

———. *1982 Survey of Minority-Owned Business Enterprises: Black*. Washington, D.C.: U.S. Government Printing Office, 1979.

———. *1977 Survey of the Minority-Owned Business Enterprises: Black*. Washington, D.C.: U.S. Government Printing Office, 1979.

———. *The President's National Urban Policy Report: 1980* Washington, D.C.: U.S. Government Printing Office, 1980.

———. *Provisional Estimates of Social, Economic and Housing Characteristics*, Washington, D.C.: U.S. Government Printing Office, 1982.

———. *The Social and Economic Status of the Black Population in the United States: An Historical View, 1790–1978*. Washington, D.C.: U.S. Government Printing Office, 1979.

———. *State and Metropolitan Area Data Book 1982*. Washington, D.C.: U.S. Government Printing Office, 1982.

U.S. Commission on Civil Rights. *The Federal Fair Housing Enforcement Efforts*. Washington, D.C.: U.S. Government Printing Office, 1979.

U.S. Department of Housing and Urban Development. *Report of the President's Commission for a National Agenda for the Eighties*. Washington, D.C.: U.S. Government Printing Office, 1980.

———. *The Land Use and Urban Development Impacts of Beltways Case Studies* Washington, D.C.: U.S. Government Printing Office, 1980.

Walker, Jake, "Negro Voting in Atlanta: 1851–1961." *Phylon* 24 (Winter 1963): 379–87.

West, Richard. "Only the Strong Survive." *The Texas Monthly* 7 (February 1979): 94–105.

Wheeler, Kenneth. *To Wear a City's Crown: The Beginning of Urban Growth in Texas, 1836–1865*. Cambridge: Harvard University Press, 1968.

Williams, Bruce. *Black Workers in an Industrial Suburb*. New Brunswick, NJ: Rutgers University Press, 1987.

Wilson, Franklin D. *Residential Consumption, Economic Opportunity, and Race*. New York: Academic Press, 1979.

Wilson, William J. *The Declining Significance of Race: Blacks and Changing American Institutions*. 2d ed. Chicago: University of Chicago Press, 1980.

———. "The Black Underclass." *Wilson Quarterly* 8 (Spring 1984): 88–99.

———. *The Truly Disadvantaged: The Inner City, the Underclass, and Public Policy*. Chicago: University of Chicago Press, 1987.

Contributors

DELORES P. ALDRIDGE is a professor of sociology and chairperson of the African American and African Studies Program at Emory University. She is the past chairperson of the National Council for Black Studies.

ROBERT D. BULLARD, editor of *In Search of the New South*, is currently a visiting scholar at the University of California-Berkeley. He has held appointments as an associate professor of sociology at the University of Tennessee in Knoxville and Texas Southern University in Houston. He is the author of *Invisible Houston: The Black Experience in Boom and Bust* and numerous other articles and monographs on urban life.

ROBERT A. CATLIN is the dean of the College of Social Sciences at Florida Atlantic University. He is the former chairperson of the Political Science Department at the University of South Florida in Tampa. He has written extensively in the area of urban politics, public policy, housing, and community development.

ERNEST PORTERFIELD is an associate dean of the College of Social Sciences and professor of sociology at the University of Alabama at Birmingham. He is the author of *Black and White Mixed Marriages* and coauthor of *Perspectives on Marriage and the Family: A Reader*.

E. KIKI THOMAS is an associate professor in the Department of Mental Health at Georgia State University in Atlanta. She has worked extensively in the areas of housing, clinical education, skill development, and job functioning among low-income and black residents in Atlanta.

SANDRA VAUGHN is an associate professor of political science at LeMoyne Owen College in Memphis. She is codirector of the Memphis Writer's Workshop. Much of her research has focused on equity issues and the black Memphis community.

BEVERLY HENDRIX WRIGHT is an associate professor of sociology at Wake Forest University. Her former appointment was with the University of New Orleans. She is the author of a series of articles and essays on racial group identification, achievement motivation, social stratification, and quality of life issues in New Orleans.

Index

Alabama, 4, 5. *See also* Birmingham, Alabama; Mobile, Alabama
Alabama and Chattanooga Railroad, 121
Alabama Penny Savings Bank, 137
Aldrich, Truman H., 122
Alexander, Avery, 68
Allen, Augustus, 16
Allen, John Kirby, 16
American Missionary Association, 62
American Missionary Society, 92
Antioch Baptist Church, 17, 28
Apartheid: protests against, 29
Arkansas, 4
Arrington, Richard, Jr., 132, 139, 140
Askew, Reuben, 159
Atlanta, Georgia, 6, 7, 75–97; black-owned businesses, 34, 81, 89–92; black politics, 93–95; community responsibility in, 135; economic change, 80–92; employment rate, 83, 88–89; federal employment in, 81; geographic expansion of, 76; historical background, 75–77; housing in, 77–80; income patterns, 93; industrial expansion and, 76; in-migration, 85; metropolitan growth, 77; minority contracts, 94; population growth, 77; poverty rate, 89; public housing, 80; residential patterns, 77–80; school desegregation, 92–93; social change, 80–92; substandard housing, 79; suburbs of, 86; as trade center, 81, 83; transportation and, 80–81, 86, 88; voting divisions, 86; white flight and, 77

Atlanta Constitution, 88
Atlanta Life Insurance Company, 84, 86, 91–92
Atlanta University, 92
Atlanta University Center, 85

Baracoc-Pontiac, 91
Barthelemy, Sidney J., 54, 61, 71–72
Birmingham, Alabama, 6, 7, 121–41; absentee business owners, 123; black-owned businesses, 137–39; black politics, 139–40; convict labor, 123–24; economic change, 130–39; employment in, 135–37; hardship rating, 9; historical background, 121–25; housing in, 126–29; income gap, 135; integration in, 139; labor strife, 123; metropolitan growth, 125–26; mining industry and, 121–23; minority contracts in, 139; population growth, 125–26; public housing, 128–29; recessions and, 137; residential patterns, 126–29; school desegregation, 140; sharecroppers and, 122; social change, 130–39; white flight and, 126
Black(s):
concentrations of, 4–7; emerging industries and, 2; home ownership of, 11–13; housing quality, 14; migration patterns, 5–6, 161. *See also* Atlanta; Birmingham; Houston; Memphis; Nashville; New Orleans; Richmond; Tampa
Black, Hugo, 131

Black Enterprise, 34, 90, 114, 138, 156, 169
Black Monday demonstration, 107
Black-owned businesses:
  in Atlanta, 34, 81, 89–92; in Birmingham, 137–39; in Houston, 23, 31–34; in Memphis, 113–15; in Nashville, 34; in New Orleans, 60, 61–62; in Richmond, 34; receipts of, 169; recession and, 168; in Tampa, 151, 155–57
Black politics:
  in Atlanta, 93–95; at-large elections and, 159; in Birmingham, 139–40; gains in, 170–72; in Houston, 40–43; in Memphis, 116–19; in New Orleans, 67–73; in Tampa, 159
Blockbusting, 52
Bloc voting, 72
Bond, Horace Mann, 92
Bond, Julian, 95
Booker T. Washington Insurance Company, 137
Boutwell, Albert, 131
Boyce, Joseph N., 91–92
Bradford Industrial Insurance Company, 138
Breckenfeld, Gurney, 7–8
Brimmer, Andrew, 169
Brown, Lee P., 33
Brown v. *Board of Education*, 36, 64, 106
Buckeye Cellulose, 113
Bullard, Linda McKeever, 38
Bullock, Henry A., 18
Butler, Asberry, 41

California: population gains in, 9–10
Carrier Air Conditioning, 113
Catholic schools: black enrollment in, 67
Central Atlanta Improvement Association, 81
Central Atlanta Progress, 81
Central Life Insurance Company, 156
Church, Robert R., Jr., 116
Church, Robert R., Sr., 100
Church of God in Christ, 112
Cigar industry, 142–43

Cities:
  annexation by, 14; black populations, 6–8; crime rates, 3, 9; ghettoization of, 2, 9; housing growth, 13–14; population gains, 9–10; transportation systems, 166–67; uneven development in, 2. *See also* Atlanta; Birmingham; Houston; Memphis; Nashville; New Orleans; Richmond; Savannah; Tampa
Citizens Federal Savings and Loan Association, 137–38
Citizens Trust Bank, 91
Civil rights: federal enforcement of, 9
Civil Rights Act (1875), 62
Civil Rights Act (1964), 64
Clark College, 92
Clement, Frank, 117
Cleo Wrap, 113
Cleveland, Ohio: hardship rating of, 9
Climate: attraction of, 1
Community Chest, 130
Community Development Block Grant program, 25, 52, 154
Community Federal Savings and Loan Association, 156–57
Community Organizations for Urban Politics, 68–69
Comprehensive Employment and Training Act (1973), 25
Connor, Eugene "Bull," 131
Consumer's League of Greater New Orleans, 68
Contracts: with minority businesses, 94, 139
Cotton industry, 99
Creoles, 46
Crescent City Independent Voters League, 68
Crime rates: in cities, 3, 9
Crump, Edward H., 100, 116
Cuban immigrants, 142–43

Dallas, Texas, 6;
  housing growth, 13; population gains, 9
Davenport and Harris Funeral Home, 137

Davis, A. L., 68
Davis, Fred, 117
DeBardeleben, Henry F., 122
Dennis, Dave, 68
Detroit, Michigan: hardship rating of, 9
Dirosa, Joseph, 70
Dobbs's House, 113
Douglas, Niles, 68
Dover Corporation, 113
Drug problems, 3
Du Bois, W. E. B., 92
DuPont, 113

Edds, Margaret, 140
Education:
    black migration and, 6; teacher short-
    ages and, 38–39; underclass and, 2. See
    also School desegregation
Edwards, Edwin, 68
Elyton Land Company, 121
Employment:
    black migration and, 6; competition
    for, 9; education and, 166; marginal
    skills and, 2; occupations, 167–68; pri-
    vatization and, 25; racial gap, 162–64,
    167; regional differences, 164; South
    and, 162–64, 166, 167. See also At-
    lanta; Birmingham; Houston; Mem-
    phis; Tampa
Espy, Michael, 171

Fair Housing Act (1968), 23, 52
Faucheux, Ron, 71
Federal budget cuts, 9
Federal Express Corporation, 112, 113
Federal Reserve Bank, 76
Financial institutions: black-owned, 169–
    70
Firestone Tire and Rubber, 104
Ford, Harold, 109, 117–18, 171
Ford, John, 118
Fort Gilmer, Georgia, 75
Fowler, Wych, 95
Franklin, John Hope, 92
Fraternal Bank and Trust, 100
Freedman's Aid Society of the Methodist

Episcopal Church, 62–63
Frenchy's Po-Boy, 34
Fuller, Chet, 2–3

Gaston, A. G., 137
Georgia, 4, 5. See also Atlanta, Georgia
Ghettos, 2, 9, 14
Gifted/talented schools, 66, 172
Graves, Bibb, 124
Graves, Curtis, 41
Greco, Dick, 151
Guardsmark, 113

Hall, George, 6–7
Handy, W. C., 100–101
Hardship ratings: of cities, 9
Hargrett, James T., 153, 159
Harris, Charles M., 137
Hartsfield Airport, 80–81
Harvey, Perry, Jr., 159
Harvey, Perry, Sr., 143
Henry, Clarence "Chink," 68
Herenton, Willie W., 108
Herndon, Alonzo F., 91
Higgs, W. Otis, 118
Hill, Jesse, Jr., 84, 91
Hirsch, Arnold, 58
H. J. Russell Construction Company, 90
Holiday Corporation, 113
Hooks, Ben L., 117
Horton, Odell, 117
Housing:
    construction of, 10–11, 13–14; costs
    of, 3; ownership of, 10–14, 164–66;
    quality of, 14. See also Atlanta; Bir-
    mingham; Houston; Memphis; New
    Orleans; Tampa
Housing and Community Development
    Act (1974), 25
Houston, Texas, 6, 16–44; black-owned
    businesses, 23, 31–34; black politics,
    40–43; cost of living, 24; economic
    change in, 24–35; employment in, 27–
    29, 31; Hispanics in, 37; history of,
    16–18; housing in, 13, 19–24; income
    patterns, 24; job programs, 25; metro-

politan growth, 18–20; out-migration,
17; population growth, 9, 17, 18–20;
poverty rate, 24–25; public housing,
23–24; recessions and, 27; residential
patterns, 20–24; revitalization activities, 21; school desegregation, 35–40;
segregation in, 20–24; slaves in, 16; social programs, 24–25, 27; teacher
shortages and, 38–39
Houston Area Urban League, 37
Houston College for Negroes, 35
Houston Colored Junior College, 35

Income:
in Atlanta, 93; in Birmingham, 135;
black migration and, 6; in Houston,
24; median family, 10–11; racial gap,
167
The Informer, 17
Interdenominational Theological Center,
92
International Business Machines, 149
International Harvester, 104
International Longshoremen's Union,
143

Jackson, Kenneth, 37
Jackson, Maynard, 94
Jefferson, William, 70–72
Job Training Partnership Act (1983), 25
Johnican, Minerva, 118
Jones, Mack, 94
Jordan, Barbara, 41

Kasarda, John D., 1
Kellogg, Paul, 48
Kentucky, 4
Kimberly-Clark, 113
King, Martin Luther, Jr., 34, 92, 107,
131, 134
King, Martin Luther, III, 95
Kraftco, 104
Kuykendall, Dan, 117

Labor unions, 1
Landrieu, Moon, 58–59, 69, 72
Lavelle, James, 143

LeBlanc, Sam, 72
Lee, George W., 100
Leland, George "Mickey," 30, 171
LeMoyne-Owen College, 103
Lewis, John, 87, 95, 171
Little, Perry A., 159
Lockard, H. T., 107, 117
Logsden, Joseph, 70
Louisiana, 4, 5. See also New Orleans,
Louisiana
Louisiana State University in
New Orleans, 63
Louisville and Nashville Railroad, 122
Lowry, A. Leon, Sr., 152, 159

MacDill Air Force Base, 149
Magnet schools, 40, 66, 172
Marshall, Thurgood, 36
Marthasville, Georgia, 75
Mathews, Barbara, 38
Mays, Benjamin, 92
Memphis, Tennessee, 6, 7, 98–120;
black-owned businesses, 113–15; black
politics, 116–19; black population,
104; community responsibility in, 135;
cotton industry and, 99; economic
change, 105–15; employment in, 106,
112–13; historical background, 98–
101; home ownership, 105; housing in,
102–105; in-migration, 100, 102; metropolitan growth, 101–102; population
growth, 101–102; redevelopment in,
111; residential patterns, 102–105;
school desegregation, 106–107, 110;
sharecroppers in, 106; slaves in, 98–99;
social change, 105–15; tourism and,
111, 112; as trade center, 112; white
flight and, 110; yellow fever in, 99
Merrill-Lynch, 113
Miami, Florida, 6, 9
Midwest:
unemployment in, 164; urban ghettos
of, 9
Milner, John T., 121
Mining industry, 121–23
Mississippi, 4, 5
M & M Products Company, 90–91

Mobile, Alabama: community responsibility in, 135
Model Cities program, 25, 151, 154
Morehouse College, 92
Morehouse School of Medicine, **85**
Morial, Ernest "Dutch," 52, **54**, 58, 59–60, 69–72
Morris Brown College, 92
Mutual Federal Savings and Loan, 91

Nashville, Tennessee:
    black-owned banks in, 34;
    community responsibility in, 135
National Alliance of Postal Workers, 35
National Association for the Advancement of Colored People, 35, 68, 106–107, 135
National Business League, 115
National Football League, 149
Near-town neighborhoods, 21–22
Neosheba, Tennessee, 98
Netters, James, 117
New Orleans, Louisiana, 6, 7, 45–74;
    black-owned businesses, 60, 61–62;
    black politics in, 67–73; Creoles in, 46; economic change in, 58–62; Economic Development Corporation, 59; ethnic divisions, 46–47; Fair Housing Program, 52; free blacks, 45, 47; French influence, 45; French Market renovation, 59; hardship rating, 9; history of, 45–74; housing in, 49, 51–58; institutional racism, 64–65; labor force, 58, 60–61; metropolitan growth, 49–51; population growth, 49–51; poverty rate, 60; public housing, 54, 56–57; public transportation, 48–49; residential patterns, 51–58; school desegregation, 62–67; slaves in, 45; unemployment in, 60; voter registration in, 68; white flight and, 52
New Orleans University, 63
Nike, 113
Norment, Lynn, 118
North:
    black homeowners in, 12; growth periods, 148; out-migration from, 161;
unemployment in, 164; urban ghettos of, 9
North Carolina, 4, 5
North Carolina Mutual, 91

O'Conor, Robert, 40
Oil glut: effects of, 9, 34, 162
Orleans Parish Progressive Voters League, 68

Padgett, Reubin, Jr., 159
Pat Carter Pontiac, 114
Patterson, J. O., Jr., 117, 118
Peirce, Neal R., 111–12
People's Defense League, 67
Pettiford, W. R., 137
Pinchback, P. B. S., 63
Plessy v. Ferguson, 36
Poe, William, 154
Politics:
    progressive, 1; sexism in, 41. *See also* Black politics
Population growth, 4
Portman, John, 81
Pratt Coal and Coke Company, 122
Private schools: black enrollment in, 67
Protective Industrial Life Insurance Company of Alabama, 137
Public services, 3

Racism: institutional, 2, 64–65
Recessions:
    Birmingham and, 137; black-owned businesses and, 168; black progress and, 3; effects of, 9, 162; ghettos and, 15; Houston and, 27–29, 31
Recreation opportunities, 1
Report of the President's Commission for a National Agenda for the Eighties (1980), 1
Republic Iron and Steel Company, 123
Retirement population, 1
Richmond, Virginia:
    black-owned banks in, 34; black population of, 6, 7
Ridgeway/Germantown, Tennessee, 98
Riverside Bank, 32–34

Robinson, Judson, Jr., 41
Robinson Cadillac-Excalibur, 91
Ross v. *HISD*, 40
Row houses, 26
Russell, Herman J., 90

Savannah, Georgia: black population in,
    7
Schering Plough, 113
School desegregation:
    in Atlanta, 92–93; barriers to, 166; in
    Birmingham, 140; class-based differ-
    ences and, 172; in Houston, 35–40; in
    Memphis, 106–107, 110; in New Orle-
    ans, 62–67; in Tampa, 149, 151, 157–
    59
Sexism: in politics, 41
Sharecroppers:
    Birmingham and, 122; Memphis and,
    106
Sharp Manufacturing Company, 113
Shores, Arthur, 139
Shotgun houses, 26
Singleton ratio, 37, 38
Singleton v. *Jackson Municipal Separate*
    School District, 37
Skinner, Thomas, 159
Slavery:
    in Houston, 16; in Memphis, 98–99;
    in New Orleans, 45; in Tampa, 142
Sloss, James Withers, 122
Sloss-Sheffield Steel and Iron Company,
    123
Small, Leonard, 115
Smith, Erskine, 131
Smith, Milton Hannibal, 122
Smith and Gaston Funeral Homes, 137
Smith Pipe Companies, 34
Smith v. *Allwright*, 40, 116, 150
Solvent Savings Bank, 100
South:
    black homeowners in, 11–14; defining,
    3–10; demographics, 4–10; growth pe-
    riods, 148; home ownership, 164–66;
    housing trends, 10–14; in-migration to,
    161; poverty in, 161–62; unemploy-
    ment in, 162–64, 166, 167; urban

ghettos, 9. *See also* Atlanta; Birming-
    ham; Houston; Memphis; Nashville;
    New Orleans; Richmond; Savannah;
    Tampa
South African Airways, 29
South and North Railroad, 121, 122
South Carolina, 4, 5
Southern Organization for United
    Leadership, 68, 69
Southern University, 63
Southern University in New Orleans,
    63, 65
Spelman College, 92
Standard metropolitan statistical areas
    (SMSAs), 6
Steffey, Joan, 142
Straight College, 62
Student Nonviolent Coordinating
    Committee, 95
Surgarmon, Russell, 116, 117
Sweatt, Heman, 35–36
Sweatt v. *Painter*, 35–36

Tampa, Florida, 6, 142–60; black-owned
    businesses, 151, 155–57; black politics,
    159; cigar industry in, 142–43; Cuban
    immigrants, 142–43; economic change,
    150–57; employment rate, 144; histori-
    cal background, 142–43; home owner-
    ship, 144; housing in, 13, 145–50;
    metropolitan growth, 143–45; popula-
    tion growth, 143–45; port industry,
    143; poverty rate, 144; public housing,
    155; renovation in, 151, 154; residen-
    tial patterns, 145–50; school desegrega-
    tion, 149, 151, 157–59; slaves in, 142;
    social change, 150–57; voter registra-
    tion, 159
Tampa Tribune, 158
Tax base, 3
Tennessee, 4. *See also* Memphis,
    Tennessee; Nashville, Tennessee
Tennessee Coal Iron and Railroad
    Company, 123
Terminus, Georgia, 75
Texas, 4, 9. *See also* Dallas, Texas;
    Houston, Texas

Texas Southern University, 35–36
Texas State University for Negroes, 35
Thayer, Ralph, 48
Thurgood Marshall School of Law, 36
Tri-State Bank, 114–15
Turner, Jessie, 117

Underclass, emerging, 2
Unemployment. *See* Employment
United States:
    Bureau of the Census, 4; Department
    of Housing and Urban Development,
    25, 52, 57; Justice Department, 135
United States v. *the State of Louisiana*, 64
U.S. Steel, 125
Universal Life Insurance Company, 115
University of Houston, 36
University of New Orleans, 63, 65
University of South Florida, 158
University of Tampa, 158
University of Tennessee, 113
University of Texas, 35–36
Urban Development Action Grant, 154
Urban League, 37, 130
Urban renewal programs, 24–25, 151

Vann, David, 131
Virginia, 4. *See also* Richmond, Virginia
Voter registration, 68, 171

Voting Rights Act (1965), 41, 68, 117,
    139, 171

Wagner Act (1937), 54
Walker, A. Maceo, 115
Washington Shores Federal Savings and
    Loan, 156
West:
    black homeowners in, 12; unemploy-
    ment in, 164
Westinghouse, 149
White(s):
    home ownership of, 11;
    housing quality, 14; white flight, 52,
    66, 77, 110, 126
White, Alton, 154
White, Hattie Mae, 40–41
Willis, A. W., 117
Wilson, Charles L., Jr., 159
Wood, A. Baldwin, 48
Woodfork, Warren, 53
Wood pump, 48, 49
Woodward Iron Company, 123
Wright, Ernest J., 67
Wright, Frances, 98–99

Yates, John "Jack," 17
Yellow fever: outbreaks of, 99
Young, Andrew, 82, 94, 95